Luminos is the Open Access monograph publishing program
from UC Press. Luminos provides a framework for preserving and
reinvigorating monograph publishing for the future and increases
the reach and visibility of important scholarly work. Titles published
in the UC Press Luminos model are published with the same high
standards for selection, peer review, production, and marketing as
those in our traditional program. www.luminosoa.org

Migrant Conversions

1. Jinsoo An, *Parameters of Disavowal: Colonial Representation in South Korean Cinema*

2. Sungyun Lim, *Rules of the House: Family Law and Domestic Disputes in Colonial Korea*

3. Erica Vogel, *Migrant Conversions: Transforming Connections between Peru and South Korea*

Migrant Conversions

*Transforming Connections between
Peru and South Korea*

Erica Vogel

UNIVERSITY OF CALIFORNIA PRESS

University of California Press
Oakland, California

Suggested citation: Vogel, E. *Migrant Conversions: Transforming Connections between Peru and South Korea*. Oakland: University of California Press, 2020. DOI: https://doi.org/10.1525/luminos.86

Library of Congress Cataloging-in-Publication Data

Names: Vogel, Erica, 1978- author.
Title: Migrant conversions : transforming connections between Peru and
    South Korea / by Erica Vogel.
Other titles: Global Korea ; 3.
Description: Oakland, California : University of California Press, [2020] |
    Series: Global Korea ; 3 | Includes bibliographical references and index.
Identifiers: LCCN 2019040148 (print) | LCCN 2019040149 (ebook) |
    ISBN 9780520341173 (paperback) | ISBN 9780520974579 (epub)
Subjects: LCSH: Foreign workers, Peruvian—Korea (South)—Social
    conditions.
Classification: LCC HD8730.5 .V64 2020 (print) | LCC HD8730.5 (ebook) |
    DDC 305.868/8505195—dc23
LC record available at https://lccn.loc.gov/2019040148
LC ebook record available at https://lccn.loc.gov/2019040149

29   28   27   26   25   24   23   22   21   20
10   9   8   7   6   5   4   3   2   1

*This book is dedicated to my loves, Omar, Zoe, and Ian,
and to the memory of my father, Vince Vogel*

CONTENTS

ILLUSTRATIONS

FIGURES

MAP

TABLE

ACKNOWLEDGMENTS

I am grateful for the many people who have helped me complete this project by sharing their time, knowledge, resources, and friendship with me. I wish I could thank everyone by name, but the following is just a partial list.

First, I am deeply indebted to the many Peruvians in Korea and their families in Peru who welcomed me into their lives and homes and bravely shared their stories. I cannot name them here in order to protect their anonymity, but I am truly grateful for the time and energy they gave to help me complete this research. I would also like to thank the many Catholic and Protestant clergy in Korea who supported my research from the beginning, let me chat with them on long subway rides from Seoul, and helped me stay connected to the community even while I was far away. Thank you for allowing me to conduct research in your churches and for fearlessly supporting your parishioners. Thank you also to the consuls of the Peruvian embassy who gave me hours of their time and provided me with an insider's perspective on the history of the Peruvian community in Korea.

This ethnography would not have been possible without the support and encouragement of my mentors at UC Irvine. Foremost, Mei Zhan championed this project from the beginning, and her comments and critiques helped me develop my ideas from a hunch into a book. Susan Coutin's astute comments on multiple drafts inspired me to look for unexpected connections. Leo Chavez's passion for anthropology and expertise on transnational migration sparked my interest in doing fieldwork and translating it onto the page. Rachel O'Toole motivated me to find miracles in impossible situations and appreciate the power of my informants' beliefs. I also developed key parts of this project in inspiring classes with Victoria Bernal, Karen Leonard, Bill Maurer, Tom Boellstorff, and Michael Burton.

I am grateful for the chance I had to work with Nancy Abelmann as a Korea Foundation Postdoctoral Fellow at the University of Illinois at Urbana-Champaign. I always seem to remember her advice or stumble onto something she wrote whenever I need it most. At UIUC, Jungwon Kim, Elizabeth LaCouture, Adrienne Lo, and Jason Petrulis welcomed me into a wonderful community that inspired me as I started moving this project into book form. I continue to benefit from discussions I had with Laila Amine, Jessi Bardill, Shane Barter, Alex E. Chávez, John Cho, Laura Sachiko Fugikawa, Ju Hui Judy Han, Yoonjung Kang, Dohye Kim, Sujung Kim, Chamara Jewel Kwakye, Alex Jong-Seok Lee, Kyou-ho Lee, Robert Oppenheim, Andrew Orta, Karen Roybal, Josie Sohn, Jesook Song, and Anantha Sudhakar. Carla Jones first helped me learn how to ask anthropological questions. Hyun Mee Kim and Teofilo Altamirano gave me astute advice in the field. I am grateful to Sharon Dilworth and the late Hilary Masters at Carnegie Mellon University for encouraging me to write and see the world.

Some of my most enjoyable moments during the research and writing process came alongside friends doing the same thing. I continue to value the friendships of and learn from fellow researchers, including Nanao Akanuma, Andrea Ballestero, Kimberly Chung, Caitlin Fouratt, Nalika Gajaweera, Philip Grant, Sharon Heijin Lee, Alexandra Lippman, Connie McGuire, Caroline Melly, Sheena Nahm, Cortney Hughes Rinker, Neha Vora, and Lien Vu. Friends and family helped make my world more fun and full of love, including my grandma, Colleen Celani, and Lorraine Celani, Collette and Neil Celani-Morrell, Minda Berbeco, Emily Merz, Britt Nehyba, Rivelino Pacheco, Rosa Pacheco, Lila Rodriguez, Bonni Sanford, Caitlin Sanford, Stephanie Tsang, Courtney Vogel, and my grandparents who have passed away, but whom I still love very much, Bernetta Vogel, Thomas Vogel, and Frank Celani.

I would like to thank Bill Nelson, Deborah Hawkins, Laurie Helmrath, and Scott Selin for help with designing my methods diagram in chapter 1. Thank you also to FXTop.com for letting me use their historical conversion graph in that diagram. Thank you to all of my students at Saddleback, UIUC, Soka, and UCI for being wonderful interlocutors in my process of learning how to communicate this story.

My Peru-based research was funded by grants from the Fulbright Hays Doctoral Dissertation Research Abroad Fellowship and a Dissertation Research Grant and Mini Grant from the Pacific Rim Research Foundation. My Korea-based research was funded by a Fellowship for Field Research from the Korea Foundation and the Center for Asian Studies at the University of California, Irvine. A Libraries Access Grant from the Center for Latin American Studies at Stanford allowed me to finish the research for this book. I want to thank Molly Aufdermauer, Elizabeth Saenz-Ackermann, Alberto Diaz-Cayeros, and the library curators for welcoming me to campus and giving me access to the amazing Stanford library collection. Debbie Armstrong, Jenny Langrell, Carolyn Seaman, and Lydia Tamara always got me what I needed from the Saddleback Library.

A special thanks to Claire Cesareo, Christina Ghanbarpour, Margot Lovett, and Zully Vielman for creating a supportive and intellectually stimulating work home and championing me to finish the book. I am lucky to have many friends and colleagues who make Saddleback a wonderful place to work, including Allison Camelot, Deidre Cavazzi, April Cubbage, Kathy Damm, Suki Fisher, Renée Garcia, Caroline Gee, Nicole Major, Tracey Magyar, Jennifer Pakula, Brenda Plascencia-Carrizosa, Christina Smith, Maureen Smith, Barbara Tamialis, and more. I am thankful for having Christina Hinkle as my dean; she inspires collaboration and excellence in teaching and finds resources whenever I need them. Thank you to Yvonne Belardes, Karen Yang, and Katelyn King for helping me and being great company during the summer days in the office. Thank you to Marina Aminy, Laura Harris, and Saddleback's Online Education and Learning Resources for assistance with indexing and completing the manuscript. I appreciate Bridget A. Bohorquez, Eduardo E. Bohorquez, Amy Godoy-Guerra, and Yourim Lee's help in understanding how people talk about *respuestas* in other places.

This book would not be here without John Lie and Jun Yoo of the Global Korea series inviting me to participate in a manuscript workshop. In this process, the advice and comments I received from Jessica Cobb, Susan Coutin, Alyshia Gálvez, Caren Freeman, Eleana Kim, John Lie, and anonymous reviewers inspired me and helped me to figure out how to give this story life. Thank you to Reed Malcolm and Archna Patel and the University of California Press for answering my myriad questions and expertly guiding this book to production.

Erin Hayes and Seo Young Park have given me incredible friendship, support, and scholarly critique throughout every draft and iteration of this project. My research and life have overlapped and intertwined with theirs in countless ways, and they are now family to me.

I want to thank my mom, Deborah Hawkins, who is the best person to hang out with and the first person I want to share my news with. To my dad, Vince Vogel, who passed away before this book was complete, but whose sense of adventure and kindness continues to inspire me. To Pam Vogel and Russ Hawkins, thank you for loving Zoe and Ian. To Juana, *gracias por cuidarnos*. To my brothers, Matt and Geoff Vogel, whose love and support make me who I am. And a very special thank you to Omar Pacheco, whose sense of direction helped us travel the world—even to places we had never been—and we hardly ever got lost. I am grateful for his love of life, laughing, and family. Finally, thank you to my little loves, Zoe and Ian, who have transformed my world for the better.

Part of chapter 4 comes from my article "Predestined Migrations: Undocumented Peruvians in South Korean Churches" and is reproduced by permission of the American Anthropological Association from *City & Society* 26, no. 3 (2010): 331–51. Part of chapter 5 comes from my article "Ongoing Endings: Migration, Love, and Ethnography" and is reproduced by permission of Sage Publishing from *Journal of Contemporary Ethnography* 45, no. 6 (2016): 673–91.

Introduction

Constructing "The End"

Pastor Andrés caught the attention of the Spanish-speaking congregation of Seoul's Nazarene Church—the majority of whom were undocumented migrant workers from Peru—when he compared their lives in Korea to a party that was about to end. "You are afraid of Peru," he told them.[1] "The problem is that we are too comfortable here [in Korea]. But now it's time. We are ready. *It's over. The party is over.*" He meant that the Peruvians' work in Korea (mostly doing manual labor in factories or selling jewelry on the street) was both easy and inconsequential in comparison to the work that lay ahead of them—working with Nazarene to start a mission in Peru and converting their friends and families to Protestantism. Unlike much of the congregation, Pastor Andrés had a valid visa to be in Korea, which also allowed him to travel freely in and out of the country. He had just returned from a trip to Peru. "Peru is a field of disaster," he said. "Those are your compatriots and families who are suffering." As he told it, the very economic and spiritual salvation of Peru was at stake, and the migrant workers in Korea were the only ones who could save it.

On this August afternoon, the chapel was filled with men, women, and a few children, and as was usual at this evangelical church, most of the adults sat in their own pews to maximize their concentration on the day's sermon. Although they had been sitting with their spiral notebooks open for over an hour, ready to take notes on what would now be their second sermon of the day, I did not see anyone move to write down what the pastor said. Nearly all of the Peruvian migrant workers I met in Korea told me they preferred Korea to Peru—mainly because Korea had more employment opportunities, and it was safer and cleaner than the neigh-

1

borhoods where they were from in Peru—but I would have been surprised to hear any of them refer to their lives here as being anything like a party.

The part of Pastor Andrés's statement that seemed to make the parishioners uncomfortable, however, was not that life in Korea was a party, but that their time in Korea was *over*, that they had reached "*the end*." Nazarene church leaders and the Peruvian parishioners had laid plans to build a new religious center called Cristo Vive in the city in Peru where many of the parishioners came from. It seemed Pastor Andrés knew that the Peruvians had little hope for remaining in Korea, so he wanted the migrants to return to Peru as quickly as possible to begin the new mission. While the Nazarene Peruvians were enthusiastic about Cristo Vive and considered themselves to be leaders of the new mission, they had no intention of leaving Korea any time soon. Some Peruvians had been in Korea since the mid-1990s, and despite declining earnings, being separated from their families, and living under a constant threat of deportation, they did not want to return to Peru where they saw themselves as having even fewer opportunities for work and travel. In fact, rather than making plans to leave, many Peruvians I knew were making plans to bring their family members to Korea, not just so they could make money, but so that they could do things like "learn the value of work," convert to evangelical Protestantism, and study to be pastors or find a route to a new migration destination. No matter their plans, and despite the fact that they could be detained and deported at any time, "the end" seemed like a long way off. However, delaying the end—and their return to Peru—came at a cost.

For example, that morning when I arrived at the church for the main Korean-language service, I said hello to Ximena, a woman from a poor *pueblo joven* of Lima, and immediately noticed that she looked distraught.[2] Just a few days earlier, we had spent the afternoon hanging out in her apartment in Seoul while she cheerfully evangelized to me and told me about her life in Korea. Her apartment was so tiny that the platform just inside the front door—which in typical Korean style was also where she kept all of her shoes—doubled as the shower. She showed me how it worked on our way out the door. "I just move all the shoes and hang up the curtain." Then she pointed out the nozzle attached to the wall and the drain on the floor. The toilet was communal and located in a small building away from the apartments. She liked her small apartment though and felt lucky to have a place for her young daughter, who had been born in Korea, to play and sleep. However, this morning at church, when I asked her if she was OK, she started to cry. "I am worried about my children in Peru," she said. She had two young children in Lima whom she had left in the care of her mother. She sent them money for school, clothing, and food but had not seen them since she arrived in Korea four years earlier. I was immediately concerned that they had gotten sick from swine flu, which was moving through Peru at the time and had infected the children of another woman I knew.

"They aren't sick," she told me. The problem was that she had just had a fight with her mother on the phone about how to raise them. Like many Nazarene members, Ximena had recently converted to Protestant Christianity and now in addition to worrying about her children's financial welfare, she was also suspicious that her mother was not raising them to be good *Cristianos*.[3] She felt angry but helpless to do anything from Korea. However, even with these problems, she felt an urgency to stay. Only in Korea could she give herself enough time to complete plans she had started: saving money for her family, finishing her training to become an evangelist, and converting others.

Ximena was not alone. Although 2009 had been a difficult year for all Peruvian migrants in Korea, few wanted to leave. Starting in September 2008, when the effects of the global financial crisis hit Korea, there had been a sharp increase in the number of deportations of undocumented migrants, a decrease in jobs, and an unpredictable conversion rate between the Korean won and the US dollar that made the remittances migrants sent home worth much less.[4] A common topic of conversation among the Peruvian migrant workers I knew in Korea—whether I saw them in Protestant churches with Peruvian congregations, like Nazarene or Friendship Ministry, or at Catholic Masses, or in Fandango salsa club—was how, in the face of rising deportations and the economic crisis, they found it increasingly difficult to support themselves and their families in Peru. While they had originally come to Korea looking for a temporary place to make money, through the course of their migration those plans had converted into something new. Rather than prompting them to leave, the threat of "the end" had intensified their efforts to stay in Korea and realize their new plans.

Pastor Andrés's sermon was not the first time I had heard someone declare that Peruvian migration to Korea had ended. The first time was in 2004, after I had finished a four-year term of teaching English in South Korea. I received an email from a Peruvian friend in Seoul telling me that the Korean government had put an end to Peruvian migration. "Peruvian migration to Korea is finished," she wrote simply. "*Ya se acabó*. It's over." This was right when the Employee Permit System (EPS), Korea's nationality-based quota guest worker program, was being implemented, and it was becoming apparent that Peru would not be included.[5] Peruvians and other migrant workers (both undocumented and those with valid temporary E-9 unskilled labor visas) were ordered to leave Korea in order for the government to start the new policy with a clean slate. Under the EPS, "unskilled" migrants were required to leave the country, and then only certain documented migrants would be allowed to return with new temporary work visas. The policy was part of creating "the end," a clear point in time where undocumented migration would cease to exist and documented migration would begin.

"The end," however, kept moving forward, as many undocumented workers—including Peruvians—refused to leave the country despite the efforts of immigration officers to round them up and deport them. The implementation of the Employee Permit System—and the exclusion of Peruvians—was a particular kind of imagined "ending" that united the various players concerned with the story of Peruvian migration to Korea: specifically, the Korean Ministries of Justice and Labor (the creators and enforcers of the Employee Permit System), the Catholic Church in Seoul (the church with the longest experience in helping migrant workers in general and Peruvians in particular), the numerous Korean Protestant churches that began Spanish-language ministries specifically targeting Peruvian members in the 2000s, and Peruvian migrants. For all groups involved, "the end" was a place in time that was constantly under construction, but whose looming presence had inspired people to develop new possibilities for the future. They each had stakes in creating different endings, and those stakes created a sense of urgency that was productive for making changes.

MIGRANT CONVERSIONS AND GLOBAL PLANS

This is an ethnography of conversion and global plans—not only of converting from one religion to another, but also of converting ends into beginnings, of converting unexpected migrations into predestined routes, and of converting impossibilities into previously unimaginable possibilities. It considers what happens when the global plans and desires of people from vastly different legal positions, geographic origins, and economic means converge through religious, policy, and labor channels. This book follows a community of Peruvian migrants as they attempt to navigate the global world from their positions as undocumented migrants in South Korea or potential/former migrants in Peru. It examines how the Peruvians who form a small and yet resilient group of "temporary" laborers in South Korea live unauthorized lives and refashion their identities as they are permanently in transit in global labor and religious circuits. It shows how migrants, churches, and policy makers contribute to the formation of new routes, blockages, and precarious global subjectivities in both hidden and established transnational networks between Asia and Latin America.

Peruvian migrant workers first came to Korea in large numbers in the mid 1990s on the heels of a larger return migration of ethnically Japanese Peruvians to Japan. Many Peruvians lacked the family history, money, and documentation to enter Japan—and other popular routes for Peruvian labor such as the United States and Spain—through authorized routes, yet they still wanted to work abroad. Korea first emerged as an ideal transitory destination because of its proximity to Japan. It was also one of the few countries with a visa-waiver agreement with Peru, which allows Peruvian citizens to enter as tourists without having to apply for a visa prior to arrival. Most early migrants originally planned to save money and travel elsewhere, but found well-paying factory jobs in Korea's newly booming economy, overstayed their three-month tourist visas, and funded the migrations of their family and friends. By the early 2000s, there were more than 4,000 Peruvians in Korea—just a fraction of the total estimated 243,363 migrant workers in Korea at that time (ethnically Korean Chinese and Han Chinese made up the largest numbers)—but a larger number than other groups of non-Asian migrant workers.[6] There are also Peruvians in Korea who hold student and professional visas, but according to estimates by the Peruvian embassy made in 2007, they only accounted for about 15 percent of the total number of Peruvians in the country.[7]

While the Peruvian community may seem small, given the difficulties of their journeys and that they are ineligible for work visas in Korea, the community stands out as being unique, fairly large, and with impressive staying power. Unlike the more numerous groups of migrants in Korea, Peruvian migrants were neither ethnically Korean nor even Asian and had to fly sometimes for over forty-eight hours to arrive (since the September 11, 2001 attacks, they cannot transit through the United States, Mexico, or Canada without a visa, so travelers must fly around the other side of the world, through South Africa). However, outside of the sending communities where the majority of Peruvians in Korea come from, the migration flow is not well known in either Peru or Korea.

While Peruvian laborers in Korea may seem like an anomaly—even to the Peruvians themselves—I use the concept of conversion to show how through their migrations, and often because of their legal exclusion, they come to see Korea as a place full of previously unimaginable possibility. Some who convert to a religion or change religions while in Korea even come to believe that their migration was actually predestined from God. I demonstrate that through remitting money and new values about work and religion, they attempt to convert themselves and their families into people who have greater access to global networks. I explore how faced with an end to their time in Korea, Peruvians are inspired to create relationships with others also in transit and surpass their roles as economic migrants to become transnational pastors, lovers, entrepreneurs, and cosmopolitan travelers who create and deepen cultural connections between Asia and Latin America. As Peruvians help carve out social spaces in South Korean churches, factories, and the migrant community, they change the value of their migrations and statuses, and they create a complex and uneven transnational connection from Peru to Korea, thereby challenging and redefining a global hierarchy of nations and migrants.

I use *conversion* as an analytic tool for thinking about the ways movement and imminent departures promote transformative changes for migrants and their communities. I use the frame of conversion as a way to explore people's complex migration motivations beyond economic gain, and how they and their worlds change as a result of their migrations.[8] I suggest that conversions are processes of self and world (re)making that are sparked and fueled by transnational journeys and negotiations.[9]

I explore the intersections of three types of conversions—with regard to money, religious beliefs, and cosmopolitan plans—to argue that conversions are the way migrants negotiate the meaning of their lives in a constantly changing context of place, statuses, and relationships and continue to make meaningful impacts on their worlds even when their money has run out. Their contexts are constantly changing because of their own transnational movements and connections between Peru and South Korea, their unstable legal statuses in Korea, their relationships with others also in transit and at home, and their own changing worldviews and plans. As migrants work in Korea, send remittances to Peru, and attempt to influence their worlds on both ends, Peruvians act as *transnational migrants*, or people who "take actions, make decisions, and feel concerns within a field of social relations that links together their country of origin and their countries of settlement."[10] Focusing on the processes of these conversions and exploring how they are all informed by their positions within transnational journeys not only shows the ways seemingly disenfranchised migrants and their families understand, navigate, and even affect the most powerful of global forces, but also how transnational connections between Latin America and Asia can come to be deepened and redefined through an unauthorized and relatively small migration.

Each of the types of conversion—monetary, religious, and cosmopolitan— happens in a particular transnational social field and within a global capitalist system, a global theological system, and a global discursive system. The overlaps, connections, and disruptions of those fields become visible through the process of migrants moving and negotiating the value of their migrations among these planes.

MONETARY CONVERSION

When speaking of monetary conversion (in Spanish, *conversión* or *tipos de cambio*, meaning exchange rate), I am specifically referring to the fluctuating conversion rate between the Korean won and the US dollar since the 1990s, but especially during the global financial crisis of 2008 when the salaries that migrants earned in won became worth much less when converted to dollars. For example, while in 2006 a salary of one million won converted to about $900, by November 2008, that same salary was only worth $666. With prices of food and schooling in Peru staying the same or increasing, even migrants who had managed to keep their factory jobs during the recession found that their remittances had much less buying power. Currency conversion brings the global hierarchy of migration destinations and legality into relief and illustrates the marginality of Peruvians in Korea. While migrants in more mainstream destinations, like the United States, can earn, remit, and spend in the same currency (because there is an infrastructure set up in Peru to process dollars), migrants in Korea must first convert their earnings into a world currency—like US dollars—before they can send them home. Depending on the day's conversion rate, migrants stood to lose a little or a lot of the value of their earnings in the conversion.

Just as there was no way to get money home without first converting it into dollars, the migrants themselves changed while undertaking their journeys and remitting. Remittances alter these social fields in unexpected ways because money gains meaning and status depending on its context of exchange, and migrants and families do not always share the same "regimes of value."[11] When people convert their money to send home, they do more than just move from one currency to another.

RELIGIOUS CONVERSION

By religious conversion (*conversión* in Spanish), I am referring to the significant number of Peruvians who either changed from one religion to another, started attending church for the first time, or experienced a renewal of their faith and church participation while in Korea. Most Peruvians arrived in Korea as either nonpracticing Catholics or Protestants with only high school educations, but since the 1990s, many have converted to or renewed their faith in Protestantism, become leaders in Korean churches, and launched, or planned to embark on, missions to Peru with the support of their Korean churches. Peruvians who identified as Catholics also felt a sense of rejuvenation to their faith in Korea, becoming leaders and/or completing baptisms or confirmations they had missed in Peru as children. By 2009, the Catholic Church offered Masses in Spanish specifically for migrant workers at four locations in Seoul and factory towns in the surrounding Gyeonggi Province, and there were at least four different Protestant churches in Seoul with Spanish-speaking congregations.

Rather than thinking of conversion as the act of experiencing a complete reversal of belief, Diane Austin-Broos writes, "to be converted is to reidentify, to learn, reorder and reorient."[12] Through learning the framework of their churches and experiencing their own migration journeys, some converts begin to reidentify experiences in their past and present—including their failure to make money in Peru, or become pregnant—as answers or signs from God (*respuestas* in Spanish). These respuestas are like epiphanies or clues of information to questions migrants did not even know they had before their journeys (chapter 3). As they shared their respuestas with me, their migration and conversion journeys became intertwined and guided by an effort both to reveal and fulfill the plans God created for them long before they were born as well as to demonstrate to me that they were important migrants in Korea. When Peruvian migrants start to "reidentify and reorient" their pasts, presents, and futures, it is within a framework similar to what Susan Coutin calls "re/membering," where migrants negotiate their membership in both Korea and Peru through reflecting on their pasts in Peru as well as their migration and conversion journeys. In Coutin's work, young people re/member their lives in El Salvador and the United States through their sharing of *testimonios*, writing poetry, and sharing their experiences with her as an ethnographer. Coutin writes,

"Re/membering is temporally complex in that it entails revisiting the past with an eye toward achieving a more just future . . . the past haunts the present."[13] In my book, I explore cases of Peruvians both re/membering and reorienting their migration and conversion journeys through identifying and sharing the respuestas they have received, recreating themselves as cosmopolitan travelers rather than undocumented workers, and through sending home social and economic remittances that they hope will convert their family members and themselves into people who are on a higher rung of the global social hierarchy. However, rather than having a linear narrative, their interpretations of events keep changing over time as their context changes.

COSMOPOLITAN CONVERSION

Finally, by cosmopolitan conversion, I am referring to the various creative projects or plans that Peruvians developed in Korea in the effort to help them change their lives and those of their families. I see these projects as cosmopolitan because not only did migrants want to use them to gain the skills and abilities of cosmopolitanism—to "feel at home in the world" and achieve "infinite ways of being"—but they also hoped to be recognized as worthy and deserving of that status by others.[14] Their efforts challenge the notion that cosmopolitanism is only the territory of rich "flexible citizens" because Peruvian migrants also hoped their migrations would lead to a personal transformation to their worldview and opportunities.[15] Most migrants I spoke with arrived in Korea with a goal of saving money for opportunities for themselves and their families—by funding future migrations, educations, or businesses in Peru. However, I focus on how their cosmopolitan conversion projects emerged and took new directions given their situation of being undocumented and Peruvian in Korea at a time when the world economy was in flux and they were surrounded by many other migrants and groups who were also trying to lay out global plans.[16]

Looking at these three forms of conversion shows the relational impact various global and transnational networks have on one another. When viewed in isolation, a migrant's choice to remain in a destination that is unprofitable and potentially dangerous might seem irrational. However, when those choices are placed in a larger perspective that includes global, transnational, and individual connections like global capitalism, Protestant and Catholic networks, and local and family histories, those choices start to make sense and clarify both individual migrant motivations and how globalization works. Exploring migration journeys and choices as conversions helps to show how people, things, places, and ideas change over time and in relation to one another. Further, the concept of conversion provides a way to study globalization even when the players in a particular "global encounter" are relatively invisible or have departed.[17] The book not only discusses the peak of the migration flow into Korea but also the ways in which that migration continues to play a role in the lived experiences of migrants after they have returned to Peru. Looking at conversion as a transnational journey reveals how globalization—and being active parts of global processes—continues to affect people's lives and ideas about their futures and pasts long after they have stopped moving, or once that particular global convergence has come to an end.

CONVERSION AS A JOURNEY AND NEGOTIATION

I draw on the following definitions of *conversion* to explore how these three types of conversion include developing a new cultural language or worldview through which to interpret or reinterpret experiences and the ways things and people change in form, character, or function as a result. As is reflected in the origin of the word *conversion* itself, which means "to turn around, send in a different direction," there is a sense of change through movement, *intentional* rather than passive change, and *multiple directionalities* rather than linearity built in to the word.[18] There are also possibilities for *multiple positions* in conversion, of which I use three: (1) the process of being converted; (2) the act of converting others; and (3) causing things (like money, family, nations) to change in form, character, or function. A person can do all of these things simultaneously, and while they may do them with intention, such actions can have unintended consequences. I bring together these definitions with literature on transnational migration, religious conversion, money and value, and cosmopolitanism to explore the changes that happen to migrants and their home and destination communities through the process of their journey, and also how the journey (migratory, spiritual, and cosmopolitan) inspires migrants to see the world and their own lives in a new way, and how that affects the choices they make and their communities.

Scholars of religious conversion have long argued against what is known as the "Pauline paradigm," which depicts conversion as an unexpected, radical reversal of belief enacted on a passive convert.[19] I agree with those who, rather than seeing conversion as a sudden and totalizing event, consider it a *process* that "takes place over time, interacts with institutional religious, network, and cultural contexts, and does not necessarily proceed in a linear or chronological fashion."[20] This makes religious conversion similar to transnational migration in that both have seemingly distinct beginning and ending points, yet the points are not bounded and the journey between them is not bipolar. Further, migrant conversions often have unexpected results, because while it may appear people are making direct journeys or negotiations between their point of origin and destination, one currency and another, or an old belief system and a new one, there are myriad other global, transnational, and local factors and forces influencing the choices and significance of the conversions. As a result, any attempt to understand the nature of the conversion and its effects must consider their context in place, in time, and to one another.

As I will show, however, part of converting is learning to see the world in a new way, and since people and their environments are also changing over time, they may not only interpret events in the past, present, and future differently over time, but they may try to influence the ways others interpret them as well. Like transnational migration, religious conversion is "a type of passage that negotiates a place in the world."[21] These conversions are types of power negotiations that could result in fracture, but they are also formations of new beliefs and a change to the way people understand the world and how it is connected.

There is a large potential for loss in these projects of conversion. In his discussion of conversion in "The Forms of Capital," Pierre Bourdieu points out that when attempting to convert economic capital into social capital, there is always the risk of incommensurability and therefore the loss of value.[22] For example, if a remitting migrant's family is ungrateful for the gifts sent and they do not comply with the sender's wishes, even the economic capital is lost. There is also the chance a migrant will be deported before she can complete her plan, and truly transformative institutionalized cultural capital—such as gaining a visa to a coveted destination, gaining covert embodied cultural capital that can be converted into economic capital, or being respected as a religious leader—takes a long time to accumulate.[23]

However, with any conversion—to money, religion, or plans—there is always loss. The loss can come in the form of fees, physical and emotional distance from family, and perhaps most importantly, the inability to pursue other potentially beneficial migrations or plans. I show that through conversions, loss itself could become valuable.[24] In fact, separation, loss, and sacrifice were intertwined with a successful migration. The longer migrants stayed in Korea, and were separated from their families, the more time they had to complete their projects. Other times, they reframed loss into what Nancy Munn calls a "desirable outcome" in an exchange.[25] For example, migrants who shared their stories of loss received invitations to present at prestigious church meetings and converted loss into valuable social and cultural capital.

AT THE CONVERGENCE OF GLOBAL PLANS BY SOUTH KOREAN CHURCHES AND THE STATE

In the mid-1990s, Peru was experiencing an economic downturn and political instability that was increasing out-migration while South Korea was experiencing a booming economy that contributed to an increase in immigration. While I imagine many of those migrants, as well as people everywhere, were embarking on their own cosmopolitan conversions, the situation in South Korea infused the Peruvian migrants' conversions with unique possibilities for changes to their mobility and status—as well as put them at great risk for loss and deportation. That is because Peruvian migrants arrived in Korea during a historical moment that landed them in the midst of a convergence of other large- and small-scale cosmopolitan conversion projects headed by the Korean state, churches, and the Koreans and migrants with whom they interacted.

For example, the Korean state had various ongoing cosmopolitan conversion plans including *seghyewha*, an organized effort started in the 1990s to make South Korea globalized, partly through a promotion of English-language learning and welcoming and capitalizing on the skills of Koreans who had lived overseas.[26] The first decade of the 2000s also saw an increase in the interest around the idea of multiculturalism, with a push by the state and NGOs to manage the growing numbers of foreigners in Korea, including workers attracted to jobs and foreign brides brought in to marry bachelor farmers.[27] Finally, I interpret the implementation of the Employee Permit System and its promotion in other countries as part of a state strategy to show evidence of Korea's rising position on the global stage and to be recognized as a country with a clean and enviable migration record.

Since Peruvians were a small group of unusual foreigners in Korea, their refusal to leave despite being legally excluded made them both an insignificant and an urgent problem for the state agencies trying to regulate migration. Most people did not even know they were there, but their continued presence contradicted the story that Korea had a successful, and therefore enviable, migration policy. It made them "impossible subjects" or people "who cannot be and a problem that cannot be solved."[28] For example, when I met with Ms. Kim, a member of the Korean Ministry of Justice, and asked about the ministry's plans for increasing deportations, she pointed out that the state could only fully protect migrant workers who were documented, implying that undocumented workers were doing themselves harm by staying outside of the benevolent gaze of the state. When I asked if Peruvians were being targeted for deportation, she told me there were no Peruvians in Korea as far as she knew. I hesitated before correcting her, not wanting to give too many specifics, but not wanting to miss a chance to advocate on the community's behalf. Regardless, effects of these state-led cosmopolitan conversion plans—including the EPS, the amnesty that preceded it, and multicultural projects—resulted in an unstable environment for foreigners who, during the time of my fieldwork, were alternately welcomed, tolerated, targeted, mistreated, protected, given documentation, or told they were excluded indefinitely.

Peruvians' looming departures accelerated their membership in various social circles, including Korean churches, which were also undergoing their own cosmopolitan conversion plans. Various Korean Protestant churches, running out of potential converts at home, had turned to evangelizing to Korea's rising numbers of foreign residents as well as launching missions abroad. In her research on these foreign missions in Africa, Ju Hui Judy Han found that evangelization techniques included linking Korea's rising economic prowess to its high numbers of Protestants and promising the same for foreign nationals who converted.[29] For churches with Peruvian members, having an unusual group of converts in their pews who wanted to work with churches to launch foreign missions added to the churches' own cosmopolitan cachet.

Because they were at the convergence of these other cosmopolitan plans, Peruvians were included because of exclusions, welcomed because of their foreignness, and eligible to become key members in a church or families because of their ineligibility to stay. For example, partly because the Peruvians' departure from Korea was regarded by most as being certain, they were fast-tracked in networks that gave them "pathways of incorporation" or access to symbolic capital such as prestige and personal connections, which they could spend to launch migrations to other destinations as educated pastors.[30] Since Peruvians were excluded from legal pathways, such as sending their children to public school, churches helped them find even more desirable alternatives, such as scholarships to American-run schools (chapter 4). Clergy intensified their leadership training and other benefits and gave them a platform for conducting a type of "politicized spirituality"[31] where they promoted issues in Peru and themselves as important leaders. At numerous events I saw Peruvian church members speak alongside ambassadors—and receive equal billing on the program—and when a Korean bishop who was also a *nuncio* (a papal ambassador) visited Korea from Rome, he made a special trip to perform sacraments for migrants at the Catholic Mass (chapter 3).

I explore how in pursuing their cosmopolitan conversion projects while legally excluded, Peruvians and their churches and communities created unexpected social practices because of their resulting experiences of liminality. Unlike migrants whose desired end point is legal and social inclusion, or asylum seekers who are in a "liminal legality" struggling to live with temporary but renewable visas that give partial rights in comparison to full citizenship, most of my interviewees were not straddling documented and undocumented statuses.[32] Rather than waiting for legalization, they were in what Melanie B. E. Griffiths calls a "temporal liminality" where they were simultaneously waiting for an imminent deportation and had the support networks in place to "[reconceptualize] the present as a meaningful time in itself."[33] I am not looking at this story from the perspective of how "illegality" is used as a flexible governing tactic to keep a labor force vulnerable.[34] Instead, I am interested in how through their efforts to create a space for themselves in Korea despite their exclusion, and influence the world despite their lack of money, Peruvian migrants become what Victor Turner calls "liminars."[35] As liminars, they work to transform into people in transnational relationships, who "know how to work," as saviors of Peru, providers for their families at home, and cosmopolitan travelers with the ability to transport themselves to other social spheres and global locations. However, in attempting to defy their legal exclusion and become recognized contributors to Korea, as good workers and as important members of churches or transnational families, they also risk becoming entangled in the very social and legal barriers they want to overcome—through being deported or legally "stuck" in bad marriages (chapter 4).

I look at how Peruvian migrants' efforts to negotiate the meaning of their lives through multiple forms of conversion—monetary, religious, and cosmopolitan— while at the convergence of other individual and groups' cosmopolitan conversions—helped to shift their value in Korea and at home. As David Graeber writes, value is the "way in which actions become meaningful to the actor by being incorporated in some larger, social totality—even if in many cases, the totality in question, exists primarily in the actor's imagination."[36] In order to get others to see them and their actions in a new way they need them to participate in their cosmopolitan conversion. I explore how initially many hoped to influence their family members through sending economic remittances; however, this became increasingly difficult during the global financial crisis when stable jobs decreased and the conversion rate of the dollar fluctuated wildly. Anthropologist Julie Chu looks at circulations of credit, desire, and migrants to discuss how mobility reveals the "differential value of various people and things entangled in webs of increasing transnational exchange."[37] Here I explore how migrants found a way to continue engaging their family members in their cosmopolitan migration plans by converting their economic remittances into other forms of capital they hoped would be regarded as more valuable. For example, in chapter 2, I present cases of migrants who tried to convert their family members into people who were financially independent by evangelizing to them over the phone, or trying to get them to pursue educations in Peru. I found that the systems of value they had created in Korea and were trying to relay to family members in Peru were not always compatible, and so the results of these strategies ranged from tangible successes (in the form of converted family members, completed houses, and educational certificates), to successes "primarily in the actor's imagination," to family dissolutions through divorce and deception.

A SNAPSHOT OF GLOBALIZATION

I think of this story as a manageable snapshot of globalization, where focusing on the participants and tracing their origins, motivations, and imagined destinations reveal larger stories of the formation and reinterpretation of global hierarchies. A snapshot captures a particular configuration of the relationships of people, things, and places together at one moment in time. When families try to re-create iconic family photos, for example, with siblings in a favorite hangout or parents holding a new baby, it is never exactly the same. The original members are older or absent, the nature of their relationships has changed, and so has the meaning of the place. Yet, the snapshot is useful in that it informs the viewer about the meaning of the present. It infuses things and people with value by showing us what has changed and what has converted into a loss or gain.

When thinking of globalization I follow the lead of scholars who see it as being a series of unequal and uneven encounters, engagements, and connections.[38] To avoid the idea that globalization is inevitable, and making all corners of the world the same, Mei Zhan uses the term "worlding" to refer to the "emergent socialities entangled in dynamic imaginaries of pasts, futures, and presents" that combine to create the world(s) in which we live.[39] The story of Peruvian migration to South Korea, how it began, why it is coming to an end, and the enduring impact it has made on everyone involved, is a complex, but manageable, series of worlding socialities. It is of a relatively small scale and its peak lasted for about twenty years, but it involves countless individual, transnational, and global forces and imaginaries that are entangled in the past, present, and future.

Plans for globalization and cosmopolitan conversions cannot ever truly fail because they are ongoing projects that emerge in conversation with the plans of other people and groups. They constantly change direction depending on the particular barriers and opportunities that emerge as people make their way through the world. Also, the process of pursuing a cosmopolitan conversion has already made you cosmopolitan, even if the project does not go as planned.

By looking at the configuration of the overlapping cosmopolitan plans and projects of migrants, governments, and churches, I hope to depict a global moment in the making. By *configuration*, I mean the ways people imagine the world to be connected, the particular routes and destinations open and closed to them, and the ways migrants themselves participate in creating the routes they travel. These are the perceived beginning and end points, routes and barriers around which people imagine and orient their journeys. I think of it as the infrastructure for these conversions as well as the "hierarchically ordered global pathways" or routes of things, people, and ideas that migrants help create through their migrations and participation in transnational networks, including sending remittances.[40] Remittances are not only constitutive of globalization, but as Michele Ruth Gamburd argues, they also "simultaneously [map] and [obscure] a social reality of labor and exchange relations between people."[41] I am interested in exploring the configuration of the tangible and imagined world that migrants, their families, their churches, and the Korean state all played a part in creating at this particular moment through their overlapping attempts to influence the world around them.

SALSA DANCING IN SEOUL

My own thread in this story helps to illustrate the larger geopolitical and historical forces that both brought Peruvians to Korea and made their arrival seem like an accident. From the year 2000, when Peruvian migration to Korea reached its peak, to 2004, when Peruvians lost their visas through the EPS, I was also a migrant worker in Korea. However, my cultural capital as a college graduate with a US passport gave me access to a renewable visa and work protections as an English teacher. Although we had traveled on very different routes, we were contributing to the same global moment.

When I decided to move to Seoul to teach English, I had just finished my undergraduate degree and knew that I wanted to travel, but I had no resources to do so on my own. After months of talking about going to China, but not having found a real way to get there, another recent college graduate said to me: "You should go teach English in Korea. Everyone I know is doing it." She told me the name of a school where she had done a phone interview, and that night, after looking at the school's website on the internet, I was amazed to learn how simple they would make my trip. Within a few months, I was on a plane to Seoul, a place that until July 2000 had never even entered my global itinerary.[42]

While it may have felt like I went to Korea "on a whim," so had thousands of other people who found jobs in Korea's "highly gendered and racialized" English teacher market.[43] This was an important time in the economic and migration history of Korea. In 2000, the year I arrived, the nightmare of the 1997 Asian financial crisis and IMF bailout was fading, Korea was becoming one of the strongest economies in the world, and the country had accepted more migrant workers than it had in any other time in history. In 2000 the estimated 243,363 migrant workers in Korea included professionals with visas (such as teachers, chefs, and businesspeople), laborers holding "trainee" visas, and undocumented migrant workers.[44] In comparison, just thirteen years before, there had been only 6,409 migrant workers in Korea.[45]

The booming economy starting in the late 1980s left a shortage of Koreans willing to do 3D factory jobs (dirty, dangerous, and difficult) and soon attracted foreign migrant workers not only from Asia but also from as far away as Latin America, Africa, and Eastern Europe.[46] Since until recently Korea had been a labor exporting country, it had visa waiver agreements set up with many other developing countries—including Peru—that allowed people to enter as tourists without having to secure a visa before arriving. In less than ten years, hundreds of thousands of people had entered Korea this way. Initially there was no system in place to regulate them, so as soon as their three-month tourist visas expired, they became undocumented. As a way of figuring out how many undocumented workers were in Korea, and where they all came from, the government offered undocumented workers amnesties on a limited basis. This was done in preparation for the Employee Permit System. Many Peruvians (and migrants from other countries) became temporarily documented during this amnesty.

Although the Latin American population in Korea is small in comparison to other groups of foreigners, Latin Americans had a very strong presence in various international spaces in Seoul. On weekends I went to areas like Itaewon (a former camp town next to Yongsan US Army base) and Hongdae (a college area) that had nightclubs and restaurants specifically catering to foreign customers and young Koreans. Two of the most popular places to go among my group of friends were salsa clubs: Fandango in Itaewon and Tropicale in Hongdae. The most exciting thing about these clubs was that they attracted a wide variety of people with different socioeconomic backgrounds, legal statuses, and nationalities who were living and working in Korea. Every Saturday night, Koreans and foreigners would gather in these clubs to drink cheap mugs of Hite beer (only 2,500 won, or about $2.50); dance to salsa, merengue, and reggaetón; and try to communicate in Spanish, English, and Korean. Saturday night regulars included Latin American embassy and consulate personnel; English, Spanish, and German teachers; Korean office workers; US soldiers from Puerto Rico, Colombia, Mexico, and the Dominican Republic stationed in Korea; and factory workers from places like Peru, Ecuador, and Bolivia.

By far, Peruvians were the most prominent group of Latin Americans in the clubs, and in Korea as a whole. By 2000 there were more Peruvians in Korea at one time than ever before. There were entire families of Peruvians living together, including parents, children, aunts, and uncles. Nearly everyone in the family—from fifteen-year-olds to sixty-year-olds—worked in small- and medium-sized factories, or on construction sites. My interviewees worked at a variety of jobs, including in factories making things like cabinets, cardboard boxes, metal parts, plastics, mannequins, chemicals, *makgeolli* (rice wine), mattresses, and jeans.[47] A few people I met worked at recycling plants, where a fringe benefit was free access to still-usable items Koreans had discarded, like rice cookers and TVs, before they were recycled.[48] Some of the least-desirable jobs involved working at industrial laundries washing fabric for the construction of jeans or other clothing items, because they required heavy lifting of wet fabric and frequently caused back injuries.[49] However, the worst jobs were those with abusive bosses, dangerous equipment, or where a person worked for a few months and never got paid, either because of a dishonest boss, a bankrupt factory, or even in a few cases where a factory exploded or burned down.[50]

The Peruvian community continued to grow until 2004, when the Korean government implemented its own global plan to try to control undocumented migration with the Employee Permit System. Full-time factory jobs became difficult for undocumented workers to find after the EPS, and people started selling small jewelry items in the street and in the subway. They referred to this as selling *accessorios* (accessories) or *chaquira* (beaded jewelry). They also looked for *arbeits* (part-time jobs) at factories and restaurants, and for jobs cleaning Korean and foreign people's homes.[51] Most arbeits lasted from a few days to a few weeks helping factories fill rush orders, but a few people used social connections from their churches and skills learned in previous careers in Peru or the United States to get long-term arbeits as chefs, house cleaners, Spanish or salsa teachers, or electricians. Like *arbeit*, there were other Korean terms Peruvians used frequently, even when speaking Spanish, including *sajangnim* (boss), which sounded something like *soyangni* in their Spanish-accented Korean. Terms like these linked Peruvians to Korea and united factory workers from different countries who could speak the common language of the factory when they came together during church services or other social functions.

Many of the Peruvians who came to the Fandango and Tropicale nightclubs left their factories right after work on Saturday night and stayed out until the subway opened around five in the morning. Most literally lived on their factory grounds—in shipping containers that had been converted into living quarters. Others rented apartments in the towns near their factories or churches. Like other groups of factory workers, the majority of Peruvians lived in cities located hours outside of Seoul, such as Dongducheon, Uijeongbu, Osan, Gunsan, and Suwon. In addition to having factories, many of these cities were also US military camp towns, or places that became boomtowns after the US military set up installations near small agricultural villages by the 38th Parallel (the present-day site of the Demilitarized Zone) during the Korean War.[52]

Dongducheon, a city of about 82,000 people near the border with North Korea, was a hub of the Peruvian community. There you could find formal and informal Peruvian restaurants as well as migrant worker soccer tournaments on summer weekends complete with trophies, custom-made uniforms, and championship rings. In addition to the neighborhoods, apartment buildings, farms, and churches that looked similar to my other field sites in Korea, there was also a carnivalesque feel to the streets near the US military base, which were lined with clubs catering to foreigners. In her ethnography about Filipina entertainers who worked in Dongducheon clubs, Sealing Cheng points out that camp towns are "host to several groups of border-crossing people who have experienced different degrees and temporalities of dislocation," including undocumented and documented migrant workers and the Koreans who work and live with them. On the way from the Catholic Church to the main Peruvian restaurant in the area, I passed Filipina club workers sitting outside of their clubs smoking cigarettes and chatting with their friends, and couples from different countries having dates along the streets of shops near the gate of Camp Casey army base.[53] Peruvian children who lived there went to American-run Christian schools, and a soccer tournament I attended there had players from Peru, Nigeria, Russia, Romania, and the United States. Dongducheon was often the backdrop to love affairs with foreigners—I heard stories of men going to the clubs to see their Filipina girlfriends and of Peruvian women who had left their husbands for their US soldier boyfriends (see chapter 4).

Dongducheon's thriving community of foreigners had also made it one of the most dangerous places for undocumented Peruvian migrants. Camp towns were targets of frequent and aggressive immigration raids, which sociologist Hae Yeon Choo describes as being part of a disciplinary mechanism, disproportionately targeting those who "stood out" for being "racial others" or for otherwise "violating the implicit rules of community conduct."[54] Yet, despite the raids, Peruvians and other undocumented migrants continued to live and create communities there. For many Peruvians I knew, Dongducheon simultaneously represented something foreign and familiar, exciting, and scandalous. It was a place where danger originated and a place with situations and people worth risking danger for.

The cosmopolitan landscape where Peruvians interacted with other foreigners from all over the world extended far beyond Dongducheon, however. On their factory floor as well as in their dormitories, Peruvians lived and worked with Koreans and with undocumented and documented foreign workers. There were numerous interethnic hierarchies based on language, gender, and nationality. In 2007, when factory jobs were scarce, I visited the factory of a Peruvian woman named Diana and received a cold welcome from the other migrants who thought I was Peruvian and there to work. Except for Diana and a Korean woman, all of the workers at this particular factory were men. They were from Peru, Bangladesh, Vietnam, and Myanmar, and some were documented with the EPS, but a few were not. Diana told me they were jealous because undocumented workers made more per month than documented workers.[55] When she introduced me to her boss and his wife and told them about my research they said they wished Diana could get a visa because she was the only foreigner at the factory who could speak Korean well enough for them to understand. Besides that, she was the only one who could understand the English words and Korean pronunciation of the other workers.[56] On my visit to her factory, she spent the day darting around the workshop, translating for workers and her bosses amid the din of loud machinery pounding out metal parts.

Other spaces that were both diverse and segregated in various ways were the churches Peruvians attended. During worship at Friendship Foreign Ministry, Korean church leaders organized parishioners by nationality: Filipinos in the front left pews, Mongolians at the back, and Peruvians on the right. One day I came in late and an usher I did not know asked my nationality and then sat me with Nigerians—who spoke English. The Peruvians in attendance saw me and waved me over to their side. Worshippers sat separately to get simultaneous translation of the sermons in their own language, but they mingled with other foreigners during meals, on retreats, and outside of the church. However, I heard more than one story of Korean church officials discouraging migrant workers from Peru from dating migrants from other countries. I do not know if this was based on their opinions about age differences, but it is one example of how they tried to control the migrants' personal lives. In addition to language, some of the divisions between groups in churches were based on class. For example, in Seoul there were other Catholic Masses given in Spanish, but a priest told me they were attended by diplomats and professionals who he said would never consider attending one of the Masses directed at migrant workers.

In exploring the ways migrants experienced and navigated localized, transnational, and global hierarchies in their daily lives, I show how their actions and perspectives created links and divisions between the transnational social fields of their churches, workplaces, and families in South Korea and Peru. This book is about what happened when the global plans of migrants, their churches, and the Korean government converged and diverged.

Although I cannot say whether the migration flow has ended, it has definitely slowed. Between 2006 and 2011, when I did the bulk of the field research for this project, the number of Peruvians in Korea had reduced to an estimated 815 to 2,000 people. The reason for these varying figures was due to the difficulty in tracking down how many Peruvians were actually in the country. In 2006, the Peruvian embassy calculated 815 using official arrival and departure information from Gimpo and Incheon airports. That figure included people holding student visas, workers with temporary visas, and those who had entered as tourists and had not yet departed. The larger figure came from the Catholic Church, which kept a census of all the Peruvians they served and determined that there were closer to 2,000 Peruvians working in the country. By now many of the Peruvian migrants who appear in this book have left Korea. Some of them were able to find work in Peru, but others migrated again, primarily to Chile and Argentina. Others, though, have stayed, either because they are married to Koreans and became Korean citizens, or because they have been able to evade deportation and continue working. In 2016 I interviewed three former migrants on the phone, and all of them said they wished they could return to Korea but knew it would be difficult or impossible. However, even after migrants depart Korea, their time there continues to affect their lives and attitudes about the world. I try to capture these lingering global conversions through the stories in this ethnography.

TRANSNATIONAL FIELDWORK

To understand the changing significance of money, religion, and migration for migrants and their families, I conducted twenty-four months of ethnographic fieldwork in both South Korea and Peru. Between 2006 and 2011, I took four trips to South Korea and three to Peru, where I spent from one to twelve months at a time. On my first two research trips I spent one and a half months (August–September 2006) and (June–July 2007) in South Korea. In August 2007, I spent one month in Peru with the family members of people I had met in Korea during my first two trips. In 2008, I spent three months in Peru (October–December 2008) reconnecting with families I had met on my first trip and former migrants I had initially met in Korea, but who had either decided to return to Peru, or more commonly, had been deported during the increased immigration stings in Korea at the end of 2008. After a brief visit to California, I then traveled to Seoul where I stayed twelve months (December 2008–December 2009). My final trips were a two-week visit to Seoul in July 2010 and then five months in Peru (December 2010–May 2011).

Making numerous trips between the United States, South Korea, and Peru starting in 2006 gave me a unique vantage point from which to see how the circulation of people, money, and religious ideas shifted along with the rising tension of the global financial crisis and the resulting unstable value of the dollar. My first three trips were before the crisis, when a salary of one million won (which was average for my interviewees) was worth between $1,000 and $1,100 when converted into dollars. Some Peruvians still had valid E-9 visas, and the Peruvian embassy was still trying to negotiate for Peru to be included in the Employee Permit System. My field notes and interview transcripts from these initial trips showed that the key concerns my Peruvian interviewees shared with me were their chances for becoming documented and devising ways to bring their children, siblings, or spouses to Korea to join them.

Starting in 2008, however, nearly every conversation I had with Peruvians in Korea or their families in Peru touched on the day's *tipo de cambio* or conversion rate between the Korean won and the US dollar and speculation about what it would mean for the families in Peru who depended on remittances. When I arrived in Peru in October 2008, the value of the dollar was plummeting, and people dependent on remittances felt it sharply. Migrant families who received remittances now had empty refrigerators, and a number of my interviewees from my time in Korea were deported and arrived in Peru while I was there (see chapter 2). When I arrived in Korea right before New Year's Eve, 2009 conversion rates were not only terrible, but unstable, and the worth of one million won fluctuated between $600 and $850. In my final trip, the value of the dollar had stabilized, but never returned to the rates of 2006. The biggest shift before and after the global financial crisis was that people had stopped hoping to be documented, and had started planning for an end that had an unpredictable date, but was now seen as inevitable.

In the years that followed these field trips, I have continued to interact with my interviewees through social media and Skype calls. My long-term engagement with the community gave me the advantage of seeing the rise and decline of the migration pattern and with it how migrants, their families, and the situation of Peru and South Korea changed over time. Although former migrants tell me it would be financially risky for them to try to migrate to Korea now, since they would most likely be turned away by immigration officers at the airport, it still comes up in people's plans. They say they would like to find a way to return.

In addition to participant observation and many casual interviews, I conducted formal interviews with seventy-five people in individual and group settings (fifty-six people in Korea and nineteen in Peru). I worked with about twenty key people in Peru and Korea who welcomed me into their homes and lives and also allowed me to formally interview them between two and five times, sometimes over the span of a decade and in multiple countries. In Korea, I interviewed and conducted participant observation with Peruvian migrants, international and Korean Catholic and Protestant church leaders working with migrants, three consuls general from the Peruvian embassy, and a member of the Korean Ministry of Justice

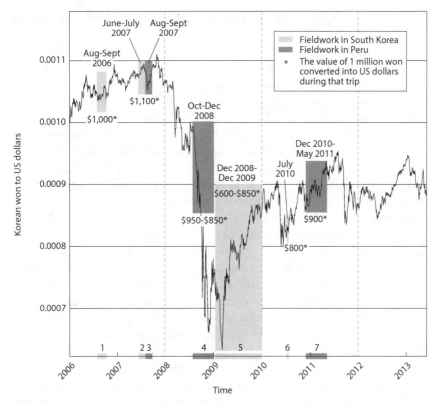

FIGURE 1. Methods and conversion rates: A timeline of my seven field trips (four to South Korea and three to Peru) superimposed on the conversion rate from Korean won to US dollars between 2006 and 2013. Note that my fourth and fifth trips coincided with some of the worst effects of the global financial crisis when the value of the dollar plunged and then fluctuated. Graph source: Fxtop.com.

working with the Employee Permit System. The majority of my fieldwork was in Seoul and four areas about 1–2 hours outside of Seoul by public transportation where Peruvian migrants lived and attended church.[57]

While in Peru, I interviewed and did participant observation with the family members of migrants in Korea including their parents, spouses, and children as well as numerous former migrants, some of whom I had met in Korea during previous trips and others who I met through snowball sampling in Peru. I worked with nine extended families who had family members in Korea. Six of the families lived in central Lima or in surrounding *pueblos jóvenes*, and three of the families lived 200 kilometers north of Lima in an area known as Norte Chico.[58] During two stays in Norte Chico I lived with the mother of a migrant I had met at a Catholic Mass in Korea. She kindly welcomed me into her home and introduced me to more interviewees in Norte Chico. In Lima, I lived in apartments in the area of

San Miguel, which provided a somewhat central base to reach families in different pueblos jóvenes.

Due to my previous experience of teaching in Korea, from the beginning of my project I had multiple points of contact with the Peruvian community. While my knowledge of Korean was useful, especially to navigate the area and contextualize the topics people discussed in Spanish or English, without my fluency in Spanish and long-term connection to Korea as an English teacher, I doubt I could have gained such a quick entry to this community and project.[59] The vast majority of my interviews and fieldwork took place in Spanish, as this was the preferred language of most of the Peruvians I met in Korea, although some of them knew English and/or Korean fairly well. Most of the Korean clergy and government officials I interviewed had studied in the United States and dealt with their international congregants or constituents in English, and we conducted interviews in that language. Each time I arrived in Korea, I met with old friends and found new contacts through snowball sampling and by hanging out in places where Peruvian migrants went in their free time, including salsa clubs and Latin American restaurants.[60]

The Catholic clergy working with Peruvian migrants, however, proved to be my most significant point of entry to the community. When I asked my Peruvian friends about who they went to for help, they all mentioned two names: Padre Ignacio, a French priest from the Migrant Help Center in Seoul, and Hermana Pilar, a nun from Spain.

I called Padre Ignacio, and by the next weekend I was traveling with him and Hermana Pilar on a bus on our way to the Spanish-language Mass in Dongducheon. Both spoke Korean and Spanish fluently (in addition to other languages) and between them had worked in Korea off and on since the 1970s.[61] They had long participated in the church's defense of laborer's rights—originally focusing on Korean laborers and now primarily helping foreign migrant workers.[62] In addition to running the Spanish-language desk of the Catholic Church's Migrant Help Center, they also offered spiritual services. Hermana Pilar was particularly beloved by migrants. As required by her order, every article of clothing that she wore was gray: her habit, her tennis shoes, and even her cell phone—a little flip phone that was always ringing at full volume. I could only imagine the kind of help people on the other end needed from her.[63] Over the years I saw that she and other Spanish-speaking Catholic clergy were the first point of contact not only for migrants but also for the Peruvian embassy and the Korean Immigration office dealing with Peruvian migrants. They connected migrants with lawyers, doctors, travel agents to get tickets home, jobs, and places to stay when they had nowhere to go. They helped families in Latin America track down incarcerated or detained migrants, and they knew inside information on immigration laws and policies. They also seemed to know nearly every person from Latin America living in Korea as well as any trouble those migrants experienced in Korea or had tried to leave behind in Peru—including bad marriages, debts, or drinking problems.

Throughout that summer and the following years, I accompanied them to the Masses they offered in areas with large Peruvian communities. Hermana Pilar asked me to write an article about my research for the monthly newsletter she published and circulated to migrants during Mass. The newsletter usually included a couple of pages of religious teachings (about things like marriage or Lent) and articles written by the clergy about the arrival or departure of Spanish-speaking clergy and religious or recreational retreats the community had taken to places like Seoul Grand Park. Each issue also had numerous articles written by migrants sharing their reactions to the retreats or their experiences of preparing for sacraments, like First Communion, in Korea. The back cover of the newsletter listed contact information for the clergy and the schedule of Masses and catechism classes in various communities for the upcoming month. From my March 2007 newsletter article, which asked those who were interested to contact me via email, as well as by attending weekly Masses and other church events, I met hundreds of migrants from Latin America—primarily from Peru, but also Bolivia, Colombia, Mexico, and Venezuela.

During the first Mass I attended with Hermana Pilar and Padre Ignacio in July 2006, we arrived to find about twenty people waiting to enter the church. There were numerous families at this Mass, including three families with school-aged children. In one family, the children worked in a factory with their parents, and in the other families, the children attended an American-run Christian school. As we walked in, I received a few smiles and looks of curiosity, but no one had time to ask who I was. It had taken us about two hours to get there via subway and bus from Seoul and we had arrived just in time to begin the Mass. As Padre Ignacio disappeared into a room by the altar to prepare, Hermana Pilar hugged a few of the members and paused to talk to a girl about her upcoming confirmation.

Hermana Pilar asked us to take a seat and reminded everyone to come forward when it was time to take communion. "You don't go to a party without food!" she joked, referring to the wafer and wine. Years later, Padre Diego, a priest from Colombia, told me that at the daily Masses he led for Korean people, nearly everyone took communion, but at the Spanish-language Masses for migrant workers, almost no one did. He thought it was because they felt guilty about not having confessed, about living with people who they were not married to, or for not having gone through their confirmation in Peru.

"Where is everyone?" Hermana Pilar asked once we were settled in the pews. There were hundreds of Peruvians who lived near Dongducheon, she had told me on the bus, but it was difficult to get them to show up to Mass. "Tell the others that Sundays are safe," she said. "Korean immigration has promised us they won't patrol on Sundays," she said.

This was the first and only time I heard her relay a promise of a "safe" Sunday. There seemed to be an implied respect for people going to church in this message from the immigration office. However, the reprieve must have been short-lived, because even that same summer, Peruvians I knew were detained and deported on Sundays while working or walking in their factory towns.

The fear of being detained by immigration officers—even as surveillance became more intense over the years of my fieldwork—did not stop people from living their lives. After Hermana Pilar asked again where everyone was, one man finally cleared his throat and said, "There is a big soccer tournament today." Hermana Pilar looked annoyed but did not comment. Later, I accompanied friends to some of the nonchurch events held in Dongducheon, including all-day soccer tournaments that started over beer and food at one of the area's migrant-owned Peruvian restaurants and finished at one of its Latin nightclubs.

Hermana Pilar then introduced me to the group. I stood up and smiled nervously as everyone stared at me. She told them that I was an anthropologist from the United States who was doing research about the Peruvian community in Korea. "She is not here to turn you in to immigration," she said straightforwardly. Then she said, "She is going to Peru next year too. If you want to share your stories, or give her your contact information, please say hello after Mass." Detecting basically no reaction from the crowd, I sat down awkwardly. I hoped I could at least meet one or two people before we returned to Seoul.

After Mass nearly everyone stayed to talk with me. The families and couples at the Mass had gathered on some benches near the church to wait for me as I left with the clergy. It was dark, and the muggy summer night was thick with mosquitos and the screams of cicadas in the trees around us. The parishioners had saved me a seat in the middle of the bench, and when I sat down they began asking me questions. They were curious about why I was there, and why I cared about Peruvian migration in particular. When I told them about my project and explained that I had also worked in Korea as a teacher, they embraced me as a fellow foreigner in a strange land. Almost like a ritual, at this and other first meetings I had after Masses, immediately everyone wanted to exchange stories of the trials and tribulations of living in Korea. "Have you been here during the winter?" they asked. Then they would tell me their arrival stories and describe arriving at Gimpo Airport in January when it was minus 9 degrees Celsius; they told me they were dressed in the lightweight clothes they had previously considered to be "winter" clothes in Lima (where a typical low winter temperature was 17 degrees Celsius). "What do you think of Korean food?" they would ask. When I said that I liked it, most shook their heads in disbelief and said they thought it was inedible. "*Demasiado ají!* [too spicy!]," they said. Then one person would say they liked some kinds of kimchi, or *gamjatang* (a spicy pork and potato soup), or appreciated that Koreans ate a lot of vegetables, and others would agree.

"I was so surprised when you read the prayer in Spanish!" one of the older men told me, referring to the prayer Hermana Pilar had asked me to read during the Mass.[64] Few non–Latin American foreigners they met in Korea spoke Spanish. "The Filipinos speak a little Spanish!" one woman told me. A few Filipinas who had Spanish-speaking boyfriends from the nearby US military base attended their Masses. They were happy that I spoke Spanish, albeit with an accent. "It's not an American accent, though," they said reassuringly. Then they tried to figure out what kind of accent it was. "French? Italian?" I told them that my family was not from Latin America, but that I had learned Spanish in college and spoke it at home with Omar, who was soon to be my husband.

They wanted their stories to be told and were happy that I was interested in hearing them. Their legal instability added to the urgency with which they wanted to talk to me. More than anything, they were frustrated with being regarded as unimportant. They saw themselves as contributing to the Korean economy and as examples of successful migrants, yet their presence was both ignored and actively challenged in Korea and Peru.

From this meeting and others like it I received invitations from migrants to visit their homes, spend the night at their factories, and attend their church- and non-church-related events, including soccer games, parties, and shopping trips. Catholic migrants later introduced me to the Protestant community, and people from both groups asked me to visit their families in Peru.

In Peru, I spent much of my time hanging out with families in one of the most visible examples of Korea I found: family homes or businesses built with remittances. We also spent many hours preparing Mexican and Peruvian meals together, shopping, communicating with their family members in Korea with online messaging and over the phone, and attending special events, such as birthday parties and block parties.

In Korea, I visited numerous churches with Peruvian members, but eventually I focused on three: the Spanish-speaking Catholic community, Friendship Foreign Ministry (a small community mission outside of Seoul), and Nazarene (Ximena's megachurch in Seoul). I concentrated on these groups because while the members from these churches knew one another and sometimes interacted, they all had different attitudes toward the significance of their migrations, their religious participation or conversions in Korea, and their responsibilities toward Peru and toward their families, especially after the global financial crisis hit.

Although both Friendship and Nazarene shared many similarities, they also had important differences. First, even though Friendship was a nondenominational mission church, it was affiliated with some of the most powerful (and rich) mainstream evangelical Protestant churches in South Korea. So, while the members were migrant workers, they had regular contact with Korean church members who would visit with food and clothing donations and would also help migrants access scholarships from more economically powerful churches located around the world. In contrast, Nazarene was a megachurch, and Peruvians attended the main service with Koreans (seated in a specially designated foreigner section listening to simultaneous translation delivered via headsets) and then retreated to a smaller hall where they held a separate service entirely in Spanish. Nazarene was

Presbyterian, but the founder was a charismatic Korean pastor whose views and teachings were admired by the Nazarene Peruvians and seen as extreme by some of the other churches I worked with.[65]

To learn more about these three churches, their infrastructures, and their current and future plans for serving or working with their congregations of Peruvian migrants, I interviewed Peruvian members and their leaders, read documents and pamphlets produced for and by Peruvian migrants, and regularly attended services, Bible studies, and special events. Each church was based in Korea but had differing levels of transnational ties. All the churches had launched missions to the Peru-based hometowns of their respective congregants.[66] This included the Catholic Church. The day I arrived in Korea in 2008, I called Hermana Pilar to see if we could meet. She told me she was actually on her way to the airport to leave for Norte Chico, where her order had decided she should relocate and set up a new chapter. In Lima, I joined a few families as they attended their churches, including one of the mission churches started by Friendship members who were former migrant workers trained to be pastors. This helped me to compare churchgoing in Korea with churchgoing in Peru in order to see how the transnational churches adapted to a Peruvian framework.

MY RECEPTION AND POSITIONALITY
IN THE FIELD(S)

Since I moved among so many different sites, families, and churches in Korea and Peru, there was a lot of variation in how others saw me and how I tried to position myself over time. My reception as a researcher and an American was different in Peru than it was in Korea. Whereas in Korea, Peruvians treated me as a fellow foreigner or potential member of a church, in Peru I was mostly welcomed as the friend of their family member in Korea, but I was also distanced because of my foreignness and class status. When I told families that I was staying in the middle-class area of San Miguel they were shocked I could afford something so expensive. In contrast, when I told other researchers in Lima where I was staying, they seemed shocked I would venture out of the tourist-friendly area of Miraflores. Many of the families I met in Lima owned taxis and offered to give me rides to and from their houses, or to my next interviews. However, I frequently found myself trying to figure out if I should pay for these rides or treat them as a favor. Some families happily accepted (and expected) a flat daily fee; others refused (and looked offended) when I asked if I could give them some gas money. In the end I tried to take *colectivo* buses or combis instead of taxis to avoid this dance, during which I always felt I had taken some kind of misstep.

I married Omar, who is from Mexico City, in the United States in between my trips to Korea and Peru in 2007, and he accompanied me on most of my subsequent field trips to Peru and Korea. I mention that because I noticed that being married to

Omar changed the ways people treated me. Before getting married, people seemed curious about my motivations for traveling alone and conducting research—I was asked more than once about whether I would consider marrying someone to help them get a green card. However, after Omar came with me to the field, it seemed to make my personal life less a topic of interest and my presence less suspicious. He was popular among my Peruvian interviewees; they told us they loved Mexico, having felt a familiarity with it from *telenovelas*, and some migrants had been there on their way to Korea or other destinations. Whenever he accompanied me to an interview, the opening conversation was invariably about Mexican food, and if he did not come, the opening conversation was asking when he was coming to visit.

My foreign accent in Spanish also carried a different meaning in Peru than it did in Korea. In Peru, on a few occasions after calling the numbers my contacts in Korea had given me for their family homes, the person on the other end hung up on me after hearing my voice, thinking I was trying to scam them. Not only were migration-related phone scams common, but also a few people had already been scammed out of thousands of dollars while arranging their trips to Korea. After emailing my contacts in Korea to confirm that their family members wanted to speak with me, someone from the family would call me back, welcome me to their homes for meals and stories, and often treat me like a friend or daughter.

Being treated like a daughter had its benefits and drawbacks, however. Although I was welcomed into Peruvian homes and included in family events, people were worried about my safety to the point that they did not want me to walk outside alone. In fact, while staying in Norte Chico, my hostess would only let me go outside "alone" if I was in the company of one of her granddaughters—girls who were nine and twelve years old at the time. My nine-year-old chaperone provided an excellent narrated tour of the places I wanted to go—especially places she frequently went, like the local bakery to pick up rolls for our dinner—but limited my ability to explore new leads in fieldwork. My freedom of movement increased dramatically on my second and third trips when Omar came with me to Peru. I either brought him with me when I went out, or told people that I had so they did not worry about me. However, the families in the pueblos jóvenes were also worried about his safety there as a foreign man. Petty thefts were common. They would give us specific instructions regarding which streets to walk down and which to avoid. Nothing ever happened to us, but we witnessed a few robberies in Lima. In one instance we were in a taxi, stuck in traffic, when a group of men began walking among the idling cars and combis. They tried to get on a combi, but the driver locked the door in time. Then they turned to the taxi directly in front of us, reached through the open passenger window and grabbed the purse of the woman who was sitting inside. They ran off with the bag, and I was reminded of the warnings about this very crime that I had heard from my Peruvian friends in Korea. This—and more serious violent crimes they told me had escalated in Peru after the global financial crisis—is what they meant when they said they preferred Korea's safety and calmness, even though they were constantly in danger of being detained by immigration officers and deported.

In Korea, I also found difficulties in focusing on three different churches simultaneously. First, logistically, it was somewhat difficult to balance attending three different main church services, all of which primarily met on Sunday and were dispersed around Gyeonggi Province. However, with planning I could attend two in one day: one in the morning and one in the afternoon. Second, I was treated either as an honorary member or potential member at each of these churches, and so I sometimes felt like I was betraying one group over the other.

Although I told everyone the purpose of my research, seeing me participating in so many different groups sometimes raised suspicions about what I was doing. For example, after Mass one Sunday, a few members of the congregation, as well as two priests and three nuns from Latin America, gathered in a room at the back of the church to share the meal of *ají de gallina* [a spicy Peruvian chicken stew served with white rice]. I was helping her serve the food on paper plates when one of the nuns looked around and asked where Antonio, one of the men who had been at the Mass, had gone. A few people laughed and said they had seen him get on his moped and drive off to "the other church" [the Protestant Friendship Ministry] right after service.

"People really go there?" one of the nuns asked in disbelief. "Why?"

A parishioner commented that she had heard they served a large Korean meal after services and hinted that they had cute Vietnamese members who Miguel might want to meet. Then she paused and said, "Well, we should ask Erica. She goes there."

The whole room turned to me with surprised looks on their faces as if to say, *You do?*

After a moment, I said, "Yes. I am a spy," and they all laughed and continued chatting.

I had been joking, but as an anthropologist, I could not help but feel a little like a spy. I kept notes on what everyone did and said and what they thought of each other. Not only did I have notes on what they thought at the time, but I could compare them with notes I kept on what they had said years prior. I knew what their parents thought of their conversions or migrations. I visited their children when they could not. Further, in interviews I conducted with different Peruvian consuls general over the years, I nearly always personally knew the "anonymous" cases they described to me with regard to things their constituents had done, including being arrested for drug use, and the man who had sought asylum in the Peruvian embassy on the basis of being gay. I learned that his request was denied, but the consul general had felt bad about not being able to help him. Each story I heard or took part in was a moment for me to enhance my research and a moment where I faced a moral choice: Do I admit I already know a little of this story, or pretend that I do not? Do I wait to see if the story unfolds on its own, or do I ask for more information? Selectively withholding information was crucial to protecting people who trusted me with their stories.

Further, as an academic from the United States, I felt conflicted about the numerous forms of mobility I had that my interlocutors lacked. Not only could I move around Korea without fear of being detained and deported, but as long as I received grants and was able to put remaining expenses on credit cards, I could also move between the destinations they wanted to go—Korea, Peru, and the United States—without becoming stuck because of a lack of visas or money. Additionally, as I moved among groups, I found myself shifting my class association, religious orientation, and loyalties, by choosing to speak up or stay silent on different issues, including my own politics and (lack of) religious beliefs. George Marcus notes that ethnographers doing multisited fieldwork become "circumstantial activists" who must navigate situations where "the politics and ethics of working in any one reflects on work in the others." This, as he points out, "generates a definite sense of doing more than just ethnography."[67] The various mobilities that I experienced were crucial to conducting my research but also troubling.

Despite my own misgivings about feeling like a spy, I was still surprised when Ximena confessed to me that there were rumors circulating at Nazarene that I was an *actual* spy in the employ of a smaller church. When she canceled a couple of lunch meetings with me, I had not thought anything of it because last-minute arbeits often came up. However, one afternoon when I ran into her in the subway station near her house, she held back tears as she told me that her Peruvian pastor at Nazarene had forbidden the congregation from seeing me. Apparently, the pastor had left this smaller church without saying where he had gone and thought I had been sent to collect intel on the new church, and perhaps even turn in the congregation to immigration. Eventually this rumor was cleared up when Imelda, a woman I had met while living in Norte Chico the year before, migrated to Korea and joined Nazarene. After she vouched for me, I was included in more church events, but never became a favorite of the pastor.

Finally, although I tried to be forthcoming with everyone about not being religious, I had to creatively and delicately respond to ongoing questions of how my faith was developing. After all, I had been attending church with them for years. With Catholics and members of Friendship, my religious beliefs were rarely the focus of any discussion. I participated in church services, and occasionally they would ask me to interpret a piece of scripture, but no one ever sat me down and asked me to explain my religious beliefs. They also did not evangelize to me. Only after years of knowing them did the Peruvian leaders at Friendship say that I had been attending church long enough that it was about time I started to convert or at least share my experiences of conversion. However, with the members of Nazarene, my religious beliefs, and my knowledge of theirs, was a central topic of conversation. When I told them about the purpose of my research, they told me that I was wasting my time trying to study them when I should really be studying the gospel. When I explained my fieldwork, they explained *their* fieldwork, literally their *trabajo de campo*, where they went to places like Dongducheon and evangelized to other Spanish speakers. I would ask to conduct interviews, and people would invite me to their houses or a café and pull out a piece of paper or even a whiteboard with markers and explain the gospel to me for an hour. They were surprised when I listened and even took notes and asked questions for clarification. "Americans are arrogant," I heard more than once. "But you are not as arrogant as most of them." I tried to take that as a compliment. At one extreme, some members of Nazarene saw me as a *respuesta*, literally an answer to the prayers they had been making in church for months for a Spanish to English translator, whereas others, primarily their Peruvian pastor, saw me as a problematic interloper, at best wanting to study them, at worst trying to get them deported.[68] After a few months, some of the women I spent a lot of time with—hanging out at their homes, cooking together, participating in prayer circles—were happy to tell other church members about the signs that I was successfully converting, because as Susan Harding points out, "If you are seriously willing to listen to the gospel, you have begun to convert."[69] The more I listened, the more I found that their own experiences of conversion, and their interests in converting others, were intertwined with every aspect of their lives, both as migrants in Korea and with their families in Peru, and that was part of the transnational story I had been looking for.

CHAPTER OUTLINE

Chapter 1 investigates why Peruvians wanted to come to Korea, and what was happening in Korea to both welcome and exclude them. I include ethnographic data of migrant arrival stories in Korea as well as provide historical context about migration and churches in Peru and South Korea.

Chapter 2 discusses money conversion and remittances and how, during the global financial crisis, migrants had less money to send than ever before. I also show migrants' efforts to temper their economic and social remittances in the hope of transforming their family members into people who could thrive with fewer remittances and become more self-supporting.

Chapter 3 explores religious conversion and discusses the significance of South Korea to undocumented Peruvians with respect to accelerating these conversions and infusing them with the potential to change one's status. In particular, I focus on how migrants attempted to convert themselves and others as well as to recast their migration as being less about the pursuit of money and more about actions predestined by God and identified through respuestas.

Chapter 4 focuses on cosmopolitan conversion, and on how looming departures inspired people to make new plans and connections with others that helped them to defy their statuses and create unique transnational worlds. I discuss how developing these projects in Korea placed them at the convergence of cosmopolitan conversion projects led by the state, churches, and other people in transit, which resulted in migrants both transcending and becoming entangled in barriers and new identities.

In the epilogue, I summarize and bridge my key points and present stories of what migrants do after they leave Korea to discuss how cosmopolitan conversions and plans cannot fail because they are continually emerging.

1

Peru, South Korea, Peru . . .

"They have the Bangladeshi," Karina said. She had been at work but came rushing in to the small cottage where she lived to tell us that immigration officers were raiding the area. This was the second time in one day that the area had been raided. "I had to run from my factory earlier today and hide in the house for two hours," she told me.

Everyone in the house—including her father and five other Peruvian men who had gathered to talk to me about their lives in Korea—started making calls on their cell phones. They were trying to contact the other Peruvians in the area to find out the location of the officers and determine whether the Bangladeshi man was someone they knew. "*Pasa la voz,*" they said to the people on the other end. Spread the word. Hide or run.

It was nine on a Thursday night in August 2007 and pitch-black outside the one-bedroom cottage Karina shared with her father, Victor, in a semirural area on the outskirts of Seoul. The hills around us were dotted with small factories about the size of temporary buildings used in American schools. These factories each employed a handful of Korean and foreign workers and produced things like mannequins, candles, small plastic products, and cardboard boxes. Some of the foreign workers were documented, but many others, like the Peruvians in this room, were not.

I had met the father and daughter pair a few weeks before at the Spanish-language Mass provided once a month for the Peruvian migrants working in this town. They had invited me to come over and see where they worked, and also to meet other Peruvians who worked in the area. They were from a pueblo joven in

Lima, and Victor was a central figure in the Peruvian Catholic community, having been in Korea since 1995, longer than many other Peruvians who were still there. For the past few days his factory had been working on a rush order, and he looked very tired. He was going to return to work that night after I left. In her early twenties, Karina was a cheerful person who was well loved by the Catholic clergy. She regularly cooked Peruvian food in the kitchen in their house and brought it to Mass to share with the other parishioners. I am not sure if that idea was hers or the nuns' to encourage attendance at the Mass. I asked her where she got hard-to-find ingredients like cilantro and *ají amarillo,* a yellow chili used in many Peruvian recipes. She told me she either substituted local ingredients, such as Korean green chili peppers, or had her mother send her spices in the mail. She got cilantro from a Bangladeshi man who had a small farm and store nearby. She cooked most of the food she and her father ate, as neither of them particularly liked the Korean meals provided for free at their workplaces—usually spicy kimchi, a clear soup, and rice.

Their stand-alone house with a full-size kitchen was not a typical place for migrant workers to live. Most of the other migrants I met rented small apartments or lived rent free in shipping containers located inside their factory walls. This house had been the factory owners' residence before they moved their family to a newer apartment in a better location. Victor was quick to point out that his Korean employers did not do anything for him out of kindness—and that included letting them live here. Factory owners were charged a fine of twenty million won per undocumented worker they were caught employing. It was in both the workers' and factories' best interests that the migrants remain hidden and continue working.

This cottage was in the shape of a square and divided into two rooms: a kitchen and a living space they used for sleeping and relaxing. The wood-paneled walls were decorated with things like a free calendar from the local bank and large framed photos of Karina and her sister and brother at different ages. Karina's younger siblings were in Peru with their mother. Victor hadn't seen his son in person since he was a newborn.

We were all sitting in the living space, which had two twin beds on opposite walls, a TV, and a computer with an internet connection. When I asked Victor if he was able to communicate with his wife and children in Peru, he said, "Almost every day. And we have a camera." He explained that this was a huge advance in the available technology from when he first arrived and had to wait in a long line to use the only pay phone in the area.

"When I first got here it cost 5,000 won for a phone card and you could only talk for ten minutes, or even three minutes if it was a bad card," he said. "There would be like ten or fifteen [foreigners] in line waiting to talk on the phone. Sometimes there were fights. [Other foreigners and Koreans] abused the Peruvians and even hit them," he said. "[When I first arrived] this area was all Bangladeshis. They didn't want to have any other foreigners. It was bad. The Peruvians decided to have a meeting. We decided to walk together in a group to demonstrate that we weren't alone. To show that there were a lot of Peruvians here."

"It doesn't seem like I have been here that long because the weeks go by so fast," Victor said.

Victor and his friends sat on the floor, on kitchen chairs, and on the beds. Karina leaned against the door frame and occasionally disappeared into the kitchen to answer her cell phone. I was sitting in front of everyone on the swivel computer chair Victor had offered me when I arrived.

"You need that chair so you can take notes," Aldo, one of Victor's friends, said. He was a serious man who did not speak much, at least around me. His comment indicated to me the importance he was placing on this meeting. Everyone in the room looked exhausted from having worked all day in their respective factories. At their insistence we had begun the interview, but our conversation kept pausing as phone calls came in with updates.

During one of the pauses in conversation, I turned to Victor, who sat calmly on the floor. "People are outside right now?" I asked him quietly, imagining armed men blanketing the hills and winding roads. This was my second month of fieldwork, and one of the first times I had visited migrants in their home. I felt dread at the thought that everyone here might get caught because they had gathered in one place to talk to me. We had already rescheduled this meeting twice. Why did I have to come today?

"They are on the next hill over," Victor reassured me. "If they come over here, we can turn the lights out." As he had alluded, there did not seem to be anything more substantial than darkness separating us from the officers. We were close enough to see the glowing eyes of the dogs protecting the factories scattered among the hills, structures not much bigger than the house we were in now.

I had arrived by bus from Seoul around dusk. Victor's friend Javier had picked me up from the bus stop on his moped. In the fading light, I had seen that the road leading from the main street to the factories was dotted with low walls made of stone and concrete that divided the small farms and factories. After driving for about ten minutes and deftly avoiding the arms of lush foliage that reached out over the walls into the road, Javier parked the moped. He led me up a steep dirt path to the house. Big flying insects I had never seen in the city hit me in the face and buzzed by my ears. Victor's factory and house were adjacent to each other, and between them was a stack of boxlike cages holding five dogs, all of whom barked furiously at us as we passed. They ranged in size from what looked like large Korean jindo mixes to tiny lap dogs. Ernesto, a Peruvian man who lived in Seoul, but who had insisted on joining us for this meeting, laughed when I stopped to look at them.

"Don't you know, [the Koreans] are going to eat them when they get a little bigger," he said. I looked back at the dogs skeptically—especially the little Maltese mix.

Javier ignored Ernesto's comment and told us that the dogs were set up outside the factory along with security cameras to alert workers when immigration officers, or other people, approached.

Now as I sat in the small cottage, hoping the dogs outside would not start barking, I remembered naively thinking that they and the terrain had seemed quaint to me earlier in the day.

Javier told me raids like this were frequent here.

"Last week immigration officers parked at the mouth of that road and just waited for foreigners to come down the hill," he said. At the time there was a single road that ran above and below the hilly area where everyone lived and worked. That road was the only way to get out of town, or reach the town's churches, restaurants, and small local supermarket.

"We called friends and they told us 'Don't go to the church to hide! ¡Pasa la voz! Because there were three combis of immigration officers waiting right in front of the church," Javier told me. "We could see the flashing red lights from their vehicles all the way up here" he said. "[Immigration officers] are very abusive. They hit people in the head with big sticks."

They described how plainclothes officers would walk along the streets and grab people as they shopped or waited for the bus in front of the church.

"The bus stop in front of the Catholic Church is actually the most dangerous place in town!" Karina said.

"Why did you ask me to wait there?" I asked, thinking about the extra danger Javier had faced by driving his moped there. "I could have waited somewhere else."

"It's safe for you!" Karina said, smiling.

Paulo, who was sitting on the floor, told me about how his friend had been detained right at that bus stop. "She looked like a regular, nice, Korean lady," he said, describing the plainclothes officer who had caught his friend. "She said hello, and when he responded, she grabbed him."

They told me that during raids officers wore "sticky gloves," which they described as work gloves that were coated with a substance that increased their grip. With these sticky gloves, an officer could grab a person's shoulder from behind—even someone who was running away—and pull them to the ground.

Angel, a man who worked with Victor, told me about his own near deportation. It was one Sunday when he was grocery shopping. Officers had parked paddy wagons on the main road and loaded them up with the people they detained over the course of the day. "I heard a Filipino man just screaming and crying from inside the paddy wagon," he said. Angel had hidden in time, but had to watch as his neighbors were taken away.

I could feel my own anxiety rise as we sat there. I was waiting for what seemed like an inevitable knock at the door, but hoping none would come.

"How long can you take the stress of this?" I asked.

"Until we get deported," Javier said frankly.

Then Aldo spoke up again. "Two years ago it was so peaceful here. Immigration was a rarity, once in a long time."

Both he and Victor had been in Korea for twelve years, spending all but the first three months—when they had valid tourist stamps in their passports—without legal status. They told me that prior to the IMF, the streets of their rural town were full of people from all over the world—including groups of Peruvians. Sometimes over a hundred Peruvians would gather from all over to Korea for activities like soccer tournaments, *parrilladas* (barbeques), and *polladas* (events where people sell grilled chicken to raise money for a particular cause, such as a new baby or a person in immigration detention who needed a plane ticket home). However, they now dealt with the reality of immigration officers watching them from the roads above and below their factories and homes, waiting until the right moment to detain and deport them.

When I reviewed my field notes from this night, I was struck by how it was filled with both moments of normalcy and fear. Discussions of food, people's first impressions of Korea, and their expressions of pride for their jobs were interlaced with phone calls and warnings of imminent danger. Their need to be invisible—keep the lights out and stay hidden to remain in Korea—was put into relief by their stories of being visible and making their mark on the streets of their rural area. Victor and Aldo's daily lives in Korea had changed dramatically since they had arrived, and that experience was inextricable from the turbulent political and economic situation of Peru and South Korea between the 1980s and the first decade of the 2000s.

In this chapter I explore the ways migrants' journeys and travel itineraries overlapped and converged with the global plans and political economies of Peru and South Korea to discuss how the migration pattern began and has been nearly stopped—all while remaining fairly unknown outside a few sending and receiving communities. I present various arrival stories of Peruvian migrants to discuss how the trajectory of people's lives and plans changed within this unstable transnational context and depending on the ways they interacted with global plans of the Korean state and various churches as well as others they met along the way. I pay particular attention to the ways Peruvian migrants experienced the effects of the Employee Permit System, the push for multiculturalism, and practices and policies that gained traction as a result of Korea's rising numbers of foreign migrants. I argue that by migrating to Korea and continuing to participate in life there and transnationally in Peru despite facing multiple barriers, they created and elucidated transnational ties between the two countries, and in turn changed the significance and value of Korea in Peru. However, since they did this while under multiple forms of surveillance, they had to negotiate between constantly changing levels of freedom and fear and inclusion and exclusion, which resulted in the creation of uneven transnational spaces and ties, and changes to the significance of their migration.

The geography of the worlds and transnational ties migrants created is most visible in Norte Chico, the area where many Peruvians in Korea originated from, as well as, at least symbolically, in Dongducheon, an imagined Korean-based hometown for many Peruvians. I present scenes from those areas to talk about how while the migration from Peru to Korea was not well known in either country, it becomes visible and takes on meaning when placed at the neighborhood level and can be compared to other migrations, experiences, or even tangible evidence of migration such as homes or businesses catering to or built by migrant families.

ARRIVAL STRATEGIES AND ITINERARIES: 1990s TO 2000s

Immigration officers never came to Karina and Victor's house that night. When calls came in from their friends in town confirming that the officers had left, and no one they knew had been detained, everyone appeared to relax, including me.

The people gathered in Victor's house started to tell me about their migration journeys and the strategies they had taken to successfully pass as tourists at the Korean airport. The people who had arrived in the mid-1990s, like Victor, had a much different arrival experience than those who came later, like Victor's daughter Karina, who had arrived in 2003. These differences were due to their varying levels of knowledge about Korea, changes to the Korean economy, and also the changing profile of Peruvians and other foreigners in Korea.

"It was easy for me to get in, but now it's really controlled," Victor said. He had arrived at Seoul's Gimpo Airport on the same plane with twenty other Peruvians who were all looking for work. "Now, many people are unable to get in and have to go back to Peru. But some also just change their last names and try again," Victor said.

What he meant was that in the mid-1990s, the migrant population in Korea was relatively new, and it was fairly easy for Peruvians to enter by posing as tourists. Since Peru has a visa waiver agreement with South Korea, Peruvian citizens do not need to apply for a separate tourist visa prior to arrival, but instead they are given a three-month tourist stamp in their passports on entry. Peruvians were not the only migrant group in Korea to do this, and overstaying three-month tourist visas is common for groups with many undocumented workers like Nigerians and Filipinos.[1] However, Peru was one of the few countries in South America with a visa-waiver agreement with South Korea. This was one reason that I met a few Bolivians and Colombians who were working as undocumented laborers, but their numbers were tiny in comparison to the large community of Peruvians.

In order to get past the immigration checkpoint in the airport and receive a tourist visa, passengers have to prove they are actually tourists and not intending to find work and overstay. To present themselves as "authentic" tourists, many people told me they had worn their best clothes to go through immigration and tried to carry at least $1,000 in cash, which they called their *bolsa de viaje* (travel money). Although this money was supposed to prove they had sufficient funds to support themselves while visiting South Korea, most migrants feared having to actually spend this money. That is because they had usually borrowed it, along with money for their plane ticket and broker's fee, from family members, friends, or moneylenders prior to leaving Peru. The hope was to find a job on arrival and never have to touch the bolsa de viaje. Anticipation over whether a migrant would successfully pass through immigration and thereby be able to repay their travel debts figured into nearly every arrival story I heard.

Aldo, who arrived in the mid-1990s, described how for the people on his flight, the stress of arriving and not knowing if they would be admitted was both a shared and isolating experience. "There were fifty Peruvians on my plane," he said. "When we left Peru, everyone was dressed normally. Then the closer we got to Seoul, they went to the bathroom one by one and came out nicely dressed. In the plane we were friends, but when we arrived, the friendship disappeared," Aldo continued. "It was like a bomb exploded. Everyone ignored each other, and just looked for the best [immigration] window."

Most everyone I met who had arrived in the 1990s mentioned there was a good chance most of the Peruvians on a given flight would be permitted to enter Korea. This was perhaps because immigration officers did not yet know that Peruvians were most likely intending migrants. Similarly, Peruvian migrants who wanted to migrate to Korea in the 1990s also did not know much about the country, which set them up to be easily preyed on by people looking to profit from their partial knowledge.

In my research I found that the majority of Peruvians who arrived before the 1997 IMF (discussed briefly later in this chapter) had learned about Korea through unscrupulous brokers, and in undertaking their trip they were each scammed out of between $1,000 and $4,000. While countries like Nepal had organized systems of recruiters that charged migrants fees for help in getting employment visas to Korea, the brokers in Peru were laypeople who had no actual ability to secure visas and often had no real job contacts for their recruits.[2] Many of these brokers either had connections to earlier migrations to Japan or had just been lucky enough to hear about Korea before their neighbors. They took advantage of the lack of awareness in Peru about Korea, and the excitement about migrating to Japan, to get people to pay them for basic or false information.

Angel, who was from Norte Chico, said, "In Peru we didn't know anything about Korea. There were people who had been in Korea and these people took advantage of the situation to bring people to work there. They brought us in a group. They tricked us. I met a woman of Japanese descent who told us that she was with a job agency in Korea. 'You know about Korea, don't you?' she asked us. We had to pay her $3,000 for the paperwork [and $1,700 for the ticket]. Well the day came to travel, we got to Korea and found out everything was a lie."

"There was no job?" I asked.

"No, she only *knew* a man who worked here. This guy sold accessories in the street. She knew him but there wasn't any job at all. She took us to a hotel in Chongno-3ga and left us there. It was November. We didn't know the language, and we didn't know anything about Korea. And we didn't even know what the food was. The only food we had was *Kentucky* [Kentucky Fried Chicken]; breakfast, dinner, and lunch was *Kentucky*. This was our food. We didn't know!" he said laughing.

"Can you stomach *Kentucky* now?" I asked, laughing.

"I still like it for a special occasion," he said, smiling.[3]

"Were all the other people still with you?" I asked.

"Yes," he said. "There were six of us. We were waiting for a contact to give us work. We waited for one week. We realized that our money was running out. We had a *bolsa de viaje* that was very small. It was hardly anything at all, so we decided to find a hostel. There we met Iranians and other foreigners. Americans working as teachers too. We were there only one day because the atmosphere was very dangerous. People came and went. We were afraid we would get something stolen. But there we met a Peruvian. And he told us about [this town]."

Victor was also scammed by a broker he met in his pueblo joven who promised to get him a visa and job for a fee. "I paid him $4,000 before we left Peru. He told us we would make $1,000 USD a month. But in the end, it was actually one million won, which at that time was [worth much less]." Only after Victor arrived in Seoul did he realize they were getting a free tourist visa through the visa waiver agreement, not a work visa. He worked at that job for a few days before finding a new job through word of mouth.

Many Peruvians told me they eventually heard about reliable work through chance encounters with other Peruvians on the street or public transportation. These new friends would tell them where factories with lots of Peruvians were— sometimes insisting on a broker's fee in exchange for this information. In fact, one man I talked to in Norte Chico laughed when he told me a man who had told him about a factory job fifteen years prior was still trying to collect a large broker's fee from him. Neither of them had been in Korea for years.

Those who were able to find employment despite these scams were only able to work a couple of years before the Asian financial crisis shook the economy. Factories closed and migrants lost their jobs. Many Peruvians left, but according to one of my interviewees, some nearly starved to death trying to remain in Korea until the economy recovered.

When the Korean economy recovered in the 2000s, however, the Peruvian community grew bigger than ever before. For those who arrived in the 2000s, their arrival stories were usually more about chain migration and family reunifications and less about scams and brokers. However, since undocumented migrant workers were gaining visibility in Korea, it also became much harder to successfully pass through immigration as a tourist. As a result, migrant lay expertise about how to enter Korea grew during this time. In his work about migrants crossing the US-Mexico border, anthropologist Jason De León found that migrants and merchants developed their own technologies to evade the US government's vast surveillance technologies. He points out that these migrant strategies—such as painting water bottles black to avoid detection or rubbing garlic on one's shoes to avoid snake-bites—persist despite lacking empirical evidence of their success.[4] Peruvians also drew on their own migration journeys and their growing knowledge of Korea to develop creative strategies and technologies to help their family members coun-teract surveillance at the airport and successfully pass as tourists—but with incon-sistent results.

For example, on her father's advice, Karina had memorized a few phrases in English—about where she was from, or sites in Korea she was planning to visit—to prove she was prepared to travel internationally. Some travelers even made fake reservations at hotels—like the Hamilton in Itaewon—or bought tickets to upcoming events, such as the 2002 World Cup. These strategies did not always work, though, and intending migrants who failed to pass as tourists were refused entry, handcuffed, and forced to wait in a room in the airport, sometimes for days, until there was an available flight home.

Karina told us about her experience of nearly being turned away. "I didn't think I was going to make it through," she said. Like many other Peruvians, Karina had strategically planned her arrival in the Korean fall or winter months, hoping that immigration officers would be more lenient or understaffed during the holidays of Chuseok and Lunar New Year. November to January were warm summer months in Peru, so another commonality was that people arriving at that time were largely unprepared for the harsh Korean winter. For example, a woman from Norte Chico told me that the hotel owner where she first went in Seoul, shocked to see her arrive in the jeans and light jacket that she had considered to be "winter clothes" in Peru, gave her some clothes to wear from her own closet.

Upon advice from her dad, Karina had bought a two-week round-trip ticket instead of a ticket for the full three months allowed for someone coming as a tour-ist. She told us she thought this strategy had worked in her favor for passing as a tourist.

"There were five other Peruvian girls on the flight, and I think only two had real reasons for being there. The rest of us were planning to overstay," she said. She picked an immigration line and ended up being the very last person from her flight to get to an immigration officer. All the other girls got through with no prob-lem, but Karina got sent to a secondary check station—a back room where she had to answer more in-depth questions about her trip. She had heard this meant she would probably be refused entry. The immigration officers wanted to talk to the person who was going to pick her up. There was a Spanish translator in the room and Karina finally gave him Victor's phone number.

"I was waiting at the airport and was getting more and more nervous," Victor said. People from her flight had stopped coming out, but Karina still hadn't appeared. My phone rang and it was immigration!" They wanted to know his name and relation to her. He said that Karina was his friend's daughter and that he had agreed to take care of her because the friend had been so good to him before in Korea. They finally let her through, and she had been working at her factory ever since.

PLANS FOR MIGRANTS IN SOUTH KOREA:
THE EMPLOYEE PERMIT SYSTEM AND
MULTICULTURALISM

The differences in Peruvian arrival stories from the 1990s and 2000s reflected massive changes happening in South Korea during this time. As the economy improved in the late 1980s, the number of foreigners in Korea rose. Over the next twenty years, the state developed various surveillance and control mechanisms in the form of migration policies and multicultural programs. As atypical migrant workers in Korea, Peruvians were both included in and excluded from these policies, which resulted in them having experiences like that night at Victor and Karina's house—filled with both freedom and danger.

In comparison to the other migrant-receiving nations, Korea has had a relatively short experience of migration. The Korean economy was not in the position to receive labor until they had an increase in exports after hosting the 1988 Olympics. Prior to this, South Korea had been a labor-exporting country, sending laborers to places like Saudi Arabia to do construction and to Germany to work as nurses.[5] Starting in the late 1980s, foreign migrant workers arrived to fill the gap between the increasing availability of low-skilled jobs in small- and medium-sized factories and the shortage of Korean workers.

In the early 1990s, the number of undocumented workers in South Korea started to balloon, partly due to a policy the government implemented in hopes of securing a cheap source of foreign labor. This policy, the Industrial Technical Trainee Program (ITTP), was modeled after a similar program in Japan and stayed in effect from 1991 to 2006. The ITTP was an abusive system where foreigners were classified as "trainees" rather than laborers, which blocked them from having many rights earned by Korean laborers such as collective bargaining. Foreign "trainees" were given pocket money rather than wages and were prohibited from changing factories, no matter the working conditions. Since ITTP trainees could make more money as undocumented workers, many abandoned their positions and found other factory jobs—thereby increasing the overall numbers of undocumented workers in Korea. They joined other foreigners who had overstayed tourist visas, including men and women from an estimated fifty-four different countries, including China, Congo, Nigeria, Russia, Afghanistan, Brazil, and even Jamaica.[6]

The number of foreign workers in South Korea had been growing rapidly until the Asian financial crisis (known as the IMF for the subsequent interventions of the International Monetary Fund) hit in December 1997, reducing jobs and gutting the value of the Korean won. During the IMF, an estimated half of all undocumented workers who had been in the country either voluntarily departed due to job shortages or were detained and deported.[7] Just as the Peruvian community grew again along with the economy—reaching an estimated four thousand people,[8] so too did the overall number of foreign workers in Korea. By 2002, Korea's number of foreign migrants had surpassed pre-IMF numbers.

Until the 1990s, for both trainees and undocumented workers, there had been frequent reports of violence and abusive treatment, unpaid wages, and serious injuries in Korean factories.[9] In an attempt to manage the growing numbers of migrants and raise their global profile, Korea implemented a guest worker policy, the Employee Permit System (EPS) in 2004, which I see as part of Korea's cosmopolitan conversion project—promoted as a cutting-edge solution to simultaneously protecting the human rights of migrant workers and meeting Korea's need for unskilled labor. It was referred to by a Korean publication as "the most advanced in the world."[10] It was also promoted to other countries, like Malaysia, as an enviable solution for them to adopt. Apart from the EPS, the Korean government promoted at least one more of its immigration practices to other countries as innovative and worthy of replication. In 2006 the Korean Ministry of Justice invited Peruvian embassy personnel to the inauguration ceremony for KISS (the Korea Immigration Smart Service), which they said had "won the best scores for Customer Satisfaction in the world" and was an "innovation of Border Service." The ceremony to celebrate a brand name for this innovation and share it with the world was held on the significant date of September 11.[11]

Although billed as innovative, only certain migrants were allowed to participate in the EPS, and the criteria were based on nationality (primarily from Asia), gender (male), and age (eighteen to forty years old). The eligible countries were chosen based on proximity to South Korea or the prominence of the population already there, but a member of the Ministry of Justice I spoke with mentioned that the factory owners also had a racial preference for Asian workers because they felt uncomfortable disciplining non-Asians. Therefore, citizens of countries like Peru and Nigeria were not included in the Employee Permit System. While a few Peruvians I met had other visas—business visas, unexpired tourist visas, student visas, or had married Korean or US citizens and adjusted their status through them—after 2004, many of the Peruvians in Korea were undocumented with no apparent chance of becoming documented.[12]

Some Peruvians who opted to remain in Korea after 2004 were relatively easy for immigration officers to find because they had registered their whereabouts during the temporary amnesty the government implemented in preparation for the Employee Permit System. The terms of the amnesty were that no matter their country of origin, an undocumented person could apply for an E-9 Unskilled Labor visa, which allowed them to work in certain industries in Korea for "up to two years, if the total period of his/her stay does not exceed five years," granted they had "stayed in Korea for less than three years as of March 31, 2003."[13] The idea seemed to be that at the end of the amnesty period, all of the undocumented migrant workers would be first documented, and counted, and then they would return to their home countries—either by choice or by force. Those who received the E-9 visa enjoyed a year or two of documented status in Korea and even had a chance to make short trips to Peru and return to their jobs. However, the E-9 visa came with consequences. I heard from numerous Peruvians that immigration vans had arrived in front of their factories soon after the Employee Permit System went into effect, and officers had lists with the names of people who had registered for the E-9 visa but failed to depart on time. In trying to attempt a cosmopolitan conversion and gain institutionalized cultural capital, those Peruvians who received this visa contributed to the state's surveillance apparatus and their own exclusion.

Padre Ignacio and other clergy had told me that immigration officers seemed to have a quota on the numbers of undocumented migrants they detained in a given period—with surges of deportations in the summer and the holidays. I had a chance to ask Ms. Kim, a member of the Ministry of Justice, about this during the summer of 2006. I was curious how they could promote themselves as being exemplary in their humane treatment of migrant workers and simultaneously launch aggressive raids to round them up.

Ms. Kim denied the existence of a quota for deportations. Then, I did not detect a hint of irony in her voice when she told me that undocumented migrants were being deported for their own protection—and for the well-being of all migrants in Korea. She said that documenting all migrant workers was the only way to ensure they were "under the umbrella" of human rights protections, which included things like health care, regular wages, and protection from abusive, exploitative, or unsafe conditions in factories.

"If we can't see them, we can't protect them," she said. This sentiment was similar to the one presented by the director general of the Immigration Bureau in his opening remarks for the Ministry of Labor's 6th Immigration Policy Forum in April 2005. According to an English version of his remarks: "If we successfully reduce the number of illegal stayers, it is not just for the number itself. We, [the] immigration bureau, could allocate more human resource[s] to legal stayers. . . . We, [the] Korean government, could import more foreign laborers through legal programs. We, [the] Korean people, could exchange better [warmth with migrant workers]."[14] What both he and Ms. Kim left unsaid was that documentation would certainly not be extended to all intending migrants. And Peruvians would most likely never be included in the EPS. So, in order to be able to say that all migrant workers in South Korea had their human rights protected, all the ones who were ineligible for visas needed to voluntarily depart, or be deported. That included Peruvians.

Ironically, it was often the people like Victor, who had been ineligible for any kind of documentation—because they had been in Korea too long to qualify for the E-9 visa—who were able to protect themselves by evading detection the longest. That is because they had often found a reliable job they stayed in for years, spoke some Korean, and had not made themselves visible to the Korean government since they had arrived as tourists decades earlier.

Other types of Peruvian migrants who had maintained long-term ties in Korea were those who had met and married Korean citizens soon after they arrived. Often, they continued to work in factories and socialize with undocumented friends and family members, but they had applied for and received Korean citizenship through their spouses. In some ways, like Victor, they had survived by making their Peruvianness invisible. When I asked one of my key informants why she had not attended the Peru Day celebration held by the embassy and Catholic Church, she said coldly that the embassy never contacted her since she was no longer Peruvian. When I asked her to clarify, she said that what she meant was once she had become a Korean citizen (and renounced her Peruvian citizenship), she was no longer considered part of that group.

Despite feeling removed from her Peruvian identity, she and other marriage migrants had been included in South Korea precisely because of their foreignness. In the 2000s, the concept of multiculturalism became incredibly popular in South Korea partly in response to the increasing number of foreign migrant workers and growing numbers of foreign women—particularly Joseonjok (ethnically Korean Chinese)—who were allowed in as marriage migrants to combat the rural bride shortage and a declining fertility rate.[15] In discussing the rise of multicultural fever in Korea, sociologist Nora Hui-Jung Kim calculated that the use of the word *multicultural* increased in the Korean press from 235 instances in 1999 to 19,233 times in 2006.[16] A governmental focus on globalization (*seghyewha*) had also raised the numbers of return migrants to Korea from foreign countries, with a preference for those who had gone to the United States. For example, Koreans who had been sent overseas as international adoptees were targeted to return to South Korea and bring their cultural capital with them to help fuel Korea's globalization project.[17] In writing about South Korea's transition from being a labor exporter to importer, political scientist Timothy Lim finds that their relatively "late migration" affected the way the government tried to deal with foreign migrants. The South Korean government promoted the idea of multiculturalism (*tamunwha*) as a way to distance itself from what was thought of as a non-Western backward treatment of foreigners.[18]

The new attention to multiculturalism was notable because it addressed the obvious challenges foreign brides and multiracial Koreans were making to the previously dominant narrative of Korea being an ethnically homogenous country. However, as anthropologist Hyun Mee Kim argues, rather than marking an attempt to promote understandings of multiple identities or experiences in Korea, the actual effects of multicultural projects—such as offering free Korean cooking classes—went toward assimilating foreign wives into Korean culture.[19] Anthropologist EuyRyung Jun conducted ethnographic fieldwork on some of these government-funded multicultural projects and found that they were not even really about affecting the lives of foreigners but rather aimed at preparing the *Koreans* who helped to organize them to deal with an inevitable globalization.[20]

BEATRIZ'S STORY

As Peruvian migrants continued to build their communities in Korea in the 2000s, their trajectories became interlaced with state and church projects for dealing with multiculturalism and globalization. Yet not all Peruvians had the same experiences in Korea—even those who had arrived at the same time. As sociologist John Lie points out, South Korea's multiculturalism wave was contradictory in that it simultaneously promoted the inclusion of foreign spouses and their children while excluding, and permitting the mistreatment of, foreign workers.[21]

While my vignette at Victor and Karina's house at the beginning of this chapter illustrated life in the multicultural moment as experienced by undocumented migrants, an afternoon I spent with Beatriz, a Peruvian woman from Norte Chico who had married a Korean man, illustrated life in the other side of this duality. Like Victor, Beatriz, who had arrived in 1996 as a twenty-three-year-old, was part of a broker scam. However, almost as soon as she arrived, she met and fell in love with a young Korean man who worked at her factory. She overstayed her tourist visa and became undocumented, but they quickly married and she applied to become a Korean citizen. Apart from one trip back to Peru to visit her parents, she had been in Korea for most of her adult life. She now spoke Korean fluently and was not only a member of Friendship Ministry but also part of a Korean church. When she first got married, she and her husband had lived in a very rural area, which she referred to as *la provincia*.[22] She had attended a Korean church there, as there were no churches catering to foreigners and it had been her only option. She found that she "enjoyed the way [Korean people] worshipped," and so when her family moved to this area, even though she joined Friendship Ministry, she had sought out a separate Korean church as well. She felt accepted in different ways at these two churches. At Friendship, she had Peruvian and other international friends, but it mostly catered to single migrants. In contrast, the Korean church's congregation was primarily families who could better relate to her life as a married woman with a child.

I had known Beatriz for a couple of years when she invited me over to visit her at the new apartment she and her husband had purchased with the help of a government program. When I saw her at church one day in May 2009, she told me she had just found out she was pregnant with her second child, and her husband did not want her to work. She said that since she was bored at home, I should come over for lunch.

On the day of my visit I stopped by the outdoor market set up along the main street of her town—the same streets where Victor and his friends had described plainclothes officers patrolling on the night of the raid. I did not see any other foreigners here though, probably because it was midday on a Tuesday and everyone was at work. I quickly browsed the items Korean vendors had displayed on boxes and tarps on the sidewalk—piles of apples, bananas, and large purple grapes as well as bundles of simple cooking utensils like plastic strainers and bamboo spoons. At church, Beatriz had mentioned she had pregnancy cravings for watermelon, so I picked one out and headed to wait for the local bus she had told me to take the rest of the way to her house. Once it arrived, I rode the local bus for about thirty minutes, bumping through an area that appeared to be transitioning from farmland to the suburbs. I got off the bus and almost immediately realized I had gotten off too early. After walking for twenty more minutes and sweating in the summer heat and humidity, I considered tossing the watermelon—which seemed to be getting heavier by the minute—into the bushes. I finally pulled out my cell phone to call Beatriz for help. I described my surroundings to her and she told me to wait.

"It's actually good you got off at the wrong stop," she said, giving me a hug. "On my way here I saw an advertisement for a little *arbeit*." She held up a scrap of paper with a short job description handwritten in Hangul. It was faded from being out in the sun and looked like it had been pinned to a board for a while. As we walked to her apartment building, she exchanged greetings with her Korean neighbors. I noted that while I stuck out in this neighborhood, Beatriz looked like she fit in very comfortably.

Her high-rise apartment building was newly constructed and part of a large complex. At the entrance to the building there was a small grocery store that stocked snacks and staples like rice, cooking oil, and a few baskets of loose produce items such as carrots and potatoes that still had traces of the dirt from the fields where they were grown. Beatriz was going to show me how to prepare *tallarines en salsa roja* (pasta in red sauce) from a Peruvian recipe book that her mother had slipped into her suitcase when she first left Peru years ago. She told me she had to refer to the instructions in the book because she usually only cooked Korean food.

"I love my *kinchi*, my *jjiggae*, my *ramyeon*," she said, pronouncing kimchi with an "n," which many Spanish speakers did. She almost never ate Peruvian food anymore.

She told me that she had loved participating in the multicultural projects sponsored by the Korean government—including cooking classes where she learned how to prepare kimchi and other Korean foods for her husband.

I had to contain my surprise at the unqualified appreciation Beatriz had for these classes. Before this I had only heard of these classes within a social science critique of their assimilationist mission. I also knew Beatriz to speak frankly about the experiences—positive and negative—she had in her churches and community. Her seemingly genuine gratefulness for the information she learned there as well as the occasional free food (rice and kimchi) she received from some state-sponsored programs made me understand they were also filling a real need for her family.

We went in the store to buy soft drinks to go with our lunch.

Two elderly Korean men were sitting outside of the store on plastic stools. They greeted us flirtatiously in Korean. Beatriz acknowledged them but did not greet them warmly as she had the other neighbors.

The shop owner was standing behind the register. When we brought up our bottle of Chilsung Cider to the counter, he rang us up and put it in a black plastic bag.

"Where are you from?" he asked us. "Why are you here?"

Beatriz told him in Korean that she lived there with her family. "You know that," she said. She took the bag and led us out of the store.

She sounded annoyed as she told me in Spanish that typically the owner did not try to flirt with her because his wife was usually there too. I regretted that my presence seemed to be exacerbating the differences she felt in her daily interactions here as a foreign-born woman.

As we walked to her apartment, she explained that this was uncomfortable, but nothing compared to what she faced years prior when she and her husband lived in *la provincia*. At that place she had numerous Peruvian friends—mostly men—who worked with her. Her brother had also just arrived from Peru and lived with her and her husband. After work she and the other Peruvians would go to the convenience store by their apartment to buy snacks like popsicles or chips. She could tell that the Koreans who worked there were talking about her, but she did not know what they were saying. Then over time, as she learned more Korean, she realized they thought she was having sex with all of the different men they saw her with.

Beatriz laughed as she told me this story.

"*This lady is so easy, she is always in here with a different guy,*" they said. She tried to explain that the men were just her friends, but the gossiping neighbors did not believe her. "*She is taking their money from them,*" they would say.

Then one day she went in to the store with her husband, who is short, and they were even more shocked. They said, "*Look at this poor little guy. She is robbing him of his money!*" She had to explain to them that he was her husband. However, she became serious when she told me that she had been happy when they left *la provincia* because the neighborhood children had been unkind to her family for being different.

Although they lived minutes from each other in Korea, Beatriz and Victor had become involved in two different aspects of South Korea's multicultural projects, and had each been "socially absented" to varying degrees, so were often part of different worlds even as they occupied the same space.[23]

I never saw Victor and Beatriz socialize, but they knew some of the same people in Korea and Peru. Despite having different legal statuses, Victor and Beatriz were both under surveillance and had to negotiate between freedom and fear. While he was trying to remain invisible, she was making her mark on her community in Korea. Beatriz was under surveillance as a foreign wife in Korea—her actions were watched and managed by the state through multicultural programs, and by her neighbors through comments and daily interactions. She was legally included, having obtained Korean citizenship through her husband, yet still excluded every day as she raised her family. Her neighbors treated her as if she belonged, yet she and her children also stood out. For both Victor and Beatriz, their lives and families had changed because they were in Korea, and Korea had changed because they were there—but they had helped to create different transnational networks.

Their networks intersected, however, because like most of the Peruvians I knew in Korea, Beatriz and Victor belonged to mixed-status families and social groups. They interacted with both undocumented and documented migrant workers and with Koreans at work, at church, in their towns, and even at home. Despite being part of groups treated very differently under multicultural programs—foreign wives and migrant laborers—they simultaneously experienced the inclusion and exclusion of Korea and its multicultural moment through their relationships with others. Since marrying her Korean husband and having children, Beatriz had been included in legal and cultural projects meant to help assimilate her into the Korean family. Yet, she also felt uncomfortable with her neighbors' recognition of and discrimination against her family's differences. As a Peruvian man who had managed to remain in Korea for many years undocumented and undetected, Victor was part of Korea's wave of low-paid migrant laborers and also relatively invisible within it.

LEAVING PERU: "YOU HAVE TO REALIZE ALL THESE DESTINATIONS AREN'T THE SAME"

Although they had not known each other prior to migration, it was not a coincidence that Beatriz and Victor had both arrived in Korea in the mid-1990s. At the time, out-migration was at a fever pitch in Peru, and since they were part of the lower middle class, they had fewer migration options than members of the upper class. While their limited economic and cultural capital excluded them from migrating legally to the most prestigious destinations for Peruvians like the United States, it also made them look beyond popular, but less prestigious, destinations like Argentina to find South Korea.

While in the 1980s South Korea shifted from an immigrant-exporting to a migrant-receiving nation for the first time, Peru was doing the opposite. Historically Peru had brought settlers, conscripted laborers, and slaves from Europe,

Asia, and Africa, but starting in the 1980s, Peru experienced social and economic instability that prompted an acute trend toward out-migration.[24] One catalyst was that the civil war launched from Peru's highlands by the Maoist terrorist group Shining Path, or Sendero Luminoso, left 69,280 people dead and forced people from the highlands into the pueblos jóvenes of Peru. As anthropologist Kimberly Theidon notes, Peruvians are still processing the violence committed by the military, guerrillas, and everyday *campesinos* during this conflict.[25] The conflict sparked an exodus of people escaping violence and financial insecurity and had long-term consequences on internal and external migration. Added to this were the economic policies that failed during former Peruvian president Alan García's first term (1985–90), which resulted in hyperinflation. The people who were first able to escape these problems were members of the upper and middle classes who qualified for US tourist visas. Not surprisingly then, the first wave of Peruvian emigrants primarily went to the United States and consisted of people who were wealthier and better educated than most other Peruvians.[26] Many had held professional jobs in Peru before reaching the United States, where they were forced to accept low-paying unskilled labor jobs, a phenomenon that caught the attention of ethnographers.[27] More recent studies of Peruvian migration have shifted away from these upper-class migrants to explore the experiences of other groups, including racialized Peruvian migrants from the highlands who travel to the United States.[28]

Unlike other labor-exporting nations such as Mexico and El Salvador, which send migrants to one or two main destinations (for example, 98 percent of Mexican migrants are in the United States), Peru stands out for having migrants "scattered" all over the world in at least twenty-five countries.[29] However, apart from the families I worked with in Peru, hardly anyone else I spoke to in Peru had heard that there were Peruvians in Korea. It was not common knowledge. People were not surprised to hear about it once I told them, though. For example, when I told the landlady of my San Miguel apartment that I was researching Peruvian migration to South Korea, she raised a manicured hand dismissively and said a phrase I heard frequently, "There are Peruvians all over the world." She managed our apartment for her brother who had migrated to Ireland in the early 2000s and married an Irish woman. She told me that the whole building was filled with Peruvians who had lived abroad themselves or received remittances from family members. She collected the rent in US dollars. Not just migration, but migration to widespread destinations, was quotidian.

While there were Peruvians all over the world, that does not mean that all destinations were equal. Further, however dispersed Peruvian migrants are or imagine themselves to be, there are certain points on the globe that have concentrations of Peruvians and are considered to be more desirable migration destinations than other places. The most sought-after places are the United States (1.3 million Peruvian migrants), Spain (120,300), Italy (70,800), and Japan (60,000). Those Peruvians who want to migrate but who do not have many resources go to nearby

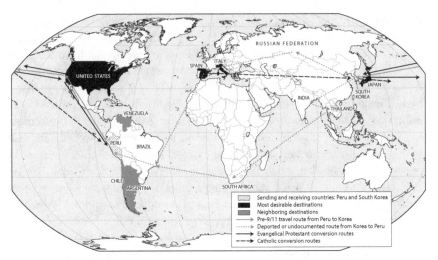

MAP 1. Peruvian migration destinations. Map courtesy of University of Texas Libraries.

places like Chile (62,000) and Argentina (100,000).[30] In his book on migrant remittances in Peru, Karsten Paerregaard argues that families with migrants and their neighbors place different values on remittances depending on which destination they come from. Remittances from Japan are valued the highest because they come from a prestigious destination with a high salary, while remittances from the United States and Europe rank lower, and then those sent from Argentina and Chile are ranked at the bottom.[31]

The popularity of these destinations also changes with the geopolitical climate. For example, given the instability in Venezuela since the installation of President Maduro's government in 2013, I have not heard of any of my interviewees talk about people migrating there for work. However, in 2006 Peruvians in Peru and South Korea told me about Venezuela as being a great option for migration not because of high salaries but because it was like a "trampoline" that let them jump to better destinations. They had heard that Venezuela offered migrants a pathway to citizenship, and Venezuelan citizenship could be parlayed into citizenship in Italy—a more prestigious destination. This was similar to what Vanessa Fong found in her research with Chinese students who dreamed of studying abroad to enhance their citizenship both abroad and in China.[32] Although the Chinese students used the term *waiguo* (abroad) to refer to all developed countries, they had ranked destinations based on their relative amount of geopolitical power and visa opportunities. Students did not always end up in their first choice. Like these students, through their years of experience searching for the best migration plan available to them, many of the Peruvian families I spoke with had become lay experts on the changing laws, economics, and political relationships of numerous nations worldwide—and they contributed to this knowledge as they shared it with others. After failing to reach other, better places, South Korea emerged for some families as the *only* destination in the world that seemed open to their family members.

In recent years, out-migration from Peru has decreased because young people have been able to find jobs in improving domestic markets, including tourism and mining. However, during my fieldwork, nearly every working-age Peruvian I spoke to in Korea and Peru felt that migrating *anywhere* outside of Peru was preferable to staying home. When I asked migrants in Korea why they did not want to return to Peru, they told me it was because there were no jobs.

"*No hay nada en Perú*," they said. "There is nothing for me in Peru."

There was a widespread belief—confirmed by economic data—that leaving Peru was the best way for people to achieve both geographic and social mobility. Leaving Peru literally allowed people and their families to *salir adelante* (leave to get ahead).[33]

In Peru, migrating abroad was a regular part of everyday conversations that I had with friends, at the local store, or overheard from strangers on the street. There were many factors that went into choosing the correct migration destination, including economics, family connections, and knowledge of risk. In 2007 I visited Señora Wilma, the aunt of one of my friends from the Catholic Church in Korea. We sat in the airy second-floor living room of the house her niece had built in a pueblo joven. When I asked Señora Wilma if many people in the area had migrated to South Korea, she shook her head *no* and then listed the many other places that people in the neighborhood had gone: Chile, Argentina, Italy, the United States. Although she had not migrated herself, she seemed to set herself apart as being more knowledgeable about the risks of migration than her neighbors, most of whom appeared to be poor.

"You have to realize all these destinations aren't the same," she told me. Her friend had migrated to Argentina to take a domestic labor job. "She was shocked that she couldn't really save or send anything from Argentina," she said. "And a friend of mine sent her son to Mexico and paid $6,000 to cross [the Mexico–United States border]. She didn't hear from him for twenty days! They crossed with nothing but a cell phone. She was terrified for him the whole time," she said. "No, I would never send my child to the United States that way."

Most people from this area would not qualify for a US tourist visa. However, like Señora Wilma, no one I met during my fieldwork ever told me they or their family members had considered crossing surreptitiously into the United States. They were very familiar with the dangers of crossing the Mexico border and had heard stories of the rising deaths on the border, especially from South American migrants.[34] The relative safety of entering Korea as a tourist versus risking a clandestine border crossing was one reason they had chosen Korea as a destination. However, for the Peruvians I interviewed, Korea emerged as a destination because of its proximity to Japan.

"MY UNCLE CALLED AND SAID, 'LET'S GO TO JAPAN!'
THAT'S HOW I CAME TO KOREA."

Between the 1990s and first decade of the 2000s, Korea changed from being a stand-in destination for Japan to a desirable destination of its own. A few migrants told me they first heard about South Korea when they saw it on TV during the 1988 Olympics, but they did not think of traveling there until after Peru established a "return migration" agreement with Japan. Organized in 1990 by then-president Alberto Fujimori, himself the son of Japanese immigrants, the "return migration" agreement allowed ethnically Japanese Peruvians to get jobs in Japan.[35] In the first three years of the program, 30,000 Peruvians, or an estimated 38 percent of Peru's 80,000-member Japanese Peruvian community, had gone to Japan.[36] The majority of Peruvians who applied for this visa and traveled to Japan were third-generation Sansei, many of whom did not speak Japanese. Particularly at the beginning of the return migration program, the ambiguity about who Japanese Peruvians were created the opportunity for Peruvians who were not of Japanese descent to enter as well. This resulted in people who were not ethnically Japanese, but wanted to migrate, to either travel to Japan or try to get as close as they could. "Japan was like the United States. It was the promise of opportunity," a man who had been in Japan before South Korea told me.

In 2008 in Norte Chico, I talked with Esteban, a man I had first met in Friendship Ministry years prior. When I asked him how he had first decided to go to Korea, he told me that he had ended up there by chance in the mid-1990s. He said, "My uncle called and said, 'Let's go to Japan!' That's how I got to Korea." Esteban went on to explain that in the end his uncle decided to stay in Peru, so Esteban went alone. To prove that he was a real tourist, he decided to spend a week in Thailand before flying to Japan. In Thailand, he heard about Korea from other foreigners and decided to go there instead. He ended up finding a job and never made it to Japan.

In some extreme cases, like that of Juan, a forty-year-old man I met in Norte Chico, migrants actually thought they *were* going to Japan when they arrived in Korea. Juan, who many people told me was one of the first Peruvians in Korea, had paid a broker to take him to Japan. But when they arrived at Seoul's Gimpo Airport, which he thought was going to be just a transfer point, the broker pointed out across the East Sea and said, "There's Japan, right over there."

After working in Korea for a few years, Juan did eventually save enough to get to Japan. Before he left Korea, he had helped to finance the trips of many of his nephews, friends, and neighbors. They all came to Korea to join him in his factory. This contributed to the growth of the community—and a concentration of Peruvians from Norte Chico.

By the 2000s, information about Korea as a destination had spread, particularly in Norte Chico and some pueblos jóvenes. Most people learned about Korea

from family members who were already there, but others learned about it seren-
dipitously, from taxi drivers in Peru. In addition to being able to enter as tourists, there were also other benefits that made Korea desirable. Since most workers lived at their factories, which provided housing, some food, and even gas for
cooking, the salary was liquid. That meant migrants could send home almost all
of their earnings. Also, unlike other destinations where the employment demand
is for males only, Korean factories employed women too. However, according to
my interviewees, men made between one and 1.2 million won per month, while
women made between 800,000 and one million won. Both male and female Peruvian migrants told me this pay discrepancy was reflective of what they saw as ram-
pant sexism in Korea. They thought Peruvian culture was sexist too, but they held
Korea up to higher standards because they saw it as being more developed than
Peru. One woman I knew told me she did the exact same work as her boyfriend,
who was employed at the same factory, but was annoyed to be paid 200,000 won
less per month.

"THERE WAS NO HERMANA PILAR IN JAPAN":
KOREAN CHURCHES AND MIGRANTS

Another reason that South Korea became a desirable destination of its own was
because of the strong presence of Christian churches—both Catholic and Protestant—and their growing interactions with migrant laborers. Peruvians who had
worked in both countries told me that the special attention and help they received
from the Catholic and Protestant clergy in South Korea actually made it a better destination than Japan. When I asked Lily, a woman from a pueblo joven, to
compare her experiences working in both Japan and South Korea, she said simply,
"There was no Hermana Pilar in Japan." In other words, when she was in Japan,
she was on her own, but in Korea, although she was undocumented, she had a
clear source of strong spiritual and institutional support. I cannot say if people
migrated to Korea specifically for the attention they received from these churches,
but it would be impossible to separate the churches' presence from the experience
of being a Peruvian migrant in Korea.

Unlike other key labor destinations in Asia, like Japan, Hong Kong, and Sin-
gapore, Korea has one of the largest Christian populations in Asia—estimated at
20 percent of the population.[37] The Catholic Church in Korea had a long history
of working with, first, Korean labor activists and then with migrant workers. A
sit-in on the steps of Myongdong Cathedral where industrial trainees from Nepal
chained themselves together and camped out for weeks in 1995 to bring attention
to the abusive conditions in their factories became a flashpoint for migrant rights
in Korea. The protest promoted a narrative of migrant suffering and response of
shame from Korean people,[38] but it also highlighted the significance of the Catholic Church as a central player in the struggle for migrant rights in Korea.

In the 2000s, Korean Protestant churches became more involved with migrants as a way to provide relief in terms of physical needs, but also to give them spiritual salvation. Proselytizing to foreign migrant workers and inviting them to join Korean and mission churches became a way for Korean churches to spread beyond the local Korean population—which had become saturated with churches. In addition to thousands of local churches, Korea is believed to be home to five out of ten of the world's largest Protestant megachurches—citing membership in the hundreds of thousands. Pastor Sarah, who founded Friendship Ministry, told me that nearly all of the large churches in Seoul claimed to be the largest in Korea, and perhaps the world. Korean churches began turning their attentions to overseas missions. Korea is only second to the United States in the number of missionaries abroad, and as of 2013 there were 19,798 Korean missionaries in over 167 different countries.[39] Many of these Protestant churches have transnational ties, due to early contact with American missionaries[40] and then to immigration of Koreans to the United States and the establishment of sister churches and their own overseas missions.

Foreign migrant workers provided a chance for churches to do "foreign missions" domestically. In her research on short-term Korean missions, geographer Ju Hui Judy Han notes that many missionaries regarded proselytizing to foreign areas "unreached" by Christianity as being equivalent to providing food or clothing.[41] This was because the missionaries considered their work with migrants to be what Han calls "an assemblage of neoliberal capitalism and the Protestant ethos of perpetual self-improvement . . . articulated with a distinctly Korean model of authoritarian developmentalism."[42] That model promised that if people accepted spiritual salvation, they would also be on track toward personal and national economic prosperity. This was a narrative that Peruvian migrants—coming from a country reeling from economic instability and trying to survive the global financial crisis—responded to enthusiastically. Migrants I worked with were also excited to be part of launching a mission to Peru and being the ones who would bring positive change to their country. This potential for changing the world, starting with themselves and their country, was the thing that seemed to draw Peruvians to their evangelical churches, more than any promise of free food or clothing.

CREATING TRANSNATIONAL SPACES IN KOREA

The real value of Korea as a destination emerged as Peruvian migrants continued to establish a community there, joining churches, forging relationships with others, and making their mark on the space.

Dongducheon was one of the only places in Korea where I could spot visible, concentrated signs that Peruvians had made a mark on the space. Someone had literally tagged "Peru" on the walls of the abandoned school where migrant workers held soccer tournaments. At one point there were at least four Peruvian restaurants and two Latin nightclubs owned and operated by migrants and located within one square mile of one another. On the weekends, the restaurants were spilling over with Peruvians who were drinking beer, eating plates of *lomo saltado*, and waiting to play soccer. There were also lots of parties: engagement parties, weddings, christenings, and birthday celebrations. On the weekends, people went out to share meals of Korean BBQ or large pots of *kamchatang* (potato stew) with their coworkers and friends.

Although I did the majority of my fieldwork in Korea in Seoul and semirural areas outside of Seoul (like the place where Victor and Beatriz lived), Dongducheon had an important symbolic presence for me and the people I interviewed. Rather than being the subject or backdrop of my ethnography, Dongducheon represents a salient global space in people's stories and memories of their time as migrants in Korea. It was often their starting point—the first place they lived or hung out when they arrived, the place they sinned and decided to convert, or the place they missed when they were deported.

Peruvians I knew were simultaneously scandalized by, attracted to, and scared of the fast life in Dongducheon. One Sunday afternoon two sisters from Norte Chico invited me to a popular Peruvian restaurant. They were so embarrassed by the men drinking and singing boisterously to the salsa music playing on the TVs above the booths that the three of us left before we had even ordered. Whenever Peruvians told me stories of migrants breaking up their marriages by cheating on spouses with Koreans, foreigners, or other Peruvians, Dongducheon was frequently the backdrop of the romance. Cristianos from Nazarene called it *el campo* (the field) and treated it a little like a foreign mission. They would borrow a van from their church in Seoul, load it up with Peruvians training to be evangelists, and make the two-hour drive out to visit people after work in their factories. Yet, whenever I interviewed former migrants in Peru and asked them what they missed about Korea, they almost always mentioned the experience of being in a place like Dongducheon and having friends from all over the world. That feeling of being part of an international community was something they could not find in Peru. Thus, although Dongducheon was not central to my fieldwork, it is significant to the story of Peruvian migration to Korea.

TRANSFORMING PERU

As Peruvians created their worlds in Korea, they simultaneously transformed their sending communities in Peru. As a result of chain migration and word of mouth, Norte Chico became a large sending destination for migrants to Japan and then to Korea. A man in Korea told me that when he arrived at the cabinet factory where his cousin had found him a job, he was surprised to see numerous people from his Norte Chico neighborhood already working there. He even met a classmate from his middle school in that factory.

There were few acutely visible marks of Korean migration in that space, however. In contrast, I frequently stumbled across signs of Japanese migration such as statues, commemorative bridges, and foundations in Norte Chico and Lima. It caught my eye one day then, when I crossed the Plaza de Armas in Norte Chico and saw a parked moped with a sign attached on the back advertising, in Hangul, a Korean pizza place. It still had the Korean license plate on it. Shipping used taxis and other vehicles from Korea was a common way that migrants earned money on the side. I guessed this moped must have been brought over or sent by a migrant in Korea, but I never got a chance to meet the owner. There were other signs of Korea in Norte Chico though, including businesses run by former migrants or the families of migrants still in Korea. I spent time with migrant families in their stores that sold things like party supplies and electronics sent from Korea.

One evening in Norte Chico I went out for coffee and cake with the woman I was staying with and her granddaughters. Although the town had a laid-back beach-town vibe, the Plaza de Armas and nearby marketplace were bustling. It was already 8:30 p.m., but lots of people were shopping in the stores, hanging out on the benches in the town square, and moving around in moto-taxis (motorcycles outfitted with a covered trailer that held the driver and two passengers). Cumbia hits from the Peruvian groups Hermanos Yaipén and Grupo 5 blasted from the *cabinas de internet* (internet cafés) and *chifas* (Chinese restaurants) on almost every street.

Since migration was so common in Norte Chico, some of the space of the central area was organized around that project. An example was *locutorios,* storefronts that were filled with phone booths where one could place local or international calls. There were several locutorios on both sides of nearly every street, and some of them were combined with internet cafés. The locutorios had colorful signs posted out front advertising how much it was to call places that had communities of people from Norte Chico: including Paterson, New Jersey, and Japan. I occasionally saw ones that advertised the rate to call South Korea.

The granddaughters were surprised that I was interested in these locutorios, which were commonplace to them. "Are these set up to call people abroad?" I asked.

"They are to call anyone, I guess," one told me. Cell phones and calls were very expensive in Peru. Eventually I started using the locutorios to call my family and arrange interviews in Peru when my cell phone ran out of credit—something that always seemed to happen at the worst time. I also accompanied families to the locutorio a few times and waited outside while they chatted with their family members who lived abroad.

In contrast to Norte Chico, the connection to Korea was more scattered in the pueblos jóvenes. People came from different areas and, besides from a few families who migrated together, had not known each other before migrating. Lima has many pueblos jóvenes, which had started out as squatter communities to

FIGURE 2. Taxi in a *pueblo joven:* A symbol of migration. Photo by author.

accommodate internal migrants coming from rural areas in Peru in the 1970s and were still struggling to improve their infrastructures. Some of the pueblos jóvenes still had dirt roads and provisional water and electricity connections, but others were developing quickly.[43] On each subsequent trip, I saw that the infrastructure had improved, with things like newly constructed traffic signals, parks, and sidewalks. The individual homes changed every time I visited too, with migrants having sent remittances in the form of cash to construct second floors or items such as electronics and clothes.

In all of my field sites in Peru, the impact of migration to Korea was more visible within the family homes than anywhere else because pursuing the opportunities of migration, as well as taking on the risks, was a family project. Of the nine families I spent significant amounts of time with in Peru, all of them had at least two immediate family members in different countries: primarily Japan, Argentina, Chile, or Bolivia. Most often their family migration history mapped on to larger migration trends in Peru; they often had a parent or older sibling who had been in Japan since the early 1990s. Many had worked in Japan or the United States themselves prior to migrating to Korea. Migrants also routinely had to leave young children in the care of their grandparents not knowing when they would return. To gather the money for the migrant to travel, family members had done things like borrow from family members already abroad or take out loans against the family home. Taxis were also a significant symbol of family migration projects. I met a few people who had sold their family taxis to finance migrations, but more hoped to buy taxis with their remittances and turn them into a sustainable source of income for the family long after the migration had ended.

CONCLUSION

The migration of Peruvians to Korea developed during a time of drastic changes in Peru's and Korea's political economies. Peruvian migrants were just one group of many to find jobs in Korea, and Korea was just one destination for Peruvian migrants. Yet, I have shown how through their actions of migrating and participating in life in Korea and Peru, they created and elucidated transnational ties between the two countries as well as changed the significance and value of Korea in Peru.

While Korea most likely never entered the ranking of desirable destinations for Peruvians in general, at one point during the mid-2000s some families in Norte Chico saw it as the only destination in the world open to them. They could arrive by plane with a temporary visa and find a familiar community of Peruvians and the possibility of joining new communities of foreigners. Over the period of twenty years, the meaning of Korea changed from being a stand-in for Japan to a desirable destination all its own. This value change happened through interactions with others, as migrants created meaningful spaces and relationships in Korea and then sent remittances to their families in Peru. These connections happened through word of mouth and within family networks, resulting in chain migration primarily from Norte Chico, but also from some pueblos jóvenes in Lima and other cities outside of Lima.

By showing the differences and parallels between the experiences of Victor and Beatriz, two Peruvians who arrived in Korea in the same year and lived in the same area, I hoped to demonstrate that the lives of migrants were affected by the ways in which their plans converged with the cosmopolitan conversion plans of the Korean state and churches. Their lives were constantly changing partly because they were there helping to create the Peruvian community in Korea and continued to participate in their communities in Peru. Despite the obvious differences of Beatriz being documented and a wife and mother in a Korean family, both of their daily lives involved negotiating between constantly changing levels of freedom and fear, inclusion and exclusion, under multiple forms of surveillance. Neighbors judged Beatriz as they also included her in their daily lives. She was treated as being both different from, and a member of, her community. Similarly, Victor was able to remain in Korea because of the invisibility his house and factory provided. While his movements were restricted, he saw them in context with the levels of freedom he used to enjoy as he helped to create and establish the Peruvian community in his area.

Although the effects of these conversions and transnational ties are sometimes difficult to spot, they made a big impact on migrants and their communities. It was visible in their homes and the ways they saw their relative places in the world—especially when viewed in comparison with how their neighbors lived. Similarly, in Korea, the spaces that emerged as symbolically "Korean" were also those most affected by Peruvians who dared to create their communities out in the open—such as in Dongducheon. However, even those impacts were fleeting and only came into relief in other areas where Peruvians made their worlds within the safety of their homes or churches for fear of being spotted by immigration officers and detained. In the chapter that follows, I explore how the multiple worlds that people like Beatriz and Victor occupy and create in and between South Korea and Peru converge and clash through the medium of the global financial crisis and unstable remittances.

2

Monetary Conversion

One afternoon, Franco, an undocumented man from a city outside of Lima, told me that although his business in Korea was booming, he wasn't making any money. We sat in a coffee shop in Hyewha, an upscale area of Seoul where he lived and sold costume jewelry from a small table he set up in an alley next to a shoe store.

"Is it because of the dollar?" I asked. We were now many months into the effects of the global financial crisis. The won-to-dollar conversion rate had been unsteady for months. The rate was still terrible but had recently leveled off. Most Peruvians I knew who had managed to keep working despite the economic downturn were still worried about not having enough money to send home.

He said the day's conversion rate was a concern, but he was talking about a bigger story. Franco was a single father in his forties, and this was his second stint as a migrant worker in Korea. While on his first trip in 1996, he had worked in a factory for a few months and managed to save $5,000, which he described as being a considerable amount of money in Peru at that time. On this more recent migration, which began in 2004, he barely made enough to support himself. This change of fortune transpired for three main reasons. First, since the implementation of Korea's Employee Permit System in 2004, there had been an increase in crackdowns on undocumented workers in factories and therefore a decrease in the numbers of jobs available. Second, since Franco's first migration, Korea had undergone two major financial crises, the 1997 Asian financial crisis and the 2008 global financial crisis, and as a result, the Korean won had significantly devalued relative to the US dollar. And finally, almost immediately after arriving in Korea

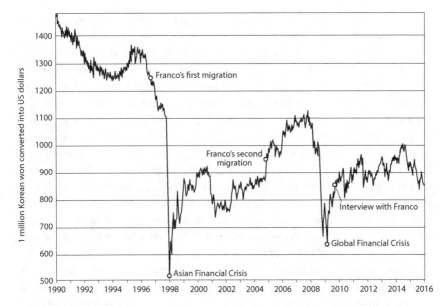

FIGURE 3. Won to dollars during Franco's migrations: Conversion rates from South Korean won to US dollars between 1995 and 2015. When Franco first arrived in Korea in November 1996, one million won equaled $1,250. When he arrived for his second migration in 2004, the value had dropped to $954. At one of the worst points in the global financial crisis of 2008, it was only worth $661. Graph source: FXtop.com.

for the second time, Franco had joined the Peruvian congregation of Nazarene church, converted to Protestantism, and his career goals and worldview had drastically changed.

While making money and sending it to his family had been his original reason for coming to Korea, in the past two years, converting his friends and family in Peru had become his primary pursuit. Franco went on to explain that despite not making money, his migration was actually very successful. He claimed that his family's financial situation had improved due to changes in their spiritual lives, which was a direct result of his efforts to evangelize to them over the phone.

I begin this chapter with Franco's story as a way to show that given the instability of the won relative to the dollar and their own undocumented positions in Korea, by 2008, migrants had fewer economic remittances to send their families than ever before. To provide for their families and to protect their own sense of self-worth as migrants, they needed to creatively convert their remittances into being worth more than they were. One way to do this was by pairing them with "social remittances,"[1] or the new ideas they had learned about religious belief, social capital, and how to manage their households in Korea, as a way to persuade their families in Peru to convert into people who required less money.

Franco's concern over the economic and social remittances he sent his family was a common story I heard from Peruvians in Korea regardless of their religious affiliation. This concern pointed to drastic changes in the global economy and the stress felt by migrants as a result of suddenly shifting from being their family's financial supporter to not being able to send enough money home. Further, the plans for financial success migrants had laid out, or had hoped to find while in Korea, were suddenly being challenged in myriad ways, which affected how migrants in Korea and their families in Peru viewed their migrations and remittances. While many people first tried to influence their families with money, this became increasingly difficult to do during the global financial crisis when even something as seemingly solid as the value of the dollar became unpredictable.

I argue that through the remittances Peruvians send their families—economic remittances in the form of won converted into dollars and sent home, and social remittances in the form of religious conversion and changing attitudes about work and money—migrants attempt to convert their family members and themselves into people who value money and work in ways that give them autonomy and choices despite their disadvantaged positions as undocumented migrants (or potential migrants) in an unstable economic climate. In attempting to influence their family members and negotiate the meaning of their own value as migrants even when the money had run out, they tried to convert their limited economic capital into other forms of capital that would be even more valuable than money. However, with every conversion comes loss, and while some of these attempts at conversion were successful, others failed in unexpected ways. In attempting to convert and remit their economic capital, they showed that while there is no direct conversion route between South Korea and Peru, new ways of being emerge in the process of attempting these creative strategies.

"LA PLATA ES INGRATA, VIENE Y SE VA" (MONEY IS UNGRATEFUL, IT COMES AND GOES)

In September 2008, the won-to-dollar conversion rate, which had been hovering between 900 won and 1,100 won per dollar since 2006, suddenly shot to 1,326 won per dollar, and by mid-November of that same year, had reached 1,500 won per dollar. However, the salaries of undocumented factory workers—which on average were between 800,000 won and one million won per month—stayed the same.[2] This meant that while in 2006 a salary of one million won converted to about $900, by November 2008 it was only worth $666. The Peruvian nuevo sol was also devaluing against the US dollar, and with prices for food, transportation, and housing in Peru rising, remittances did not go as far as they used to.[3] Around the same time that the world economy was in flux, the Korean government was preparing for the G-20 Summit to be held in Seoul in November 2010. Preparations for this event included intensifying efforts to rid the peninsula of undocumented workers by doing things such as increasing raids and charging factory owners with a fine of 20 million won per undocumented migrant caught working in their factories. Officials did this partly in response to fears that a surplus of migrants would exacerbate the damage of the economic crisis to the Korean economy, but also in an effort to protect Korea's image as a country that does not have an illegal migration problem in anticipation of the world spotlight that the G-20 Summit would bring.[4] Given these conditions, Peruvians had an increasingly difficult time finding and keeping factory work, and immigration officers detained and deported people every week.

During this turbulent period, many migrants had to decrease the amount of money they sent home. Even if people managed to send the same amount of won they had always sent, due to the conversion rate, it was now worth much less than before.

A few days after I arrived in Seoul in January 2009 I received a call from Angela, a woman from Lima, who was excited to tell me about a new route she had found for converting our remittances. Angela and I had first met years before at a Catholic Church event in Seoul, and she knew that similar to many other foreigners, I also had to remit money to cover my bills. While I received my fieldwork grant in Korean won, I had to pay my credit card bills and car payment in California in US dollars. I owed $568 each month for my bills in the United States, which I had initially thought would be difficult, but manageable, to pay with my monthly stipend. However, instead of sending 588,000 won per month for these expenses as I had initially planned, just the week before I had needed to send 790,000 won to cover the same expenses.[5] That left me with very little to live on. I worried about how to pay rent, and everyday expenses like subway fare became luxuries. I frequently checked the conversion rate online to see if it had improved. It united me with other foreigners in Korea who were doing the same thing.

"What's the route?" I asked Angela, excited for any chance to relieve some of the pressure of these expenses.

She told me that the rate for Japanese yen was looking better than the dollar and that we could possibly send money home that way. She had gotten the idea from watching a news magazine show on "Peru TV," an on-demand Peruvian media network broadcast from Japan that she accessed through her computer for $30 per month. She watched a lot of Peru TV because she rarely left her house for fear she would be detained by immigration officers. She told me that if the yen route did not pan out, her friend who was working in Italy as a maid had said good things about the euro. In order to get our money home intact, she proposed we change it first to yen, then to euros, then to dollars once it was on home soil. She had watched the won steadily weaken since 2008, and when the *tipo de cambio* improved just a little she agonized over whether or not to send her money home. Despite what the experts, her friends, or even "Peru TV" said, she knew that the won could either continue to improve, stay the same, or get much worse the next day.

I do not know if Angela's strategy actually worked. It frankly sounded too complicated for me to attempt. However, her late-night call about how to get the best
dollar value out of won through converting it into something else illustrates how
the value of money had begun to shift for Peruvian migrants at this time. With
Angela and many other people I hung out with over the next year, their conversion
and remittance plans revealed their understandings of the configuration of the real
and imagined infrastructure of the global world, their relative place in it vis-à-vis
their money, and how to navigate it. Pulling from a constellation of social, cultural,
and economic capital, they had to devise ways to avoid barriers and create new
routes to convert and remit their money.

The only way to avoid losing a large portion of their money in the conversion
was to delay sending money home and hope that the rate would get better. Few
people had the luxury to wait very long though, because their family members
needed their remittances. To judge the best time to send money home and lose
the least, migrants had to become experts at currency speculation and the relative value of the won against other world currencies. This expertise also reflected
their disadvantaged positions in a global hierarchy of currencies and migration
destinations—once they became remittances, wages earned in Korean won did not
go as far as those earned in US dollars. That is because unlike Peruvian migrants
in more popular destinations who earn and remit in the same world currency
because there is an infrastructure set up in Peru to process and even spend dollars
(and to a lesser extent euros and yen), migrants in Korea had to first convert their
won into a world currency before sending it home. Being forced to convert their
money into dollars during the world economic crisis meant that their already limited earnings lost even more value.

There is no direct route for converting or remitting money from Korea to Peru,
but this opened up the chance for migrants to make creative conversions. Not only
did they have to track their money's relative worth against global currencies, but
they also had to devise creative solutions to minimize their losses when converting
and transporting their money from Korea to Peru. As unlikely migrants in South
Korea, Peruvians also faced many practical difficulties in converting and remitting
money. They experienced language barriers when trying to exchange money and
also had to find a reliable and affordable method to transport the money from
Korea to Peru. Since they lacked valid visas, they could not send their money
directly through a bank, and they did not want to pay the steep transaction fees of
companies like Western Union. Similar to other undocumented migrants around
the world, they had to trust in more informal systems, like finding a courier (usually a returning migrant) to hand-carry their cash to their family members in Peru
or devise an alternative method of wiring the money.

They stood to lose at each step.

I saw the difficulties involved in money conversion and the multiple ways to
lose firsthand one particularly cold night in February 2009 when Señora Juana,

a woman in her fifties, asked me to accompany her to Itaewon where she needed help exchanging and transferring money. Señora Juana was a widow and mostly worked to support herself, but she was also sending remittances to her daughter and granddaughter who lived in a city in the northern part of Peru.

That night I had originally planned to accompany her as she sold accessories at the subway station by her apartment, but the bitter cold had kept customers away. I was helping her pack up her merchandise, mostly dangly silver earrings inlaid with stones that were popular at the time, when she told me that she did not need help converting the money, but that she did need help with depositing it in the bank account of a documented Peruvian woman living in Korea who would send it to her daughter. The bank's ATM was only in English and Korean—not Spanish. Although she had learned to speak Korean pretty well from watching Korean dramas and from interacting with Koreans at work and church, she could not read it. I agreed, happy I could do something for her. Before we could send the money, though, she told me we had to take the subway a few stops to Itaewon to a money exchange office that would be open late on a Monday night.

The tiny money exchange office was located in an alley running behind Itaewon's main shopping street. It was at the end of a row of hole-in-the-wall ethnic restaurants and not too far from the mosque and Yongsan army base. This area was packed with English teachers and soldiers on Friday and Saturday nights and tourists and Koreans shopping for imitation designer clothing during the day, but it was almost empty tonight. The only open place in the alley besides the money exchange office was a mom-and-pop stand displaying piles of premade Korean street foods ready to drop in a fryer.

It seemed that this money exchange office catered to tourists and to migrant workers who did not want to use the banks and travel agencies located on the main street, which were bigger, more nicely furnished, and easier to find. The windows of this shop displayed advertisements for things like international flights, pay-as-you-go phones, and money exchange services. Señora Juana told us she regularly used this particular money exchange office because they did not check her passport like many of the other offices usually did, and they had pretty good rates.

The owner, who was from Pakistan, greeted us in English as we entered the store. Señora Juana was disappointed. She had been hoping to see his wife, a Korean woman who had converted to Islam and wore a head scarf. She was the person Señora Juana usually interacted with here.

We stood in the small space between the counter and the waiting area, which held a couple of plastic chairs and a TV playing the news on mute. But the central feature in the space was a large black electronic board displaying the day's exchange rates in electrified red digits. At the top of the board was the day's date, February 9, 2009, and below that were images of flags representing world currencies the office would exchange: US dollars, Japanese yen, Chinese yuan, and Hong Kong dollars. I cringed looking at the current rate for US dollars, which was slightly better than the week before, but still terrible, at 1,365.15 won per dollar.

The owner glanced up from the ledger he was writing in and saw us looking at the board. "You aren't here to exchange money, are you?" he asked us in English. "Don't do it now. The exchange rate will get better soon."

Señora Juana looked at me and I translated.

When she learned what he had said, she scowled and shook her head dismissively. "The conversion is not going to get better any time soon," she said to me in Spanish, apparently annoyed at his suggestion that we were on our way to a secure economic situation, or that he could predict what would happen with the dollar. Everyone hoped the *tipo de cambio* would get better, but it seemed like it never would. Plus, her daughter needed the money immediately.

Señora Juana pulled out a stack of crisp one-hundred-dollar bills from the zippered pocket of her down coat.

"Wait, you want to exchange *from* dollars to won?" I asked, confused. I had assumed she wanted to buy dollars. It seemed like converting from dollars to won at this time would be great, given that you could get more won than usual.

"Where are you from?" the owner asked with curiosity. Our US dollars were marking us in a peculiar way. Were we migrant workers—who usually came in to exchange Korean won—or tourists—who came in to exchange US dollars? We were not US military because it was after the curfew and all of the soldiers were back on the base by now.

When we did not answer right away, he shrugged and told us he did not get too surprised anymore about who came in. He launched into an in-depth story of how his brother had first come to Korea as a migrant worker twenty years before and then opened a business. He owned most of this street now, he told us.

I translated the highlights of the story for Señora Juana, but she did not seem interested. When she counted out $2,000 in one-hundred-dollar bills, he stopped talking and picked up his calculator. He told her he could give her about 2.7 million won—which was about 822,000 won more than she would have gotten for the same amount a year before.[6] She accepted the rate and he counted out a large stack of bills on the counter.

She struggled to fit the stack of bills in the small envelope he had given her. He gave her another envelope for the rest and we left.

On our way to the ATM, she explained that she had actually lost a lot of money on this exchange. That was because this was the second time in two days that she had converted this same amount of money.

The money had started out being in the form of won that she had earned selling *accessorios*. The day before, she had exchanged it from won to dollars to give to the courier. But then she found out the woman who was supposed to hand-carry the money to Peru for her had already left. She had then found a Peruvian woman who was married to a Korean man and had bank accounts and assets in both Korea and

Peru and was willing to send it for her. The woman had instructed Señora Juana to deposit the money into her Korean bank account—in won—and then she would arrange to give the money to Señora Juana's family in Peruvian soles from her account in Peru. That way the woman would not lose out on wire transfer fees or exchange rates. On top of this, she charged a transaction fee. This was a common method for undocumented migrants to remit money, but there was also a risk the person would not actually send the money.

Since there was no direct route for converting and remitting her money, Señora Juana lost money each time she converted it—either from the conversion or from the commission.

Before we got to the subway station, we stopped by a bank ATM to deposit the cash in the woman's bank account. After a few failed attempts at depositing the money, she suspected she had copied down the account number incorrectly. By this time it was even colder, and she decided to go home and send the money the next day.

I told her I was sorry she had lost so much in this money exchange, but she brushed it off.

"Money is ungrateful. It comes and goes [*La plata es ingrata, viene y se va*]," she said.

I thought about that phrase all the way home and for years afterward. First off, it was catchy because it rhymed in Spanish. More importantly, it indicated that she saw these losses as part of the normal risk of undertaking a cosmopolitan conversion project like migrating to Korea and helping improve her family's situation. She was not dismissing the importance of the money. It represented many months of working, saving, and risking deportation. But, by converting the significance of the loss of money into a quotidian event—even part of the nature of money itself—she was also reaffirming her position as a remitter and family leader. When viewed in the long term, loss was just part of a successful migration.

I have come to see her phrase as eloquently describing the immediate situation of her unstable economic and legal situation and her years of experience. In this quote, she not only fetishizes money, but she also personifies it as an ungrateful lover or even negligent parent. We are all united in our intimate relationship with money. Money prevented her from helping her family, and it also allowed her to help them. In Michele Ruth Gamburd's work on the changing meaning of remittances in Sri Lanka, she finds that once female migrant workers return from the Middle East, they talk about how their money was tainted by the manner in which it was earned and as a result "burns like oil" or spends quickly. The burning money metaphor has also become a culturally acceptable excuse for female migrants to avoid obligations to extended kin and keep remittances within their immediate families. In the same way the burning money metaphor "simultaneously maps and obscures a social reality of labor and exchange relations between people,"[7] Señora Juana's personification of money as an ungrateful intimate becomes a way for her to affirm a position of control despite being an undocumented worker in a harsh and relatively obscure labor circuit during an unstable economic climate.

The saying takes the heat off the global inequality that forced her to migrate to Korea to pay her bills in Peru, but it also implicates money and capitalism as the real problems. The only dependable thing about the conversion rate was its undependability. Her agency came from not only accepting that but also having the wisdom and experience to ameliorate her losses. The unstable conversion rate forced people to negotiate the value of their money, their migration journeys, and themselves.

UNPLUGGED REFRIGERATORS AND
REMITTANCES OUT OF ORDER

The erratic conversion rate during the world economic crisis also changed the meaning of remittances, dollars, and migration for migrants' Peru-based family members.

Economic remittances are a major contributor to the economies of many countries with large emigrant populations, and Peru, as a country with over three million citizens working abroad, is no exception. According to a report by the Inter-American Development Bank, Peruvian migrants remitted three billion dollars in 2007. Migrant remittances, or "migradollars,"[8] are an important national resource and the ultimate "neoliberal currency," because even in the face of great economic uncertainty, the individual migrant must find creative solutions to get money (including traveling to Korea) and assume all risk (including being arrested, deported, or even killed while abroad).[9] In an attempt to keep migrants connected to the state and remitting long after they have left Peru, the Peruvian state has invited migrants to form advisory councils at many of its embassies abroad.[10] The Peruvian state publishes official remittance figures, with the largest percentage coming from its emigrant populations working in the United States, Spain, and Italy. However, like Señora Juana, most Peruvians in Korea lack the proper documentation required to send money home via official channels. Further, because they are not making as much as migrants in other places, figures from Korea are not included in those official reports.

Long before the global financial crisis, I noted that migrants in Korea seemed dismayed that their contributions to Peru were overshadowed by those from migrants in more well-known destinations like Japan. A few people showed me social media pages where they had uploaded videos of themselves working or hanging out in Korea. They told me they had done this specifically to compete with the multitudes of videos of migrants in Japan doing the same thing and to spread awareness of their lives in Korea.

Despite South Korea's ambiguous status in the hierarchy of destinations for Peruvians, migrants from Korea sent dollars, which were important and

FIGURE 4. Made in Japan: A house in Norte Chico built with remittances. Photo by author.

FIGURE 5. Waiting for remittances: Partially constructed and more humble homes across the street in Norte Chico. Remittances dried up during the 2008 economic crisis. Photo by author.

prestigious in Peru. In addition to being the main way Peruvians in Korea remitted their earnings, dollars were also widely exchanged for goods and services, particularly when purchasing expensive items or paying monthly rent. Dollars held an elevated status, and people talked about them as being more secure than the Peruvian nuevo sol. The conversion of won to dollars and then soles not only facilitated the livelihood of migrant families in Peru; the inflow of dollars to the household also became a tangible symbol of these families' connections to Korea and their elevated status as being active participants in "globalization" as a result of having a family member abroad.

When people showed me around Norte Chico, it was easy for me to guess which homes belonged to families with members abroad. As with other migrant-sending communities, there were stark differences between the homes of people who had migrated, or were receiving remittances, and those who had not.[11] The houses of people who did not receive remittances from abroad were usually a single story, square, and sometimes made of adobe (sundried clay). Some even had makeshift doors or roofs. Even the more permanent structures were unfinished. When I accompanied Karina's sister to her friend's house, I looked up from the couch and saw the stars in the night sky between the corrugated tin roof and the wall. In contrast, all of the homes I visited that were owned by families with members abroad were constructed with stronger materials. Homes built with remittances from Japan, the United States, and Korea were usually at least two stories, had a larger footprint, and were covered with stone or tile. Some had storefronts on the first floor, or garage doors that enclosed vehicles that had also been purchased with remittances.

During the crisis, the dollars sent from South Korea came to symbolize something dangerous in the daily lives of my interlocutors in Peru and highlighted the ways that this particular migration pattern represented an alternate route in larger paths of global movement.

I saw an example of this from changes I observed in the home of Señora Esperanza, the woman I lived with during my trips to Norte Chico before and after the global financial crisis. I first met Señora Esperanza in 2007 after spending time with her son Hugo and his girlfriend in Korea. Hugo asked me to stay at his mother's house, saying it would be good for both of us. I could meet many Peruvians who had been in Korea, and his mother would have someone to talk to. All of her children except one were abroad, and she lived alone in the two-story house he and his siblings had built for her with their remittances.

Señora Esperanza was an enthusiastic hostess and interlocutor. Before I even arrived, she had arranged for me to interview her nephews who had lived in Korea. She frequently introduced me to neighbors as an anthropologist and her friend, and she appeared to relish correcting people who said anthropologists were always coming through Norte Chico on their way to nearby excavation sites like the ancient settlement of Caral. "That's archaeology!" she would say, gleefully cutting them off mid-story, and look to me for confirmation. I would smile sheepishly, but quietly agree. For whatever reason, foreign archaeologists did not seem to have a positive reputation in Norte Chico.

When I returned to Norte Chico with my husband in 2008, Señora Esperanza asked us to stay with her again. She loved Mexico, she told us. She had never been there, but from her stories and references, it was apparent that Mexican movies, TV shows, and music had been part of her life since she was a child. Over lunch one day, she had us and her thirteen-year-old granddaughter laughing at a story she told of a mildly romantic dream she had when she was young about Pedro Infante, a Mexican movie star from the Golden Age of Mexican cinema. The story was especially funny coming from her, because she had converted to Protestantism a few years before and lived piously. Unlike her children who were Catholic, she did not drink and did not like others to drink either. Yet, she would attend family parties with us where large bottles of beer were drunk by the case.

"Erica looks like *Chapulín Colorado!*" she joked affectionately after one such party. This was a reference to a red-suited Mexican superhero (the Red Grasshopper) from a 1970s children's show and was meant to comment on how I had turned red from drinking too much beer.

Señora Esperanza was in her sixties but looked older due to her habit of wearing bulky sweaters over dresses buttoned all the way to her neck and pulling her gray hair back into a tight bun. Her daughter Yesica attributed her mother's premature aging to having had two bad marriages and a lifetime of struggling to raise her five children alone. Señora Esperanza's first husband, Hugo's father, had run off. Her second husband, whom she called "El Chucho," was an alcoholic—which may have contributed to her own choice to abstain from alcohol.[12] Although Señora Esperanza had kicked El Chucho out of her house many years prior, she begrudgingly tolerated him hanging around in the afternoons when he took care of Yesica's children.

Señora Esperanza told us that during their marriage, El Chucho had not contributed anything to the household, "Not even a teaspoon," and that if it had not been for her children migrating abroad, they would have all died of starvation. Her youngest son lived in Japan (having paid a Japanese Peruvian man to adopt him in the early 1990s), and the others were in Korea, Venezuela, and Bolivia. Thanks to their remittances, Señora Esperanza told me, she had rebuilt her house from a crumbling adobe structure to one made of brick.

In the afternoons El Chucho would ride his squeaky bicycle up to the house with his granddaughters in tow and slip into the kitchen to wait for a snack. On this particular afternoon in October 2008 though, Señora Esperanza ignored him. After a while, when no food appeared, he walked out of the kitchen and rode off on his bike. It was then that I noticed that Señora Esperanza's large refrigerator—full of food on my last visit the previous year—now sat empty and unplugged.

"It's terrible what's happening with the dollar," she told me in explanation for not running the refrigerator, itself purchased through remittances Hugo had sent during better times. Electricity, always expensive in Peru, had now become a luxury. Through the act of unplugging the refrigerator, something that had once represented a surplus of money was now converted into a symbol of the family's shortage of dollars.

I suspected that Señora Esperanza may not have used the refrigerator even if she had the money to do so. Yesica told me her mother thought the refrigerator—much larger than ones most people used in Peru—was a waste. Since she lived alone, she did not cook much for herself.

The global financial crisis and lack of dollars contributed to the refrigerator being turned off, but it might have been more of a justification for what she already wanted to do, which was to not use that particular remittance. As many scholars have pointed out, although sending remittances can elevate the status of the remitter, they are not always appreciated by the recipients, or used in the way they were intended.[13] Hugo's unstable economic and legal situation during the global financial crisis allowed Señora Esperanza to refuse his gift—by not using the fridge—without seeming ungrateful or hurting his feelings.

I also saw her attitude toward these remittances in the context of being part of a family where migration projects were long-term and always emerging. She seemed to have come to a point in her life where she no longer needed economic remittances in the way she had before, and now she wanted her children to come home. She wanted their company. When we cooked together, she always had to run around to the houses of her nephews and nieces who lived nearby to collect the things she had lent them over the years like pots, a cutting board, a blender, and kitchen knives. When Yesica scolded her for giving away her things, she said she had no use for them with no one there.

While the transformation of her home from adobe to brick had been very important to Señora Esperanza, other remittances were burdensome. Her house held remittances that were unused, half-finished, or in disrepair. She had an enormous stereo system that she kept covered in plastic and did not know how to use. Her children had installed a heated shower in the bathroom, but she never used it for bathing. Instead she used the base of the shower to store boxes and bags. Whenever her children visited, they complained that their mother did not use the shower and tried to fix it. She humored them and then filled the space back up with boxes after they left. She told me I could try to use the shower, but it had a leaky faucet. "If you turn it on, it will never turn off again," she warned.

Toward the end of 2008, even more visible signs of the financial crisis arrived in Peruvian homes: people I had first met in Korea, including Hugo, were being deported and returning to Peru without many dollars. Whereas the arrival of dollars and foreign goods into rural Peruvian homes and the departure of family members had once constituted "Korea" to these families, now it was the return of the migrants and the absence of dollars that came to represent this migration flow.

As deported migrants arrived, their family members did not talk about how they were worried about losing their remittances, but about how they were worried for how the returning migrant would see him- or herself once they were back in Peru. In her research about migrants returning to Cape Verde after years of working in Europe, anthropologist Lisa Akesson found that the community categorized and ranked returning migrants based on the remittances they had returned with and the plans they had managed to lay out for their own futures while they were gone.[14] A "successful" migrant was one who had saved enough to build a house for him- or herself in Cape Verde and had also established a pension or business that would continue to provide money after the migrant had left Europe. Anything short of this was seen as a failure. While I did not find such an openly agreed upon ranking system in Peru, the families I knew were concerned about the presence or absence of the same qualities in their migrant family members. If the migrant had set up a long-term plan for their own future income, that would have meant success. But many returning migrants I knew fell short of that, and therefore their deportations made their family members worried that all the years they spent in Korea were a waste.

The deported migrants who greeted me when I visited their family homes represented the new realities of globalization for Peruvian migrants who had been in Korea. Many had brought their Samsung and LG cell phones with them from Korea although they ran on a different system and did not function as usable phones in Peru. The children in the house liked to play games on the phones and take photos, but I heard more than one ask when they were going to get a newer model, one that worked. The disconnected cell phones, like the unplugged refrigerators, kept migrants and their families somewhat connected to Korea, but they also showed how they were disconnected from both transnational circuits and the dollars they promised. While the out-of-order statuses of these products proved that their owners had once brought in and spent US dollars as active participants in "globalization," they also illustrated their owners' new even lower positions in this already precarious global circuit between Peru and Korea. In many ways, these broken-down remittances, and their reminders of what had been and could be again, inspired migrants to try to return to Korea as soon as they were deported. Despite the insecurity of the won, their years living as undocumented migrants in Korea, and the slim chances they had of ever entering the country again, the majority of deported migrants with whom I spoke had spent their first few months in Peru planning creative ways to return to Seoul. From their seats in their mothers' kitchens in Peru, being an active member of globalization—even as a vulnerable participant with little chance for saving money or becoming legalized—was preferable to staying in Peru. They also wanted a chance to finalize plans they had tried to lay out while in Korea. Without money, they needed to find new ways to influence the world.

SUCCESSFUL AND FAILED CONVERSIONS: TWO REMITTANCE TALES

Peruvians still in Korea working to lay out future plans for themselves and their families found that money alone was not reliable; they needed to think of other creative ways to increase the value of their economic remittances. In this section I focus on the remitting experiences of two migrants who tempered their economic remittances with social remittances about work, education, and frugality in an attempt to convert their family members from disadvantaged Peruvians into autonomous people who could weather the unstable economic climate. Lily and Rafael each had worked in Korea for over six years and had been active in the Catholic community. They both were able to keep their factory jobs throughout the economic crisis and so had a more regular income than people like Franco or Señora Esperanza who were self-employed. While Lily, a single young woman, had been successful in using her remittances to establish authority in her family and to influence changes that helped her economic remittances go further during the economic crisis, Rafael, a husband and father of two, failed to get his family to accept his social remittances along with his money—and their refusal to convert into self-sufficient people had caused permanent divisions in his family.

Lily, just twenty-four-years-old when I met her in Seoul in 2007, had worked in Korea and Japan for six years and had become the head of her family in Peru after she started sending remittances home at the age of eighteen. Over the years she had sent enough money to Peru to construct a two-story home, buy two taxis, which her family members rented from her, and put her niece through nursing school. In 2008, I visited the home Lily had built in Lima. It was in a pueblo joven that was not yet developed. The streets were unpaved, and not all of the homes had access to plumbing or electricity. The neighbor's house directly across the dirt street was constructed out of scraps of plywood and aluminum sheeting and had a piece of fabric nailed across a gap in the walls that served as a makeshift door. Lily's two-story house would have been impressive in any part of Lima, but its blue stone facade and wrought-iron balconies stood out sharply in this neighborhood. Lima is humid, so to reduce the presence of mildew, people use concrete, marble, granite, and tile for flooring and wall coverings. While most migrant families I visited had been able to cover the exterior of their homes with plaster (as opposed to leaving it exposed), very few had done so with an expensive stone like Lily had used.

Lily's father, three elderly great-aunts, and her sister all lived in the two-story house. They referred to their home as "Lily's house" although Lily had never been there. As her father walked me through the home, pointing out the work he had done as his daughter's contractor, I noted that the aunts had all decorated their rooms with dolls sent by Lily and another cousin working in Korea. Dressed in Korean *hanbok* and Japanese kimonos, the dolls were kept in glass cases and put in places of honor on top of dressers as the only decorations in each room. Lily's father explained that their next project on the house would be to turn the front room into a marble-covered space that would serve as both the kitchen and a garage for Lily's taxis. After the visit, her father took me home in his daughter's taxi. "He drives it for me," Lily had explained to me when I met her in Korea. She had purchased the taxi with cash and allowed her father to operate it. He paid her a rent of 25 soles per day (about $9, which was half the going rate for a taxi rental), and then kept the rest of his earnings as profit.

Lily's economic remittances did more than just pay for the family's bills. They positioned her as a leader of her family, as an employer, scholarship provider, and caretaker of the elderly. The family showed me around the house gingerly, frequently mentioning that this was Lily's house. Her money also helped to convert her family members into the type of people who could care for themselves and would not need remittances. Her remittances gave her father a job and her niece an education in nursing—a field with real employment possibilities both in Peru and abroad. The remittances physically united the family by allowing them to live together, as opposed to spread out over the pueblos jóvenes of Lima like they had been when Lily left Peru at eighteen years old. In addition to the Korean and Japanese dolls, which were a daily reminder of the family's status in the global scheme of things, having direct access to beautiful foreign items as well as foreign money, the house itself was a symbol of "global migration" and the prestige Lily's migration gave her family. I imagined that as the neighbors peered at the home's stone-covered walls through the holes in their own makeshift doors, they received a clear message about the affluence of the family and the power of remittances. The home, education, and businesses established via Korea gave Lily inspiration to continue laboring in her factory—a place she worked twelve to fourteen hours a day under the constant danger of being injured by the ancient equipment or detected by the immigration officers who constantly patrolled the area looking for people just like her. In late November 2008, at the height of the economic crisis, and while I was visiting her family in Peru, Lily was suddenly detained in her factory and deported to Peru. While many migrants find themselves penniless when they return to Peru, Lily returned to a new home and a nearly self-sufficient family. Although Lily could have possibly made more money in other migration destinations, her money had gone very far.

Most remittance stories do not end so successfully. In some cases, like that of Rafael, who sent money to his wife, Nancy, so she could open a store in Peru, remittances lead to new divisions in the family. Rafael's idea had been that if Nancy turned the front room of their home into a profitable store, his remittances could go into savings rather than paying for their daily expenses. When I visited the family in Peru, Rafael's sister told me about how the store—and subsequently, Rafael's marriage—had failed. At first everything went according to plan. Nancy used the remittances to buy the essential items for stocking any Peruvian neighborhood store—cases of Cristal and Pilsen beer, full tanks of gas for stoves, jugs of cooking oil, and racks of candy and snacks. Many neighbors came into the store, and the stock went down quickly. However, every month, instead of turning a profit, Nancy asked for more money to buy new stock. After a few months, Rafael's sister finally told him what was happening. "Nancy's family, her siblings, her parents, her cousins, were using the store like their own cupboard," Rafael's sister told me.

Nancy's family members would come by and grab a tank of gas and promise to pay the next day, but never did. They would hang out every evening in the store listening to music, drinking beer, and eating snacks as Nancy's nonpaying guests. After a few months, the shelves were empty, Rafael refused to send more money, and the business closed. Rafael's marriage, already ailing, collapsed along with the business.

The failure of the family store shows the power that remittances have to change things; in this case, family dynamics. His wife's family may have believed that it was their right to take items from the store without paying—partly because they saw Rafael as having unlimited access to dollars, and partly because they felt they deserved a share of the remittances. The family's ability to open a business—and Nancy's generosity in giving away the stock to her friends and family—gave the impression that Rafael's job in Korea was more profitable and secure than it actually was. In a photo on the cover of Sarah Mahler's book about Latin American migration to the United States in the 1990s, a young man poses against a sports car on a suburban American street. In sending this photo to his family in Peru, and presenting the car and tree-lined street as his own (when it is not), Mahler says he is fueling a "cycle of deception" that further promulgates the American Dream as something easily attainable by all who enter the United States looking for work.[15] Rafael's store reveals other dimensions to this "cycle of deception." Rather than Rafael directly misrepresenting his own level of success, Nancy did it for him by allowing customers to consume products without paying. She made it seem that Rafael, as a worker in Korea, had nearly unlimited access to cash.

During an interview at his home in Korea in July 2007, Rafael told me that one result of having his store was that he frequently received emails and calls from his relatives and friends in Peru asking him to sponsor their own journeys to Korea. They promised that the first thing they would do after arriving would be to earn money and pay him back. However, after putting up the money for a few attempted migrations, which had all ended in the potential migrants being refused entry at the Seoul airport and immediately returned to Peru, Rafael shied away from these requests. Rafael knew that even if the sponsored migrant successfully passed through immigration at the airport, there was a very low chance he or she could earn enough money to pay him back before being deported.

Further, Nancy's continual demands for remittances, but failure to run the store correctly, showed her unwillingness to participate in Rafael's efforts to convert her into a self-sufficient person. Rafael's original plan had been to work in Korea to save money to get his family ahead; however, unless migrants can find a way to invest their earnings, they will never make enough money in Korea to sustain their families once they return to Peru. In order to make his original plan a success, his wife and family would need to take the remittances he sent and turn them into productive cultural capital, like a business or an education. However, the failed store was just one of many projects Rafael had devised to invest his remittances, only to discover that his family had not cooperated with his wishes. At his urging, in the seven years he had worked in Korea, his sons had entered expensive English academies, private high schools, and trade schools, and then dropped out after a few weeks without telling him. His wife had failed to use the remittances to fix the roof on the house or remodel the second floor into apartments to rent. In a final effort to help his youngest son learn to help himself, Rafael brought him to Korea to "learn how to work"; however, this too failed when Rafael himself was deported six months later and his son opted to leave as well, rather than stay and (learn to) work. Even the priest in Korea criticized the boy for returning to Peru with his father instead of staying in Korea.

Rafael's attempts to extend the value of his economic remittances by turning them into cultural capital for his family—a business and an education—ultimately resulted in new forms of loss. The refusal to participate in Rafael's family conversion project, and the "misspending" of his economic capital, caused new rifts in the family. Further, in Rafael's absence, an uncle was trying to assert his claim to the family's *chacra*, or farmland. "When he gets home, he will have nothing," his sister told me as we sat on her couch discussing the news of Rafael's deportation and pending arrival. Instead of setting up his financial future, Rafael would return with less money than he had accumulated before he left. His family had grown up, but also grown apart, partly through their failures to use the money he sent in the way he had intended. In this case, a small amount of money had been converted into a big problem, and his attempts at converting his family had, in many ways, failed.

"DINERO SIN DIRECCIÓN ES MALDICIÓN"
(MONEY WITHOUT DIRECTION IS A CURSE)

In this last section, I return to the conversation I mentioned with Franco at the beginning of this chapter as a way to explore how despite the success or failure of a migrant's ability to manage their family through their economic and social remittances, perhaps the most significant conversion happens to the person doing the converting and remitting.

Franco told me that since the world economic crisis started, he was sending less money than ever, but now also evangelizing to them over the phone.

"How did your family react to that?" I asked. I imagined they would be angry about getting less money and being targets of conversion.

Surprisingly (at least to me), rather than causing problems, Franco believed that this new arrangement had actually improved his relationship with his family in Peru. He became animated as he told me about it:

> All I did was give them the *evangelio* [gospel], and thank God, huge changes came to their lives. Years back I sent money here and there, but the moment the money got

there and they divided it up, nothing happened. This year, I began to give them the word of God. . . . And wow, I saw that all of my siblings, all of my family, began to change. I said nothing, nothing, only, "God just got here and you guys already want to change!" Now I can send their *propina* [pocket money] because I know what they are going to spend it on. [laughs]

Franco concluded that as a result of his evangelizing, his family had been converted into people who no longer wanted to spend money on foolish vices like drinking and partying. As a result, even though he sent them less money, it went further.

Essentially, Franco described sending his family a combination of economic remittances in the form of Korean won converted first into US dollars and then into Peruvian nuevo soles and social remittances in the form of Korean-style evangelism interpreted for a Peruvian audience. This was a version of prosperity theology: if people behave as good Cristianos by avoiding alcohol and immoral behavior such as sex before marriage, then God will reward them with economic prosperity. Franco's willingness to continue sending his family economic remittances depended on their openness to receiving the particular social remittances he wanted to send. If they did not convert according to Franco's specifications, or at least act like they were willing to do so, they would not receive any more money. And—at least from Franco's perspective—if they were really earnest in their conversions, they would become good Christians who would receive their own rewards from God and would therefore not need as many remittances. This quid pro quo mixture of economic and social remittances was mutually beneficial to his family's spiritual welfare, their economic autonomy, and the good of his own wallet.

Given that remitting was the primary—and often sole—impetus my interlocutors cited for originally migrating to Korea, suddenly being unable (or unwilling) to send money home could cause serious problems. However, according to Franco, no amount of money would ever be enough for his family unless he successfully converted them into people who knew how to value it correctly.

"Money without direction is a curse," he told me. Franco's new attitude did not mean that he had stopped thinking about money. In fact, like other Peruvian migrants, he seemed to think about it constantly. However, as opposed to focusing on money's immediate value, he was thinking of its relational value coupled with his new religious message and the potential it held to convert his family. The potential value of Franco's remittances shifted as he sent them transnationally. For example, his money gained value (at least in his eyes) as he integrated it with his social remittances, and he gained personal value as a remitter and family savior through the process of remitting. However, because he had to first convert his earnings into US dollars in order to send them home, his money lost value when he sent it to Peru.

While Franco assured me that his family had truly converted and no longer needed so much money, I did not get a chance to meet them and ask how they felt about the new arrangement. Many of the families I knew in Peru had conflicts over their converted family members' new beliefs, primarily because they did not like being evangelized to or judged for their non-Cristiano ways, like drinking alcohol or going to parties. However, whether or not his family converted, the person who was most changed through intermingling these remittances was Franco himself. When he told me that "money without direction is a curse," he could have been talking about himself.

He told me that although he had saved $5,000 on his first trip to Korea, rather than investing it, he had wasted it on partying. Of that experience, he said:

> I went back to my country and was satisfied for one month, I recall. Then I was back to my old ways—parties. You know how people are who have money but don't have direction in their lives. I went back to my same vices. I used up all the money. I was back to zero again. [laughs] God help me.

By the time he made his second trip to Korea he was no longer a single man, but a father of a two-year-old daughter. His plan for this second trip had been to save a large sum of money over a two-year period before returning to Peru to open a business. However, almost immediately on his arrival, he found out that his daughter in Peru needed emergency heart surgery. Distraught and penniless from his journey, he accompanied a cousin to a Korean evangelical church with a Spanish-speaking congregation to seek help. There, he said, his life began to change. Not only did the Korean church members help him raise money for his daughter's operation, but the Latin American congregation and lay pastor from Peru also taught him the gospel and showed him that everything in his life—including his search for money—would be a failure until he accepted Jesus Christ into his heart.

Now, six years later, Franco was still in Korea but had given up on working in a factory. His daughter was healthy in Peru, but he had not been able to leave to see her. "I listened to the message, and I changed. I found that money wasn't the solution for my life," he said.

Although Franco did not convert for money, money infused his story of conversion. His desire for money brought him to Korea where he found his true destiny—to bring others to Christ. Only by going through the experience of gaining money easily (on his first trip) and then losing it just as easily through vices such as drinking did he learn that money without direction is a curse. The particular "direction" he was following came from the evangelical church he attended, which had given him just enough economic capital to bring him to God (through the help they gave for his daughter's medical bills) but also promised him cultural capital by helping him learn to be a missionary so he could teach others (and especially his family) the value of money.

In the end, it did not matter if his family really converted or not. He only had limited money to send. The loss of money gave him the opportunity to creatively negotiate the value of his remittances, which in turn gave him a semblance of control in an otherwise uncontrollable situation. Money had both caused his problems and had also inspired solutions. It had been his downfall and the impetus for the changes he made to his life and those of others.

CONCLUSION: CONVERTING REMITTANCES

Señora Juana was right; the exchange rate got even worse before it got better. Every day it went up and down a little bit before it reached a low in March 2009 of 1,500 won per dollar—meaning one million won only converted to $688. Then it slowly got better until it leveled off. No matter how good the rate got, though, it never reached what it had been in 1996 when Franco first arrived and Peruvian migration to Korea was becoming more popular—and one million won equaled $1,250. That meant that it was never as profitable to migrate to Korea as it had been in the 1990s. These shifting rates and each family's need for money in Peru made a "successful conversion" relative as well.

The world economic crisis simultaneously destabilized and gave direction to migrants as they navigated the world and negotiated their places in Korea and Peru. When my interlocutors worked to overcome barriers and successfully convert money or other people, they simultaneously converted themselves and their understanding of their relative positions in the world. Through coming to appreciate their own relational value in global hierarchies, they also tried to improve the positions of their family members. Their conversion strategies not only changed the meaning of money but also changed the nature of their relationships with their families and their ideas about their own lives as migrants.

Whether or not migrants succeeded in converting their family members into people who valued things like sober living and frugal spending, the mere attempt at augmenting economic remittances with social remittances ultimately shifted the value of the money for the families who received it. One dollar no longer simply equaled one dollar. It was now infused with the possibility for new business and success, or the potential for failure and disappointment if spent in the wrong way. Although the dollar has regained its global footing, the 2008 crisis brought attention to a point perhaps obscured in more profitable times: just as currencies can always be converted, but perhaps never equal the same amount of money, so too can an attempt at conversion be unsuccessful, but leave the family, migrant, and nation forever changed.

In the next chapter, I explore how many Peruvians converted to or changed religions in Korea. I show how they attempted to reconfigure the meaning of their migrations and their place in a global hierarchy through their participation in Protestant churches and their identification of *respuestas* or signs from God that their migrations were not about a search for money, but were in fact predestined.

TABLE 1: Important conversion rates from Korean won to US dollars between 1996 and 2017

Date	Korean Won Equivalent to 1 US Dollar[1]	Event	Value of 1 Million Won Converted to USD
11/30/1996	800	Franco's first arrival in Korea.	**$1,250**
1/1998	1,693	Asian financial crisis.[2]	**$590**
11/30/2004	1,048	Franco's second arrival.	$954
8/24/2008	1,067	Just before won weakens.	$937
9/1/2008	1,115	Beginning of world financial crisis.	$896
10/10/2008	1,307	Discussion about the dollar in Señora Esperanza's kitchen.	$765
11/19/2008	1,455		$687
11/24/2008	1,511	One of the worst conversion rates during 2008 global financial crisis.	**$661**
12/28/2008	1,262	I arrive in Korea.	$792
1/10/2009	1,355		$738
1/25/2009	1,376	Angela calls to discuss won-to-yen conversion.	$726
2/9/2009	1,378	I visit currency exchange with Señora Juana.	$725
3/2009	1,453	Rate worsens again after brief improvement.	**$688**
5/28/2009	1,282		$780
7/5/2009	1,266		$789
10/31/2009	1,186		$843
11/3/2009	1,188	Interview with Franco.	$841
11/3/2010	1,110		$900
11/3/2011	1,127		$887
11/3/2012	1,091		$916
11/3/2013	1,061		$942
3/11/2014	1,065		$939
2/16/2016	1,225		$816
8/4/2017	1,128		$885

---

[1] Conversion rates from www.xe.com/currencytables/?from=KRW&date=2017-08-04. Last accessed July 14, 2019.

[2] Rate from www.oanda.com/currency/historical-rates/. Last accessed March 1, 2014.

3

Religious Conversion

When I arrived at the pueblo joven–based home of Camila, a member of Friend-ship Ministry, one of the first things I learned was that her conversion to Prot-estantism in Korea had resulted in disagreements with her family over how to run their businesses in Peru. Camila's mother was Catholic, and the two of them were arguing—transnationally—over the ethics of selling beer in the store on the first floor of their home. As was the case with the other Peruvians I knew who had converted to Protestantism in Korea, Camila abstained from alcohol and saw Catholicism as being lax in its moral underpinnings partly because Catholics were allowed to drink. She not only abstained, but she also wanted to help improve the spiritual and economic lives of her family and community by not providing alcohol to them.

I had met Camila just a month earlier at her church in Korea where she was an enthusiastic member of the Spanish-language congregation. At twenty-three, she was one of the younger Peruvian members. She was in love with her Peruvian boy-friend whom she had met in Korea. She was excited about my project and offered to show me where she sold *accesorios* after work on the streets of her factory town and then to arrange a visit with her family when I traveled to Lima the following month. Many people in Camila's family had worked in places like Korea, Japan, Chile, and the United States. She wanted me to see the store she had built with her remittances and visit her mother and a few of her siblings who still lived in or near the family home in a pueblo joven in Lima.

I took a long combi and taxi ride from my apartment in San Miguel, and as we approached her neighborhood, I saw that few of the streets were paved. There were signs this area was improving though, including curbs, sidewalks, and traffic lights that almost sparkled with their newness. When my taxi arrived, Camila's sister, who had also worked in Korea years earlier, came outside to meet me. We walked a short distance to the family house and storefront. Camila's mother owned the house, but the little bodega was actually Camila's store, constructed with remittances she had sent from Korea. Similar to how Lily's relatives referred to their home as "Lily's house" (in chapter 2), Camila's sister made a point of referring to the store as Camila's—even though Camila had never been there (just as Lily had never been in "Lily's house").

The store was a narrow rectangular structure made of cinderblock running alongside a wall of the house. Like many other small stores I saw in Lima, it did not have a door for customers to walk through but rather just a window where they could pass money and receive merchandise. The window was covered in metal bars to protect the store from potential robbers.[1]

I stood on my tiptoes to try to see their wares. Typically stores like this had shelves of things like snacks, individual rolls of toilet paper, and small packets of laundry detergent and shampoo displayed against the back wall. I jumped back when a woman suddenly shouted at us from inside the store.

"Who is that?" the woman yelled.

"Camila's friend from Korea, Mamá," Camila's sister said.

There was no response.

That is when I noticed their mother was inside the store. She was short and only the top of her hair was visible through the slot where customers passed their money and got their change.

Camila's sister continued chatting with me about Korea and my research and moved aside every time a customer approached the window. It was before noon, but everyone who came to the store left with beer—from single bottles to entire cases.

I probably would not have even noticed that everyone was buying beer if Camila's sister had not seemed embarrassed about it. She smiled apologetically and said, "Camila has agreed, for now, to sell beer," she told me. I guessed then that Camila must have introduced me as a friend from her Protestant church.

"If we don't sell beer, we might as well close down!" her mother yelled from behind the bars, as if she was still in the middle of the fight with Camila.

Her sister made no comment on that topic. Instead, she invited me inside the house, a two-story structure. With the store completed, Camila was now in the process of sending money to build up a second business—an internet café. They were turning the front room into a place for computers but they were also still using it as a living room. She told me Camila did not want the internet customers to look at pornography—a rule she had no problem with but thought might hurt business. Her mother flatly refused, however, to comply with Camila's directive to stop selling beer in the store.

Camila's mother came out of the store through a door along the living room wall and sat in an upholstered chair. She sat in silence as I talked to Camila's sister about her own migration to Korea years before. When I asked them who in their family had first migrated to Korea, her daughter looked at her mother.

She told me her husband had gone to Japan in the early 1990s and started another *"compromiso"* (commitment). He had apparently met a woman in Japan and stopped contacting them.

I could see how the family would have a complex relationship with the remittances sent from Camila and her siblings. Remittances had allowed the family to survive and even led to their upward mobility, but remittances also had scattered the siblings around the world and were a reminder of their abandonment.

They asked about my family, and when her mother found out that my husband was from Mexico City, she asked me to bring her an image of the Virgin of Guadalupe on my next trip. She specifically wanted one that had been blessed by a priest from the Basilica, a sacred Catholic site that luckily was located near my mother-in-law's house.

I agreed to bring her the image, but I knew that Camila might not approve. That is because in addition to alcohol, many of the Peruvians who had converted from Catholicism to Protestantism in Korea had come to believe that the importance attributed to the Virgin Mary and saints (such as El Señor de los Milagros) in Catholicism in general and Peru in particular angered God. They interpreted displaying images of saints and virgins to be worshipping false idols—and believed they had contributed to the financial and spiritual demise of Latin America.

By the time I returned to Peru the following year, Camila had also returned. When I called her family house in Lima, I had to remind her where we knew each other from because she was surprised to hear a foreigner's voice on the phone. Once she recognized me, she said how happy she was to hear from someone she had known in Korea. She told me that she had gotten pregnant and decided to return to Peru instead of trying to raise an undocumented child in Korea. She and her son were living with her mother until her boyfriend, who was still in Korea at the time, could save enough money to construct a house for them in Lima. She asked me to come to the house and then join everyone for her birthday party at a nearby restaurant. In addition to her own family, which was Catholic, her future in-laws, who were Protestant, would also attend.

As soon as Omar and I arrived at their house, Camila's mother came rushing down the stairs asking if I had brought *"Mi virgencita"* (the image she wanted of the Virgin of Guadalupe). When I took the framed image out of my bag, she unwrapped it, held it to her chest, and said happily, *"¡La gringa cumplió!* [The American girl came through!]." Camila stood by and looked embarrassed. *"¡Mamá!"* she said. It was difficult to tell if she was embarrassed by her mother's devotion to the image of the Virgin, or because she had referred to me somewhat derogatorily as "the gringa," or having done all of that before saying "hello." I never found out as we rushed out of the house to get taxis to the restaurant. They did at least pause long enough to show me that the internet café had been completed. I noticed signs posted on the wall—ones that had been typed and printed out on computer paper—that said things like, "No swearing."

During Camila's birthday lunch, held at a lively family-style *parrillada,* or bar-beque restaurant, it became apparent that something had changed in the family dynamic since my previous visit and Camila's return.

We sat at a long table that ran along the front window of the restaurant. Camila's mother, her mother's friend, and Camila's siblings sat on one side of the table, while Camila's in-laws clustered around the other end. Camila directed me to sit with her near the middle of the table. Her sister and brother-in-law had ordered the food and drinks for the table, which included several elevated metal platters overflowing with slices of roasted steak, *anticuchos* (marinated beef hearts), rabbit, *cuy* (guinea pig), and pork. Scattered between the trays of meat were platters of French fries and salad as well as big bottles of Coca-Cola and Inca Kola. When the waiter placed icy pitchers of sangria on each end of the long table, Camila gave her sister a frustrated look. I did not hear her say anything about it, but she looked miserable for most of the meal.

I guessed that pitchers of sangria were a flashpoint especially today because of the presence of Camila's future in-laws. It was one thing to have family disagreements about alcohol, but another to have people witness it. I realized that since the last time I had seen Camila and her mother, their temperaments had switched.

Camila's mother responded happily to the arrival of the pitchers and held up her glass for Camila's future brother-in-law, Elias (who told me he was the only member of his family who was not religious), to fill. Elias had also worked in Korea years prior, and while we waited for the food to arrive, he had been telling me a fascinating story about how he had managed to talk his way out of the airport in Tokyo during a layover after being deported from Korea. Once outside the airport he had found a pay phone, called cousins who lived in Fukuoka, and stayed in Japan for nearly ten years before being deported to Peru the month before this party. When he offered to pour me and Omar a drink, Camila reacted quickly.

"You don't have to drink that," she said.

I turned the drink down, touched by Camila's kind gesture to protect me.

"You don't drink?" her mother asked disapprovingly from across the table.

I paused, not sure how to answer. "I do," I said, and immediately felt Camila deflate next to me. "But not today."

An hour into the meal, the pitchers on the in-law side of the table were still full, and the outside of the glass dripped with condensation. Camila's family's side of the table, which now included Elias, was lamenting their empty pitchers between boisterously telling stories. The in-law side was quieter and more serious.

After a while, Camila's mother asked the in-laws to pass their full pitchers down the table if they were not going to drink them. To Camila's obvious dismay, they did. Ignoring Camila's embarrassed looks, her mother offered both me and Camila's mother-in-law a glass, which we accepted. In this setting, I was not sure which was the most culturally appropriate response: drink or refuse. It also seemed that since Camila had returned from Korea, it was not clear who was ultimately the highest-ranking person at the table and what the expectations were for Camila, her family, and even me as the interested visitor with muddled allegiances.

Either way, spending time with this family that was now both Catholic and Protestant and had the addition of potential in-laws was more complicated than it was prior to migration. I not only saw the ways religious conversion had transformed these families, but also how the family dynamics had changed since Camila was no longer a migrant sending economic and social remittances from abroad. Although currents of disapproval and approval still ran through everyday choices, such as how to run the family store, and how to treat guests at special events, Camila no longer seemed to have much of a voice in defending her position, even at her own birthday party. She had converted in Korea, but now that she was in Peru, it was proving difficult to live her life the way she wanted, let alone persuade her family to change their lifestyles. The stakes had changed and so had the players.

Conversions were a way for migrants to negotiate their place in the world and to influence the ways others saw them. Once Camila had left Korea, the value systems between her worlds in Korea and Peru diverged. She could not get her family to see the world from her perspective because without economic remittances she no longer had as much negotiation power over her family.

Although Camila's story was just one example of the many configurations of religious belief and family dynamics I observed during my fieldwork, I found that people's stories and experiences of religious conversion provided a window into the ways migrants understood and tried to change not only their own status but also that of their families and communities and in turn influence the meanings of their migrations and how others saw them. In this chapter, I explore the ways Peruvian migrants converted to or changed religion or renewed their faith in South Korea and discuss how in converting themselves and attempting to convert others, they negotiated and reconfigured the meaning of their migrations; their relationships with their families, peers, and churches in Peru and Korea; and their place in the world.

For Peruvian migrants, Korea provided a backdrop that infused both Protestant and Catholic church participation with more opportunities to advance one's cosmopolitan conversions than other migration destinations would have. Their exceptionalism in Korea not only allowed migrants to gain cultural capital at an accelerated rate—in the form of experiences and leadership positions in their churches—but also gave them the platform to try to influence others to see them as cosmopolitan leaders rather than as economic migrants. I discuss how some migrants interpreted events in their lives and migrations through the framework of *respuestas,* or answers from God, and in doing so, they portrayed their religious conversions as being more valuable than money. Sharing respuestas at various levels—with their families, peers, and the public—gave them cosmopolitan experiences and changed the ways others saw them in Peru and South Korea. By examining how people's understanding of things like conversion, migration, money, and transnational ties between Peru and Korea were intertwined, I attempt to go beyond a utilitarian view of migrants' religious conversion and focus on the ways conversions that happen in transnational spaces create and complicate conventional understandings of global hierarchies and configurations of power.

RELIGIOUS CONVERSION AS A PATH TO BECOMING LEADERS IN KOREA

Before the global financial crisis, I centralized my fieldwork on the various communities that the clergy from the Catholic Church visited, partly because that gave me the greatest access to the Peruvian community as a whole. Over time I noticed that Peruvian congregations from Korean evangelical Protestant churches had taken a larger role in the Peruvian migrant community, not only as spiritual centers but also as alternative sources of resources and information for migrants. As I started spending more time with Protestant groups, I expanded my focus to compare the ways Peruvians experienced religious conversion within the various religious communities.

To capture the different types and degrees of "religious conversion" people experienced during their migrations to Korea, I include new, rejuvenated, and renewed levels of belief and participation in Catholic and Protestant churches. By *new* beliefs, I mean people like Camila who told me they had arrived as Catholics, or with no religion, and then joined a Protestant church in Korea.

By *rejuvenated* beliefs, I mean people who arrived in Korea as nonpracticing Catholics or Protestants, found a corresponding church, and became more passionate about participating in events and becoming leaders. I frame rejuvenation as a form of conversion because for most Peruvians, being a Catholic or Protestant in Korea was different from being either of these identities in Peru.

By *renewed* beliefs, I mean people who came from Protestant families in Peru but felt they had found the "true gospel" in Korea.[2] Jheremy, one of the migrant leaders from Friendship Ministry, explained it to me like this, "The *Cristiano* [Protestant] in South America is a partial Christian, but the Christian in Korea is a total Christian." When I asked Peruvians with renewed religious beliefs to describe their conversion experiences, they told me they had left Peru because they were looking for something, and when they got to Korea, they "found a connection with God," "learned to let God into [their] heart," or "learned what it really meant to trust in God." Although they had started as Protestants, people who experienced a renewal of faith in Korea often saw it as being a drastic transformation or conversion.

Rather than try to interrogate the "authenticity" of these religious conversions, I am interested in exploring the transnational milieu in which the conversions happened. Migration to Korea was vital in creating the context for these religious conversions. Not only did other destinations for Peruvian labor, like Japan, not have the religious infrastructure to provide spaces for these communities to form, but since Korean churches were embarking on their own cosmopolitan conversion projects looking for global destinations and converts, Peruvians also became more desirable partners than other groups of more numerous or documented foreigners.

Korea provided Peruvian migrants numerous opportunities for conversion and religious participation not available to them in Peru—and that included being Catholic. In describing his background, one man I spoke to told me that he was Peruvian and therefore Catholic. I took this statement as a naturalization of his Peruvian and Catholic identity. To be fully Peruvian one must be Catholic. While the majority of the Peruvians I met at Masses had grown up Catholic, many of them told me it was "in name only," and they had not attended Mass regularly nor had they completed the necessary religious rites of passage to be a full member of the church, such as getting confirmed. Having missed these events as children was a source of shame for many.

However, in Korea, the Catholic clergy was openly offering the chance to remedy this problem. Above the Mass schedule in the March 2007 Catholic newsletter distributed to Peruvians in Korea was written: "Everyone who wants to prepare to receive their sacraments that they have not received yet are invited." They even included a kind of Sacrament FAQ section in the same issue of the newsletter defining and describing Baptism, First Communion, and Confirmation—perhaps questions they knew many of their parishioners were afraid to ask aloud. "What happens when we are baptized?" it begins. "Nos convertimos en HIJOS DE DIOS [We turn into CHILDREN OF GOD]." In that same issue of the newsletter a man from Norte Chico wrote an article about how while growing up his uncles had bullied him for not getting baptized, and now that he had completed the process in Korea he had ended thirty-six years of shame. He wrote, "Now I am baptized, my best Christian Catholic life begins. What I was missing, not only is joy for me but for my spirit and my family. . . . Now I'm ready, with a lot of faith to . . . renew things." Being in Korea gave participants like him the opportunity to become fully Catholic and therefore Peruvian—something they could not do in Peru.

I noticed in 2009 that fewer people seemed to be attending Mass than during my previous field trips in Korea. When I asked Padre Ignacio about it, he told me that people were now more scared to leave their houses and attend regularly, but that the interest in participating was still high. He had recently baptized twelve Peruvians—all adults—in one day in Dongducheon. That was not the first time he had done a group baptism for Peruvians in Korea, but it was the largest group he had personally done. He said he thought this enthusiasm to participate in the church was because their relatively small numbers made them feel like they were part of a community. He also pointed out that rites of passage like Baptisms or Confirmations were usually reserved for children and would have been too humiliating to attempt as an adult in Peru. In Korea, though, it seemed congregants experienced a certain religious liminality where surrounded by a small community of people in a similar situation they were permitted to break the rules of age convention and undergo a ritual that was required, but taboo for them, as an adult Catholic.

In addition to defying taboos, Catholic rituals done by undocumented migrants in Korea tended to take on a new urgency. For example, in May 2009 I attended a Mass in Seoul where a man in his seventies was baptized, confirmed, and received his First Communion all in one day. He was a quiet man I recognized from Masses where he accompanied hymns by playing the *cajón,* a Peruvian wooden percussion instrument. When I talked to the nuns about how they had spent the previous months helping him prepare for his rites of passage, I noted the sense of urgency around the process. Not only was there a risk he could be deported before completing the steps, but more importantly they were also planning this event for the day a Korean bishop, who was also a nuncio (a papal ambassador) visiting from Rome, would preside over those rituals for the migrants. Everyone who was baptized or confirmed that day not only got to do so with a nuncio but also received a gift from the Vatican—a crucifix blessed by the pope. I got the sense this type of opportunity would have been a rarity for most converts in Peru (or Korea for that matter).

When I was in Norte Chico, I attended a Mass to compare it to the Spanish-language services in Korea. There were multiple Masses held every Sunday in Norte Chico, and at the one I went to, every pew in the cathedral was full. However, the attendees seemed much less cohesive. There was no message from the priest about the community, or at least I could not hear it over the chatting of the teenagers in the back where I was seated. As soon as Mass was over, people streamed out of the church. In contrast, Masses I attended in Geumcheon and Suwon felt like lively bimonthly reunions of friends. The clergy led interactive Masses where congregants participated in the sermon by reading passages or answering questions geared specifically toward applying the day's lesson to migrant life in Korea. Congregants and clergy stayed afterward to chat over meals of Peruvian food that a rotating group of volunteers had prepared. During the end of my first summer of fieldwork in 2006, the Mass ended with a sixtieth birthday celebration, regarded as an auspicious birthday in Korean culture, for Padre Ignacio. We moved to the rooftop of the church where we ate Korean food, listened to *música tropical,* and taught the French priest to dance merengue.

At another lively, but not quite as memorable, Mass in Suwon, I ran into Hermana Luz, a Peruvian nun in her early thirties who I had met in a factory town a few years prior. As we drank Chilsung Cider from small paper cups and waited for the food to be served, I asked her why she thought so many people regularly attended Mass here when they never had in Peru. She said, "I think that they have a new religious experience here in Korea. They can be together and share. It is something special."

Rafael, who had been a church leader (*un responsable*) in Korea before he was deported, shared Hermana Luz's opinion that the religious community in Korea was special. In fact, he told me that even though the church had been a central part of his life for the seven years he lived in Korea, after he returned to Norte Chico he rarely attended Mass. When I asked him if going to church in Korea had been different from going in Peru, he said, "Yes! In Korea, they [the clergy] called you personally. It depended on the nun. The Koreans [referring to Korean Protestants who went around to factories to evangelize] supported you too. They would visit the factory and invite us to church."

As these sentiments show, being undocumented migrant workers in Korea changed the significance of workers' faith and religious participation from being something normatively Peruvian in Peru to something that made them special and gave them a productive opportunity in Korea. To practice Catholicism in Korea was to join a community, be recognized as special, and also to have opportunities that would be difficult or impossible to have in Peru—such as getting confirmed as an adult or even receiving a crucifix blessed by the pope.

Perhaps the most significant thing that set Korean churches apart from those in Peru were the leadership opportunities they created for Peruvian participants. Each of the three religious groups I worked with had leadership positions for Peruvian migrants that emerged because of their status as undocumented migrant workers from a small community.

The Catholic clergy had appointed two or three men and women in each of the communities they visited to be "los responsables de las comunidades [the people responsible for the communities]." The June 2007 Catholic newsletter featured the photos of "los responsables" with a headline stating they would "help everyone else get close to God and join together with others to help themselves." These lay leaders organized the weekly group meals after Mass and were the contact people in their area between the clergy and the migrant workers. They also seemed to receive special attention from the clergy and attended retreats where the larger group was not invited.

Friendship Foreign Ministry had various leadership positions for their undocumented congregants that had potential for upward mobility beyond Korea. While some were small rotating jobs in the Sunday service, like leading hymns, others were more permanent and included "professional assistance" where select migrants received scholarships to study theology abroad. In the December 2003 Friendship newsletter, which was written in English, Korean, and Spanish and seemed to be directed at both the internal audience of the congregants and potential Korean donors from larger churches, a Korean pastor wrote about the origins and future of the Peruvian congregation and their plans for world evangelization. He wrote that in July of that year the Peruvian congregation had gotten so large—to thirty people and growing—that they were able to offer a separate Spanish service for the first time, and he had decided to elect five leaders from the group. He and the Peruvian leaders had decided they should "learn from the Korean churches overseas" and "preach the gospel with the same courage as the Korean immigrants. At their workplace, they should consider themselves as missionaries. . . . Not only should they evangelize to their foreign co-workers, but to their Korean employers, as well." Ultimately, they decided to begin a new era of "world evangelism," making their church the hub of a "nexus of missions." By the time I started conducting fieldwork in the church four years later, two of the migrant leaders had returned to Peru and enrolled in a prestigious seminary with scholarships facilitated through Friendship's connections. I later visited one of the migrant-leaders-turned-seminary-students at the mission church he helped run alongside Korean missionaries in a pueblo joven in Lima. Another leader, Jheremy, was still in Korea and in charge of the Peruvian congregation. He was learning Korean and English and did simultaneous translations of the main sermon, which was in English. He told me he was waiting to be invited by a church in Paraguay or Ciudad Juárez, Mexico, for missionary training.[3]

At Nazarene, nearly all of the Peruvians I met introduced themselves as some kind of leader in their church and in a larger world evangelization project. Pastor David, who had been a pastor before he came to Korea as a migrant worker, had an official position with the church that other parishioners told me came with a salary and free apartment. He and his wife were even listed as the official delegates for the territory of Latin America in the megachurch's program for the annual missionary convention I attended in 2007. There were many other types of leadership positions for Peruvians as well, though. The back of the program for the weekly Sunday sermon listed five evangelists and five ministers with different jobs like programming and entertainment. Nazarene members routinely dressed formally—suits and ties for the men and dresses and heels for the women—and carried name cards with their names, contact information, and titles, such as "Evangelist." Unlike the Peruvians who worked in factories, most Nazarene members sold accessories at night and were free during the day. They attended classes at church on weekdays for things like multicultural evangelism, and they held their own bible study forums. They also played a leadership role in the church's multiday missionary conference, staging large events and carrying the flag for Peru in a parade of nations at the opening ceremony.[4] Even those Nazarene members who were not listed as official evangelists or missionaries told me they were going to be the ones to construct Cristo Vive, the religious center they planned to build in Peru.

For Peruvian migrants, attending church in Korea was different from attending church in Peru because they were undocumented and at the convergence of multiple cosmopolitan conversion plans. The state's plans—which legally excluded them partially because their small numbers made them inconsequential and their cultural distance from Korea made them undesirable—interacted with the churches' plans. In these environments, their foreignness was desirable and their imminent departures gave them a sense of exceptionalism that increased the urgency and degree to which they received services and attention.

By 2009, the attendance at and frequency of Catholic Masses had decreased, but the number of Korean Protestant churches with Peruvian migrant members had risen. Like renewing one's Catholic faith in Korea, to become part of a Protestant church in Korea was also a way to find a sense of community while accessing resources and leadership opportunities. However, perhaps more importantly, since it had become increasingly difficult to survive in Korea as an undocumented migrant, participating in Korean Protestant churches was a way to obtain some social protections while also working toward a future that was different from being an economic migrant. Korea's mission-minded churches facilitated the training of Peruvians to be pastors and missionaries and helped them launch new churches and careers in Peru and elsewhere.

PREDESTINED MIGRATIONS

One evening as I helped Paty, a member of Nazarene, carry her cases filled with costume jewelry to her usual selling spot near a subway station in Seoul, she told me that her son's birth in Korea was not just a blessing but also a respuesta, or personal message from God, that her migration to Korea was predestined. "In Peru I had so many problems," she told me. "Mental, physical, and spiritual problems. I couldn't have a child. I was barren!" she said, laughing. Her son, Julian, who had just turned two years old, was shouting tearful protests at us in Korean as we tried to get him settled in his stroller. Paty cheerfully raised her voice over Julian's cries to tell me that she saw his birth as a sign that she was on the correct path God had laid out for her. "I accepted God in Korea, and . . . I found solutions to all of my problems," she said. "Now I know that I came to Korea in order to have a child."

From an outsider's perspective, Paty's migration did not look particularly successful. She was forty-one, had been in Korea for six years, and seemed to be struggling for money. Julian's father had been deported to Peru the year before and stopped contacting them. To make matters worse, the only day care in the area that would accept undocumented children was closed during the hours when Paty could find regular employment. This left her little choice but to sell jewelry on the street to make ends meet. Despite these problems, she felt her pregnancy was part of the many respuestas she was receiving as a result of moving to Korea, converting to evangelical Protestantism, and becoming an active member of Nazarene.

Like many other Peruvians I met in Korea, Paty's story of conversion was intertwined with her story of migration. Through her conversion, Paty had come to see her Catholic upbringing in Peru as spiritually and financially toxic, and Korea, with its high number of Protestants and growing economic prowess, as particularly blessed by God. When I asked how she had chosen to look for work in Korea over other destinations like Argentina or Chile, which at the time she had arrived in Korea were more popular and accessible destinations for Peruvian labor, she looked at me incredulously and said, "I come from a family of idol worshippers." She described the way her mother displayed images of El Señor de los Milagros in their living room in Lima. In her Korean church she had come to see these images and her family's Catholicism as factors contributing to her family's poverty. She explained how after converting she now felt that her choice to migrate to Korea had not really been about looking for money but was part of God's plan to help her get away from the Catholic-dominant Peru, convert to Protestantism, and then save her family and eventually all of Latin America from spiritual and financial ruin through her evangelism.

This framework required some imagination. First, the number of Protestants in Peru had been on the rise since at least the 1950s, and while Korea was one of the most Christian countries in Asia, Catholics and Protestants only made up about 20 percent of the population.[5] However, it made sense through the lens of a type of prosperity gospel found in many Korean Protestant churches, including Nazarene, that "material prosperity is evidence of God's favor, either preordained or earned."[6] In her research on Korean-led evangelization and development efforts in Africa, Ju Hui Judy Han discussed the neoliberal and geopolitical nature of prosperity theology. She wrote, "South Korea's wealth . . . was seen as evidence for God's favor, while 'African' poverty was interpreted as a result of insufficient Christian faith."[7] While Han's interlocutors cited Islam, AIDS, and tyranny as further evidence of God's disfavor with Africa, Peruvians talked about alcohol abuse, infidelity, and the worshipping of false idols as both evidence and causes of Peru's (and Latin America's) economic and social suffering. When explaining this framework to me, one of Paty's friends, Hector, told me, "Korea is the school and we are in training." Part of this training was learning how to be better Christians and also how to interpret the world and one's past experiences within this linear geopolitical prosperity theology framework that placed Korea on top.

"Respuesta" was a term that came up a lot in my Korea-based field notes starting in February 2009 when I met the Nazarene Peruvians. They told me that if I read the Bible I would find many answers (respuestas). However, as I spent more time with them, I found they used respuestas in more creative ways too. They described respuestas as answers, messages, or signs set out for them by God, either to reward them for having made a correct life choice, or to guide them in the right direction in the future. Through reading these respuestas, they determined that not only was their migration to Korea predestined and about something more important than wanting to make money, but that Peru was actually more blessed than other nations—including Korea. And rather than being unimportant as their legal status and small numbers might indicate, Peruvian migrants in Korea were exceptional.

For example, Miguel and Jaime, two Nazarene members, told me that God had specifically protected them from deportation because they were Peruvian Cristianos. Jaime had been walking near his apartment with three undocumented friends (from Peru and Southeast Asia) when plainclothes officers suddenly appeared and grabbed his friends. Only Jaime was able to escape, but the others were detained and subsequently deported. He said that in this terrifying moment he realized that he was particularly blessed and that he needed to attend church more often. He interpreted this reprieve as a true respuesta, both a sign that he was destined to be in Korea (as a Peruvian) and that he was a good Cristiano (as an individual).

Miguel interpreted his relative invisibility as a Peruvian migrant as a respuesta and a way to avoid deportation. He described how even unauthorized Korean vendors had gotten kicked out of the alleyways where he usually sold accessories. But when the officers saw him, they just left him alone. For Miguel, other foreigners (and even Koreans) being removed around him was evidence that he was destined to be in Korea, and that he belonged there even more than some other people. Peruvians have no control over their legal status in Korea, but they can change the *reading* of their status. Their telling shifted the narrative of their migration from one of tragic invisibility, where the migrant and migration pattern is unimportant, to one of strategy, where God uses invisibility as a way of protecting and recognizing an important person.

The use of respuestas located them in larger Christian movements and also marked them as Peruvian migrant converts. It is common for other evangelical groups to look for signs from God. For example, in their article "Pathways of Migrant Incorporation in Germany," Nina Glick Schiller and colleagues found that like other "born-again modernist" churches worldwide, the West African congregants in the German churches they studied also "emphasized signs and wonders" and saw "prosperity and success as proof of a 'righteous Christian life.'"[8] In 2019, I emailed three Cristianos who had converted in Korea to ask if they had used the term respuesta prior to arriving in Korea. They said yes, and that it was a term used by Protestants and not Catholics in Peru, but that their use of it increased significantly after they converted in Korea.[9] In contrast to the frequency of the use of "respuesta" to describe these kinds of special events, no one in my field notes ever described the things that happened to them as "miracles" (*milagros*). This was perhaps a conscious decision to distance themselves from Catholic icons in Peru like El Señor de los Milagros. Since respuestas were improbable and unexpected events, they could certainly be understood as miraculous,[10] but they were foremost valued for being tangible indications of one's engagement in a successful dialogue with God. Describing events as respuestas made the recipient seem like a partner in a successful negotiation rather than a needy recipient of a chance windfall.

Friendship parishioners also used the term respuesta, but much less frequently, at least when talking to me. They also discussed finding the path God had created for them as having an economic value, but they talked about it a little differently than Nazarene members. For example, one day I was talking to Jheremy and said, "Some people told me that they thought they came to Korea to make money, but money was not really what they were looking for. They were looking for something else. What do you think?"

He scoffed and said, "The Peruvians who come to Korea come for money. Nobody comes just to experience something, they just want money. Why? Because they need to support their lives economically . . . but here in Korea they realize what God wants. Right?" Then he went on to say how being in Korea helped people discover something they could not learn in Peru—that God has a path for people that might be different from what they *think* they want. He said:

> Only leaving Peru can one realize that. We have the example of [two migrant leaders from Friendship]. They had a vision, Korea. And what was their vision? Save money! But what did they find? They did not find what they asked for. They found something else. They found the vision God had for them. [When they went to Peru] they brought money for their ticket, that is it. Why? Because the church had sent them [paid for them] to study. The church paid to help them set up their churches.

Although using slightly different terms, like Nazarene parishioners, Jheremy and other members of Friendship came to see their migration decisions as being linked to their conversions.[11] They also believed that their life paths had changed as a result of coming to Korea and that information about God's plan had become accessible to them through their partnership with their churches.

Respuestas helped migrants define the global configuration of their migration and conversion journeys in Korea because they are like virtual travelogues that record migrants' routes and roots and account for the changing cultural meanings migrants gain while creating and traveling these particular trajectories.[12] As linguistic anthropologists argue, the telling of a life story can itself be a life-shaping event.[13] Respuestas, like other narratives, "situate narrators, protagonists, and listener/readers at the nexus of morally organized, past, present, and possible experiences."[14] For transmigrants, or people whose actions, decisions, and concerns create social fields that connect and surpass national borders,[15] through their telling, respuestas reflect, constitute, and reconfigure the way communities are connected. Respuestas reflect the delicate linkages and boundaries of a person's portion of the global world and constitute social fields that not only connect Peru and Korea but also heaven and earth, and the past and the future.[16]

THE FORUM

Respuestas became like capital in many Cristianos' cosmopolitan conversion plans for improving the options available to them beyond being economic migrants and for promoting their religious conversions as being more valuable than money. They presented respuestas as evidence of being on a path chosen by God and also as a way to convince others to see them as important figures. They shared respuestas at church as part of their *testimonios* (testimonies), or personal stories of salvation, in conversations with nonbelievers, and with each other during informal occasions such as prayer meetings.

I had originally met Paty at a prayer meeting Nazarene Peruvians called "The Forum," which they held at different members' apartments on Tuesday afternoons. The first forum I attended was held at the house of a man from Lima named Juan who was in his early forties and was in a relationship with a Korean woman. I never got a chance to meet her and guessed she was at work during these afternoon forums.[17]

Their apartment was tucked back in a working-class neighborhood of villa-style apartments in the shadows of a college area of Seoul where many Nazarene members lived. The apartment was humble by Korean standards. It was cramped, and the front door was flimsy like a bedroom door. However, it had its own kitchen and attached bathroom, making it better equipped for handling a crowd than the other Peruvian-occupied apartments I had visited in this area. Most others had to share communal bathrooms, which were located in separate buildings and consisted of squat toilets and a faucet.

When I arrived around 2:00 p.m. I was greeted by three Peruvian women in the kitchen cooking Peruvian food. They invited me to go into the living room and join the other forum members who were sitting on the floor around two Korean-style tables. In addition to Paty there were about seven people squeezed into the little living room, which was already packed around the edges with things like bookshelves, big cardboard boxes, and fans. In the shuffle to clear a spot for me to sit, someone kicked off the leg of one of the tables, which was only connected with packing tape. The leg must have gotten knocked off regularly as no one reacted beyond picking it up and sticking it back in place. Many of the foreigners I knew in Korea—from Peruvian migrants to American English teachers—had furnished their apartments with used items Koreans had placed on the curb as trash. I figured this table was one of those reclaimed items.

As soon as I sat down someone handed me a plate of food, and the group began asking me questions.

"Are you Protestant?" someone asked me right away.

I said no.

"So, you are Catholic," Carlos, a twenty-two-year-old wearing suspenders said in the tone of someone who had just won a bet.

"*Tampoco*," I said, meaning I was neither of the two. Everyone looked confused.

Ximena, the woman who had invited me here, had just dropped me off and left. She had needed to take her daughter to the doctor. I started explaining my research project to them in detail, afraid they did not know what I was doing there.

"We know about your project," a woman said, cutting me off.

"This forum is about spiritual problems first, then about earthly things," Juan said. "I urge you to open your heart and accept it not like it's a story or a study," he said firmly.

I told them I appreciated them allowing me to participate and I looked forward to hearing what they wanted to share. My reason for being there did not surprise them, but they did seem to have trouble fitting me—a nonreligious American— into their geopolitical divine framework of the world where the United States was usually ranked with South Korea as a Protestant nation benefiting from God's favor. They looked truly surprised when I told them many Americans were not religious.

During this discussion Juan's brother arrived from Dongducheon with a young woman from the Philippines named Giselle. The group was very happy to see them. Something had happened to the pair that had inspired them to come here, but no one told me what it was. They both looked exhausted. Giselle looked like she had been crying.

Giselle spoke English, but not Spanish, and her boyfriend did not speak English well.

"I knew it wasn't a coincidence that you were here," Paty said to me happily. "It was a respuesta. You can translate what we say to Giselle!"

At the time, I was a little confused by this, but I understood what she meant when I started attending Nazarene's Sunday services and saw that they always included a prayer request for translators on the back of the pamphlet they created with the day's sermon and schedule. The fourth prayer was, "May God raise up [levante] translators, interpreters, and materials for the message in the trainings." They had asked for a Spanish to English translator. Instead of having to find me, I had sought them out and stumbled into their weekly prayer forum at exactly the right time. Paty saw that as a respuesta materialized.

They all got out Spanish-language Bibles and little spiral notebooks they carried with them to church to take notes and took turns sharing their *testimonios* and asking God for guidance. As soon as I realized they wanted me to translate entire paragraphs of speech at a time I quickly got out my own field notebook and pen so I could remember each person's whole message.

"Please pray that God reveals my role in His plan," each member would say in a slightly different way as they went around the circle. They shared the respuestas they had received from the previous week's prayer group or during their time of conversion. In either case, participants interpreted their respuestas as signs that they were successfully navigating the plan that they believed God had laid out for them: to travel to Korea, learn the true gospel, and change their lives (and their family's lives) for the better. Like Paty, they described their journeys to Korea as part of a path that God had already chosen for them long before they were born, but one that they did not understand until they converted to Protestantism in Korea. Their respuestas indicated that they were correctly following the plan and were also viewed as a reward for being good Cristianos. Since they had chosen the correct path, they were able to stumble on these rewards and simultaneously receive respuestas, or clues as to where God's path led next. For most, signs seem to suggest the path led to Peru where they would help to create Cristo Vive, the religious center they planned to build in partnership with Nazarene in Peru.[18]

The testimonios had the flow of well-rehearsed speeches, as though they had told them many times, but there were also some parts directed specifically at me (as a scholar from the United States with a Mexican husband) and Giselle (as a migrant worker from the Philippines), seemingly to help us see our lives and presence in Korea within God's larger plan.

In addition to telling me I could be a translator for their efforts in Korea, they told me my husband and I could study and take the *evangelio* to Mexico.[19]

With Giselle they addressed her visible sadness and the common money concerns they shared as foreign workers. Although some Nazarene parishioners talked about their lack of factory work as a respuesta because it gave them the time to study at church and do evangelizing work, this did not mean that they had stopped thinking about money. In fact, money appeared in most of their conversion narratives.

One woman thanked the forum for helping her see that God had changed her life in Korea despite struggling to make money. "The fight continues," she said. "The forum has helped me see that God has come. I am getting respuestas. Before [in Peru], I cried a lot and did not know why." This comment about no longer crying was directed at Giselle.

Some talked about the profitable work they had sacrificed in order to attend the forum. For example, Stefano, a musician who supported himself by performing Andean flute music at festivals and selling CDs and *accesorios,* told us how in order to come to the day's meeting he was missing out on a festival that would have paid $6,000. This statement did not cause a noticeable reaction in the room, although many people in attendance had been unable to find any work and were accepting handouts from their church. Part performance, part confessional, and also unverifiable, Stefano's contribution to the prayer group highlighted the ways he saw respuestas and his religious training as being worth more than money.

Others tried to help Giselle see her respuestas by locating her in their geopolitical divine hierarchy framework.

"It hurts me to hear Giselle can't be happy. But I have to say that the Philippines suffers from idolatry," one woman said. She told us she also had a Buddhist mother and that had led to her spiritual problems.

Giselle, who had been quiet until this point, interjected that the Philippines was not a Buddhist country and there were a lot of Christians there. I translated that and the woman paused, but only changed course slightly.

"No one is born bad," she said.

When it was Carlos's turn, he told a story of sin in Peru and redemption in Korea. "God is real," he began. "In Peru my life was only about beer and girls. But they only brought me one day of joy. Then I was back to misery. When I got to Korea I only thought about money. But then, I realized I had spiritual problems. Now I know that I came to Korea to find God. Respuestas are coming for me!" He finished with emotion.

The general details as well as the arc in Carlos's story were common in testimonios I heard from both men and women in Korea. Many narratives involved either indulging in alcohol and sex in Peru or in Dongducheon or Itaewon before being miraculously transformed after conversion. However, after spending more time with Carlos, I came to doubt that he had been a serious womanizer or drinker. Despite the vagueness of his story, Carlos, like the other men and women at the forum, became emotional during his turn to share. I realized that respuestas could be more symbolic than factual—and still avoid being dishonest. Respuestas helped to illustrate the overall message that converts had come to believe and wanted others to believe as well—that their own presence as a Peruvian in Korea was part of a larger, more important global plan in which their Korean church had an advantage. They were in Korea as a result of divine intervention. Further, in this version of the story they were not needy recipients of charity, but were important co-contributors guiding this plan to fruition.

EXCHANGING ECONOMIC
AND COSMOPOLITAN CAPITAL

Many of the conversions discussed in this chapter involve negotiating relationships between two or more things: Catholicism, Protestantism and "true" Protestantism, selling beer or not selling beer in the family store, understanding an unprofitable migration as a failure or as being predestined. Like all relationships, these conversions were infused with power. Identifying respuestas not only gave migrants the language to frame and position themselves in their migration journeys but also power in negotiating the terms of their transnational relationships—with their churches, families, and peers.

In July 2009, Paty told me about her strategy for creating the respuestas she wanted for herself and her family. I had been visiting Paty and Julian in their tiny studio apartment when the discussion turned to her mother and family in Peru. Between her toddler, the poor conversion rate, and her choice to become an evangelist, she could hardly afford to send her family any money. "My mother knows I have my own child to take care of now," she said.

Then she turned to a topic she frequently asked me for advice on—her plan to bring her sister Marisol to Korea. This idea had initially confused me because by mid-2009, the chances that a Peruvian could successfully pass through immigration as a tourist had become very slim. However, Paty explained that she did not want to have her sister try to enter as a tourist, but to come by way of a student visa. Paty assured me that Marisol had a degree in environmental engineering, and I had met quite a few students from Mexico and Colombia working toward master's and bachelor's degrees in Korea, so I knew that getting her a student visa was plausible. Paty called me frequently to ask about the student visa. After investigating online regarding the different options for Latin American students, I asked Paty if Marisol wanted to study the Korean language or obtain a degree in a specific topic.

"No!" Paty said, speaking in the quick laughing pace she always used. "She wants to sell *accesorios*." To me this plan sounded complicated at best and threatened to be a financial disaster at worst. Paty would have to pay thousands of dollars to arrange for her sister's documents, round-trip ticket, and living costs. Even if Marisol made it to Korea, she would not make much money selling. The financial crisis had resulted in more Koreans losing their jobs and entering the *accesorios* market, and the increased deportations surrounding the upcoming G-20 summit had made the streets where Paty and her church members sold extremely dangerous for undocumented migrants. Why would Paty invest in such a doomed plan when she had such little extra money?

"If she is in Korea, I can teach her the gospel," Paty told me finally.

This was truly a negotiation. Rather than send economic and social remittances to her family in Peru, Paty was using her economic remittances to bring her sister to Korea where she thought she would be more likely to convert. Her sister wanted to work in Korea and make money, and Paty wanted her to convert. The student visa was a compromise.

As much as this plan was about her sister being saved, I saw it being more about Paty demonstrating that she could be a successful evangelizer. Paty had been taking missionary and evangelism classes at Nazarene for the past two years, but I do not think she had been able to convert anyone. Part of the problem was that since she was a monolingual Spanish speaker, Korea offered a limited audience for her to evangelize. Basically, her main options for evangelization were her family at home and other Spanish-speaking migrant workers and foreigners in Korea (including me). She excitedly told people about the signs indicating that I had started to convert—such as looking happier at forums.

Paty's efforts to bring Marisol to Korea, and convert her, seemed to make her feel like she was doing valuable work. As anthropologist Simon Coleman points out, attempting to convert someone is a self-constitutive act that is not just about transforming others but about transforming the self.[20] If Paty's plan was a success, her *respuesta* would not be more remittances but to be able to tell her sister about God in person. Physically bringing her sister to church services on Sunday and positioning herself as the person who had saved her would be an added bonus. By attempting to convert others—whether or not they listen or are converted—the converter receives a new sense of purpose and a new way of gauging one's success and sense of power through their efforts to convert. This was a conversion of economic capital for cultural capital that was multi-directional. By sending economic capital and financing Marisol's migration, Paty stood to gain the embodied capital of becoming and being seen as a successful evangelizer. By accepting Paty's gift of economic capital with strings attached, Marisol stood to increase her own economic capital by working in Korea. These religious and economic conversions were a way to negotiate the constantly changing environment of their global worlds.

PERU DAY

I saw this power negotiation on a grander scale at various events where Cristianos interacted with Spanish-speaking clergy from the Catholic Church and members of the Peruvian embassy and consulate. There were many occasions for this to happen, including community events organized by Nazarene Peruvians who had extended invitations to the Catholic clergy and Peruvian dignitaries and the annual embassy-sponsored Peru Day celebration.

Although I heard a priest say the Peru Day celebration was not a religious event, the ones I attended were held at a Catholic Church in Seoul. They also began with a Catholic Mass and finished with entertainment and a Peruvian meal.

In 2009 there were a couple of changes. The seats of the church were filled with Catholics, members of Nazarene, and Peruvians I had never met before. I stood with Padre Diego at the back of the church as there were no seats left. He explained that this year, in addition to the embassy splurging on a pisco sour toast, they had decided to invite the Cristianos to participate in the proceedings in an official capacity. Knowing that some of the Nazarene members, like Stefano, were professional musicians, Padre Diego had asked them to perform traditional Peruvian flute music to entertain the crowd. Then Nazarene's undocumented Pastor David would be invited to say a few words alongside other leaders such as the Peruvian ambassador to Korea. The Cristianos respectfully sat through the Catholic Mass—with the exception of Paty's son, Julian, who kept getting up and running around the pews yelling. As Paty chased after him, she saw me standing against the back wall. She stopped briefly to chat and inform me that she attributed Julian's disruptive behavior to bad spirits that were flying around the church. She thought the bad spirits came in part because of the large painting of Christ on the cross behind the altar—which she thought was idolatrous. I just nodded in sympathy. It was hot and crowded in there, and Julian was one of the only children.

After the Mass, Padre Diego looked annoyed as the Cristianos began to diverge from plan and evangelize to the crowd. In the pause during which organizers passed out plates of food and trays of shot-sized pisco sours, the Cristianos walked around greeting everyone and inviting them to attend their church. They also distributed little "Good News" booklets outlining the church's teachings, which they had purchased from a small stand in Nazarene's lobby. In the preceding months I had already received four copies of this booklet—in English and Spanish—and whenever I tried to refuse a new one, they encouraged me to take it for a friend. A Peruvian woman I had not met before handed one to Padre Diego and to me.[21] He accepted it, albeit with a look of astonishment on his face.

After the meal Stefano and other members of Nazarene went up on the raised area behind the altar (which doubled as a stage) and got out electric guitars and an electric drum kit. Rather than perform Andean flute music, they proceeded to play a full set of Christian rock music. The Nazarene parishioners in the audience stood up and clapped along joyfully to the songs. The priest, nuns, and much of the audience started to leave a few minutes into the show. At the end of the event the only people left to take photos with the ambassador were the Peruvians from Nazarene.

I took this as a power play by the Cristianos to reclaim Peruvian space that was normatively Catholic. By handing out booklets even to the priest, who it seemed obvious to me would never convert, showed that this proselytization was about negotiating the terms of their relationships with these institutions: the state and church. By refusing to play Peruvian Andean music—which they knew how to play, and had seemingly agreed to play—and opting for gospel music instead, they changed the Peru Day narrative. They were not normal Peruvian migrant workers—they were changing the story and establishing themselves as leaders.

NOT JUST FAKING IT

This effort by Cristiano converts to position themselves as leaders who had made authentic conversions, rather than as recipients of charity, was something I saw on a weekly basis in Korean Protestant churches. A common critique I heard from migrants, clergy, and families in Peru was that Cristiano converts were "just faking it" in order to get financial rewards.

When I asked Padre Ignacio what he thought of Catholic Peruvians converting to Protestantism, he said, "They might go there for a free meal, but it doesn't go deep."

As Padre Ignacio's comment indicated, for many Cristiano converts and their detractors the most salient of these rewards was free food after church services. On many occasions I attended the Spanish-language Catholic Mass in Gyeonggi Province and watched, alongside the priest and nuns, as parishioners slipped out of the cathedral right at 6:00 p.m. so they could make it over to Friendship Ministry in time for an extensive, hot buffet-style meal that came complete with kimchi and dessert. These meals were purchased and prepared by a rotating group of affiliated Korean churches who came early to set up the food trays and stayed to try to socialize.[22] From my chats with the Korean visitors, this meal service seemed to be a chance for the relatively affluent members of those churches to do charity work with needy migrant workers. While Friendship also offered weekly sermons in many languages, free medical clinics, haircuts, and language classes, for many attendees the biggest attraction was the free Korean food.

To avoid characterizing the free food as a utilitarian approach to drawing new members to the church, the leaders of Friendship framed it as a potential respuesta for those who come to the church to eat. They hoped that even those people who thought they were coming just for the free food would ultimately realize God had used food as a tool to bring them to church. Ideally, they would stay for the right reasons and eventually convert because they would become true believers. For example, Jheremy recalled the behavior of Friendship's early Peruvian congregation around free food:

> They came just as the sermon ended to get in the food line. The pastor said, "Those Peruvians always come just to eat!" That's what she said! Sundays they played soccer all afternoon. They all showed up in their soccer clothes to eat. . . . The church was empty during the sermon. But at dinner, it was completely full. That actually had a huge influence on them joining the church. Food. Because from that time, many of them learned about the gospel, right? So, it's actually something that brings them to God. The food brings them.

Jheremy argued that while hundreds of Peruvians had come just for the food, dozens eventually started coming for the gospel. This system seemed to work too, because the Spanish-language congregation was constantly decreasing due to immigration raids, but the church baptized and cultivated a contingent of Peruvian parishioners who continued to identify as Cristianos even after departing Korea. Thus, free food indirectly strengthened the church's ability to expand its community in Peru.

I asked Friendship's Pastor Sarah why they had been so successful in converting migrant workers. I was curious to find out if she shared many of the Nazarene Peruvians' opinions that they had been sent by God to Korea to be converted. Her frank answer surprised me. "When migrant workers are in trouble it's easier for them to find Jesus," she said with a shrug, "It's true." Like Jheremy, she hoped Peruvians came for the food and stayed for the gospel. However, in her view food is a way of meeting the basic needs of poor, isolated, undocumented migrants first, while having the secondary benefit of making them receptive to conversion. Her response also highlighted that she was comfortable with the negotiation in converting others.

While free food attracted some migrant workers, it repelled others. In fact, as the members of Nazarene saw it, they had specifically turned down the charity from other churches—including free food—in order to show the authenticity of their conversion. Originally, nearly the entire Peruvian congregation of Nazarene had been devoted members of a small neighborhood Pentecostal church in Seoul. After a chance meeting with a Latin American pastor affiliated with Nazarene, they had all stopped attending their small neighborhood church without giving an explanation. When people talked to me about this, they seemed embarrassed about it. They justified their actions by saying that the pastor at the small neighborhood church had only wanted to meet their financial needs (by giving them food, employment, or offering to help them open a Peruvian restaurant in the neighborhood) rather than attending to their spiritual needs. "God provides!" Ximena told me when justifying why she had stopped attending his church. She was nearly crying. "The pastor doesn't understand that. He thinks it is all about free bread rolls and milk," she said, motioning toward her refrigerator, which was also a gift from his church. Although she had accepted many gifts from the small church, she appeared offended that the Korean pastor would think she would attend his church just because of the availability of free food.

What Ximena and the other members of Nazarene rarely discussed, however, is that they also received free meals at their new church. In fact, the meals were more frequent and formal than I had seen at the other churches. The church gave them tickets that allowed them to eat for free at the cafeteria across the street from Nazarene on the days of their classes and on Sundays between the Korean service in the morning and the Spanish service in the afternoon. However, they seemed to regard this food not as a form of charity or as a way to attract new members, but as a way for them to achieve their ultimate goals of becoming global leaders since having lunch available on campus maximized their time at the church. Portraying the food as a tool to help them become leaders rather than as charity for undocumented workers in need illustrates the ways they negotiated the terms of their conversions and relationships with their churches and peers.

MISSIONARY ENCOUNTER—CONTROLLING THE MESSAGE

The telling of their conversion stories helped Cristianos change the value of their migrations from being about the struggles of undocumented economic migrants to being about the achievements of global figures connecting Korea and Peru. Depending on the sites where they told these narratives, and who was present to listen, they could not only reconfigure their sense of self but also their reputations in Peru and the global hierarchies they were navigating as undocumented migrant workers.

One example of this came from an event Paty and the other Nazarene Peruvians organized in August 2009 called the "Missionary Encounter." Multiple members of Nazarene invited me to the luncheon, explaining it was where attendees could meet Latin American missionaries who were in town for Nazarene's World Missions Conference, a multiday event that would take place at a sports stadium in Seoul.

That Friday, soon after arriving at the expensive Mexican restaurant in Itaewon where the luncheon was being held, I realized that while it was a chance to meet

Latin American missionaries, it was primarily set up as an evangelizing event targeted at Seoul's Spanish-speaking population. This mainly consisted of migrant workers, soldiers serving in the US Army, foreign language teachers, diplomats, and businesspeople. However, despite heavy promotion and the promise of free food and entertainment, apart from a table full of missionaries and their spouses, a few Korean members of the church, and many Peruvians from Nazarene, the restaurant was fairly empty. I sat with Paty, who had also invited me and saved me a seat at her table. She wore a formal dress and heels despite the sweaty heat of the August afternoon.

Isac, a leader in Nazarene, was the emcee, and as the meal was served, he stood on a small stage in the front of the restaurant and gave opening remarks. There would be musical and theatrical performances as well as presentations by missionaries. The first performers to take the stage were Peruvians from Nazarene. Some performed gospel songs; Stefano played traditional Peruvian flute music; there was a one-act play about the importance of God in a marriage; and then, finally, a video the Peruvians had made about how Latin America was failing because it had not yet turned Protestant. The video, which featured images of hurricanes destroying the coast of Mexico and children drinking alcohol in the slums of Lima, spoke to their plans to literally "save" Latin America—make it more economically profitable, healthier, and free from God's wrath—through the evangelization efforts they would lead.

After the video, various guest speakers, including Nazarene's Pastor David, went up to the microphone and shared their testimonies. They described various respuestas they had received from God while in Korea as well as their experiences of conversion. As they spoke, two Peruvian teenagers who had grown up in Korea and attended an American Christian school in Dongducheon stood on the edges of the stage and provided the non-Spanish speakers in the audience with a simultaneous translation from Spanish to English.

One of the first guests invited to speak was an ambassador from a Latin American country who was stationed in Seoul. In addition to being an ambassador, he was also an evangelical pastor and was very passionate about his experience in Korea and about the luncheon. The Peruvians sitting at my table all clapped as the ambassador listed the respuestas he had experienced while living in Korea, the biggest of which had been regaining his sight in a Korean church after nearly going blind. He described how a fellow church member, a Korean man, had touched him and said, "Heal!" and he had been healed. "God has the palm of his hand over Korea!" the ambassador told us to great applause.

Although the luncheon was set up as an evangelizing event, none of the Peruvians seemed upset about the poor turnout of potential converts. The scheduling of the event—Friday afternoon—when most Spanish speakers in Seoul would be working and could therefore not attend, seemed to indicate that perhaps nonbelievers were not the Peruvians' target audience in the first place. In fact, the most important audience for their respuestas, performances, and evangelizing videos seemed to be Korean church leaders, the visiting missionaries, and each other—people who were already converted. By organizing the event—even when there was no one to convert—they positioned themselves as the leaders and spokespeople of the Spanish-speaking community in Korea, and the ones who would launch a new mission from Korea to Latin America. Rather than limiting themselves to Korea, it seemed they wanted their videos, performances, and respuestas to reach a global audience, and they brought their own translators to make sure everyone understood their message. Regardless of the initial intention of the luncheon, their Korean church stood to gain its own level of multicultural prestige by having enough Spanish-speaking members to hold such a large-scale event. Further, preparations for this multilingual event illustrated the church's potential for extending its global missions to Peru, a place that they had yet to reach, and where they could demonstrate their superior place in God's hierarchy through the Peruvians conversions.

This message even reached audiences in Peru six months after the "Missionary Encounter," when the Peruvian ambassador to Korea at the time appeared on a Peruvian-based radio show available online called "Peruanos en el Exterior" (Peruvians Abroad) to discuss the Peruvian community in Korea.[23] In this episode about Peruvians in Korea, rather than using the interview to discuss the origins of the migration pattern, or the increasing economic connections between the two countries (which would develop into a Free Trade Agreement in 2011), the ambassador highlighted the presence and activities of the Peruvian Cristianos. Even before the hosts asked the ambassador a question, she jumped into the interview by characterizing Korea's Peruvian population as consisting of three main groups: (1) a small group of professionals, (2) a large group of undocumented migrant workers, and (3) a "strong" group of Christian evangelists who work closely with Peruvian communities on social projects.

The way she divided Peruvians into these three discrete groups is significant for two reasons. First, the Cristianos were presented to the radio audience as the "strongest" and most important group despite only making up a fraction of Korea's Peruvian population. The ambassador did not mention that groups two and three were the same people: the evangelists were also undocumented migrant workers. In her telling, the Cristianos did not come across as an undocumented and therefore problematic labor force. Instead, they were characterized as worldly spiritual entrepreneurs. This is precisely the image Cristianos try to create of themselves in their recounting of respuestas. Second, the ambassador's reference to "social projects" supported by Cristianos is a little misleading. These projects include launching mission churches like Cristo Vive and spearheading plans to convert their families and combat the toxicity they saw as a result of living in a predominantly Catholic nation like Peru. Together the Peruvian Cristianos and the ambassador worked to present respuestas as selfless social projects rather than the personal aspirations of undocumented migrant workers, thereby giving the migration pattern a new level of prestige and value.

I did not get a chance to interview the ambassador, so I can only guess at her motivations for using this radio appearance to present the Peruvian Cristianos as the leaders of the entire community and highlighting the value of their contributions. My guess is that she wanted to put a positive spin on the story of Peruvian migration to Korea, and that the Cristianos had succeeded in making themselves and their activities acutely visible to her.[24] In my participant observation with the Peruvian community in the months preceding this interview, I noted that the Nazarene Cristianos had organized, were featured speakers or performers, or had attended at least three events alongside the ambassador or consul general. While the foreign priests or nuns spoke for and represented the Catholic community at these events, the Peruvian Cristianos usually spoke for themselves. They introduced themselves as pastors, evangelists, and missionaries, not undocumented workers. In this "official" capacity, and within the particular political and religious transnational networks they were helping to create, they did not seem afraid of making themselves visible in Korea.

Therefore, no matter her motivation, the ambassador's recognition of undocumented Peruvians as contributing to Korea and social progress in Peru more generally is quite significant. Through the radio program, Peruvians of Nazarene were rendered visible and credited as creators of transnational projects and leaders of their community.

CONCLUSION

In this chapter I have presented various examples of how Peruvian migrants underwent religious conversions in South Korea, and how they communicated the significance of these experiences with their families, churches, and communities in Peru and Korea to show how conversion was a way that people negotiated the value of their migrations and selves as migrants in an unstable global climate. For both Catholic and Protestant converts, unique opportunities for forming communities and establishing leadership opportunities within their churches happened because of, rather than in spite of, their status as undocumented migrants from Peru with little chance of remaining in Korea. Their conversions would have been much different in Peru, with less urgency and different stakes. Further, as Camila discovered, conversions to the value of one's status and capital were more difficult to maintain and negotiate once migrants had returned to Peru. However, as I tried to convey with Paty and Marisol's story, conversions are multidirectional and cannot fail when viewed as part of emerging, ongoing plans.

Converts did not portray their legal and economic instability as moments of failure, but rather as the inspiration for them to make creative conversions to the value of their economic capital and religious experiences. I have shown that by interpreting events in their lives as respuestas, they formed and promoted themselves as co-navigators (along with God) in their global journeys. Through taking on leadership roles in forming events like Peru Day, the Missionary Encounter, or even refusing to acknowledge the items they received from their churches as charity, and instead believing them to be respuestas that furthered their preparation to be leaders, they interacted with and shared billing at events with ambassadors and professional missionaries.

The religious conversion experiences I discuss here are also essentially negotiations in the meaning of relationships—between Peru and Korea; between Catholic and Protestant; whether a migration is predestined or doomed; whether one is a leader or a recipient of charity, a successful or a failed migrant, a daughter or a remitter. Like all relationships, these conversions were infused with power, partial truths, negotiations, and tension. Since conversions are about power, they can reconfigure the value of the self, others, things, and the relationships among all of these.

In the next chapter I take a closer look at migrants' plans and projects as cosmopolitan conversions to explore the ways people interpreted and changed the significance of their lives in Korea.

4

Cosmopolitan Conversion

After six years of attending an American-run Christian school in Dongducheon—the only school her mother could find that would accept undocumented children—Rosa spoke English better than Korean or even her native Spanish. I first met Rosa at a Mass in 2006, when she was just twelve and still a novice English speaker. As one of the few Peruvian children who had accompanied her parents to Korea, she was a favorite of the Spanish-speaking Catholic clergy, the evangelical Christian teachers at her school, and other factory workers who had left their own children behind in Peru. People from each of these groups helped care for Rosa while her mother Amanda worked long shifts at a factory, making it possible for mother and daughter to survive in Korea. Initially, both Amanda and her husband had worked in Dongducheon, but after losing their E-9 unskilled labor visas in 2004 and discovering that Amanda was pregnant with a second child, they decided it was best that her husband and infant son relocate to Peru while she and Rosa stay in Korea and try to evade deportation for as long as possible. They made these sacrifices to their family's unity and safety not just so that Amanda could earn money, but so that Rosa could finish her education in Korea, and her parents could afford to pay for it. While it was too costly for most undocumented Peruvians to raise an infant in Korea, if Rosa returned to Peru, an English-language education—like the one she received in Dongducheon for free—would be financially impossible.

"If Rosa speaks English well, she can study in America," her mother told me when I met the family again in 2009. "She can get a scholarship," she said, relaying the promises made by Rosa's American teachers. Anthropologists So Jin Park and Nancy Abelmann pointed out that for many people in South Korea working to move up social classes and help their children be citizens of the world, English was a "saturated sign" that held many promises for a cosmopolitan future and transformation.[1] It was no surprise then that in Korea Rosa and her family came to see her fluency in English as representing possibilities: to transform her from an undocumented child migrant into an international student; to serve as concrete evidence of her educational achievement; and most importantly, to open up a path for her future documented migration to the United States. So, while Amanda and her husband had run into many obstacles after coming to Korea to work in a factory—that is, losing their visas, struggling to find a school that would accept their undocumented daughter, and then becoming separated—new and exciting possibilities for education and migration had opened up as a result of having no other legal options for themselves or educational options for their daughter.

Despite these opportunities, which were made possible by their exclusion, they had to find ways to normalize the danger in their lives. I saw this firsthand one hot and humid weekday afternoon in August 2006 when Azucena, a forty-year-old woman from Lima, invited me to her apartment for lunch. Azucena was out of work and had agreed to take care of Rosa while she was on summer break from school. I had just finished the long subway and bus ride from Seoul and had escaped into the relative coolness of Azucena's apartment when her daughter-in-law, Maria, called and asked us to come over to her place for lunch. Azucena peered out of her window for a few long moments before she deemed it safe enough for us to go outside. Even though their neighborhood was nearly deserted on this weekday afternoon, nowhere in Dongducheon was out of sight of immigration officers, not even this sleepy residential street dotted with gardens bursting with cabbages, chili peppers, and flowers.

The thriving gardens were planted in empty lots between the area's many villas, crumbling two- and three-story apartment buildings that had been popular housing models following the Korean War but had since fallen out of fashion. Small handwritten signs in English posted on the villa windows, advertising vacant rooms at prices higher than those found in Seoul, were obviously meant to attract non-Korean tenants—either migrant workers or soldiers. In recent years many Koreans had relocated to new high-rise apartment buildings that were popping up at an impressive rate along the highway coming from Seoul. Few Koreans would want to live in Azucena's neighborhood anyway, given its high number of foreign residents, proximity to the street of nightclubs, and the dangerous reputation with which the entire city had been saddled since the 1950s when the US Army arrived, established bases, and the population of foreigners grew. Now, with the increase in the frequency and severity of immigration raids launched here, the foreigners were the ones who were scared.

In fact, Maria told me that just days before my visit, while out looking for work, she had been violently stopped and searched by immigration officers. Since her tourist visa had yet to expire and she was not caught while in a factory, the officers reluctantly released her. The whole family, including Rosa, had been shaken up by this incident and now rarely left their apartments. They just waited at home and hoped a friend would call with information on where to find arbeits.

As I walked through Dongducheon with Azucena and Rosa, I saw that they felt the precariousness of their place as Peruvians in the ethnic and national divisions among foreigners in Korea. As we darted along the street to Azucena's daughter-in-law's house, Azucena kept pushing me ahead although I did not know the way. "You look American, you go in front," Azucena kept saying. In Korea, and in Peru, to look American often meant to look white. By telling me I looked American and pushing me in front, she meant to say that if immigration officers suddenly appeared, I was to either try to convince them we were all Americans and therefore documented, or provide a diversion with my whiteness while everyone else ran for cover. The Peruvians in Dongducheon know that the legal status of people in this area—and in all of Korea—is largely based on race and nationality. As a white woman in this neighborhood, I was most likely taken for an English teacher, an American soldier, or a Russian migrant. Thankfully we did not have to test the efficacy of this plan because we made it to Maria's apartment without seeing anyone.

Once we were safely inside, Rosa watched Korean TV and played with the family dog. I asked Azucena what would happen if Amanda were to be detained on her way home from work. I had heard horror stories about Peruvians being locked in Korean detention centers for months or years before they were able to scrape together enough money from sympathetic friends for their plane tickets home. Unlike the US government, the Korean government (like Japan's) requires its deportees to pay for their own transportation home. This can prove problematic, as Peruvians in general have few routes open to them to get to Peru, and deported Peruvians have even fewer. At this time, the price for a one-way ticket for a deported Peruvian (who could only transit through South Africa) cost roughly $2,500—an incredible sum for people who make $800 a month and a nearly impossible figure for those who have been locked in immigration prison for months or years and have to rely on friends to collect the money.

"What would Rosa do?" I asked.

"They keep their suitcases packed at all times," Azucena told me. Since 2004 when her husband left, Amanda had realized that either she or her daughter could be detained on the way to or from work or school, so they needed a realistic plan for if and when that happened. In addition to keeping their clothes and possessions packed in a suitcase, they had hidden an envelope in the apartment with enough cash for two one-way tickets to Lima. The escape plan was set up as a temporary precaution, and they hoped the heightened deportation risk would eventually decrease. However, when I met them again in 2009, they were still waiting for their inevitable deportation.

This was not unusual. Many people I met kept their most prized possessions—photographs of family in Peru and friends in Korea, and items like T-shirts, shoes, and CDs purchased at Seoul's Dongdaemun Market—boxed up by the front doors of their small apartments. Securely taped, addressed to themselves at their parents' homes in Peru, the boxes sit for years, just waiting for friends to ship them off when and if their owner is detained. Undocumented migrants cannot be certain where their plans will take them, and the mere possibility of reaching someplace new keeps them going—or in the case of Rosa, staying. Nearly every Peruvian I met in Korea had laid out plans for future migrations where they hoped to become something more important than just factory workers.

Rosa and her family's plan to prolong their looming deportation so Rosa could complete her education is an example of what I term a cosmopolitan conversion, or the various projects or plans individuals or groups undertake in the effort to change their lives and help them be cosmopolitan. By being cosmopolitan I mean the pursuit of "infinite ways of being"[2] and "the desire to become 'citizen[s] capable of living at home in the world.'"[3] Further, people or groups who attempt cosmopolitan conversions also exhibit a desire to be recognized by others as having valid cultural capital to rightfully belong in the category of a cosmopolitan.[4] For example, they may pursue institutionalized cultural capital through things like visas, marriage licenses, or academic degrees, or embodied cultural capital in the form of being seen by others as a fluent English speaker worthy of a scholarship, a member of a successful transnational family, or even the receiver of respuestas from God. Since, as Pierre Bourdieu pointed out, it takes a lot of effort—in the expense of time and labor—for cultural capital to be recognized as valid by others, or to become covert and convertible to social or economic capital,[5] the plans and projects in cosmopolitan conversions usually take a long time to reach fruition. For example, Rosa needed to prolong her deportation from Korea as a way to put in the necessary labor to acquire the cultural capital of an English education and the social capital that would get her a scholarship to a school in the United States.

Rosa was not the only person I met who had to prolong her imminent departure from Korea in order to fulfill a cosmopolitan conversion. When I met Frank, he told me he had spent his entire time in Korea preparing to move to Spain. He had applied for a resident visa to Spain years earlier through Peruvian family members who could prove their Spanish descent. He did not know how long the visa would take to be approved, or if it would be approved at all, but he was certain that being undocumented in Korea would hurt his chances of getting this visa to Spain. So, in order to keep his Korean tourist visa valid, he had traveled to China by boat every three months for two years. While in Korea, he worked in factories to fund his future move to Spain and his costly trimonthly trips to China. Ultimately, he had to abandon this plan during the economic crisis when Korean immigration increased scrutiny and he could no longer pass as a tourist.

Rosa's parents may have brought her to Korea in the hopes of finding a way for her to receive an education, but the particular way it was happening was a family project that was still taking form and had emerged during and as a result of their situation of being undocumented Peruvians in Korea. Therefore, I focus on cosmopolitanism as a "project" or "practice."[6] This is different from an individual who recognizes his or her identity as a cosmopolitan person; rather, it is a sense of cosmopolitanism in which the form and content "is yet to come, something awaiting realization."[7] Since the barriers and opportunities in cosmopolitan conversions are always emerging and the end is always yet to come, there can never be a definitively failed plan, just a chance to change direction and start a new plan. This is how the arrival of one child in Korea (Rosa) became a reason to prolong a family's stay in Korea, while another child's arrival (her brother) became a reason to leave. Further, even if Rosa was deported before she graduated or obtained her scholarship, she had still accumulated the cultural capital of attending an American school and being an English speaker, which had the potential to open up new possibilities for her even years in the future no matter where she lives.

In this chapter, I present examples of different cosmopolitan conversions undertaken by Peruvian migrants while in Korea and explore how their efforts to develop and achieve their cosmopolitan plans helped to create a new global configuration that shifted the value of their actions, status, and the results of their plans. This is because their plans emerged within the context, and at the convergence, of other large- and small-scale cosmopolitan conversion projects by the Korean state, churches, and the Koreans and migrants with whom they interacted. For example, the Korean state's efforts to be globalized and enact multicultural policies had left Peruvians legally excluded, while the efforts of various Korean and American Protestant churches to have multicultural parishioners and global missions while promoting themselves as world changers had made them highly desirable members.

I consider how even though their cosmopolitan conversions interacted with those of multiple individuals and groups, as undocumented migrants, Peruvians faced risks and potential losses others did not, including deportation, lost time with their families in Peru, or lost chances to pursue other projects. However, I argue that they built loss into their plans, thereby changing the value and meaning of these risks and losses. For example, their status as undocumented workers simultaneously put them in constant danger of being deported and accelerated their inclusion in groups and relationships that gave them new chances to develop cultural capital. They also creatively revalued loss as a "desirable outcome"[8] through incorporating it in the narratives of their cosmopolitan plans that they presented to each other and at their churches. However, sometimes in their attempts to make themselves at home in the world, they also created new potential losses for themselves, including becoming entangled in the very legal and social barriers they wanted to overcome.

"WE HAVE EVERYTHING HERE!"

Lucia, a woman from a pueblo joven who had been undocumented in Korea for two years, asked me to come stay at her factory with her for the night and then take her sightseeing in Seoul the next day. "I want to be a tourist!" she said.

I had met Lucia and her husband Jorge at a Mass the year before. Soon after I returned to Korea the following summer Lucia told me over instant messaging that she had been in a minor accident while riding on the back of a moped through the roads near her factory, so she was off work for a few days. We were friendly, but I guessed that the main reason she had asked me to accompany her to the city was similar to why Azucena and the women in Dongducheon had pushed me to the front of the group. She wanted to use my "American" face to help her pass as a tourist in Seoul and avoid the gaze of immigration officers. She was also excited about this outing because Jorge—who was jealous because she had been on a moped with another Peruvian man at the time of the accident—would be at his job in a nearby recycling plant and had agreed to let her go with me. This was one of the first times that she would venture beyond her factory town.

It was a hot and muggy Thursday afternoon in early July 2007 when I arrived at her town outside of Seoul. Jorge picked me up near the train station on his moped and drove me to where Lucia worked. The factory was surrounded by a tall wooden fence that hid it from the view of the road. We passed through the gate and drove in front of a row of metal shipping containers that were lined up end to end against the factory wall. He stopped in front of one and told me that this was where he and Lucia lived.

This was long before the tiny-house phenomenon made converted shipping containers popular housing options in the United States, but many Peruvians I knew lived in them inside their factory walls. The containers were very small but offered privacy, and the couples and a few lucky individuals who had an entire container to themselves had positive things to say about them. However, factories often housed numerous single male migrants together in one container. Earlier that week I visited another Peruvian woman's factory and had seen the shipping container shared by all of the factory's seven documented workers—men from Southeast Asia. That factory owner had actually stacked two shipping containers on top of each other and installed a shower in the top one. The living space below had sparse furnishings and the floor was made up of a patchwork of plywood and linoleum scraps. The whole place was caked with mud the men had tracked in from the monsoon rains outside. In addition to being crowded and uncomfortable, it was hot and stuffy from the lack of good air circulation.

I was surprised then when Jorge opened the door to his container to reveal what looked like a cozy bedroom. Lucia had decorated their container with curtains on the windows and a small traditional Korean table on the floor next to the bed. A queen-size bed with mosquito netting hung around it gave the room a princess

FIGURE 6. Converted shipping containers: Home for seven documented workers. Photo by author.

look. Their bookshelves and desk displayed photos of their three school-aged children in Peru. They had installed a wall-mounted air conditioning unit that kept the temperature cool and the humidity at bay. It was cramped in there, especially with all three of us, but pleasant. Jorge explained that although he lived there, after dinner he would return to his recycling plant to sleep. He wanted to give us space.

Lucia gave me a hug and invited me to sit down on the floor by the table where she had arranged three heaping plates of the *arroz chaufa* (Peruvian-style Chinese fried rice) she had cooked for us. Joyfully, she pointed out a green mesh bag filled with five avocados that Jorge had bought on the black market for our breakfast the next day. These were part of a typical breakfast in Peru, but this was the first time I had seen them in Korea. Later I would see avocados in those same bags for sale at a Costco that had recently opened in Seoul and guessed an enterprising Peruvian married to a Korean had started selling them to migrant workers who lacked the proper documentation to get a Costco membership card.[9]

During dinner Lucia and Jorge told me about their difficult migration experience. Their broker had scammed them out of $9,000 and abandoned them at a hotel in Seoul.[10] After spending three months working at jobs that never paid them, Lucia found work here and Jorge found work at the recycling plant. They had only recently paid off their debt from their migration journey and started remitting. Although they wanted to stay as long as possible to accumulate money, it was also clear that Lucia suffered emotionally from being separated from her three children. She cried every time she talked about them to me. She told me she felt terrible leaving her children, but her parents had agreed to take care of them as long as necessary.

When I asked the couple if they liked living in Korea better than Peru, Jorge looked shocked by my question. "Of course!" he said, looking around the container. "We have everything here! A rice cooker, a TV, a computer!"

He explained with pride that his boss had let him pick all of their furnishings and appliances—like their bed and air conditioner—out of the many things Korean people had discarded at the recycling plant where he worked.

Their place was definitely nice for a container, but it was still a container. The items inside it seemed to work well but showed scuffs and dents from their use and time in the recycling plant. I imagined that their family house in Peru must be very humble in comparison for him to say that.

That night after Jorge left, Lucia worked hard to hide me from the rest of the factory. She told me she was not afraid of the Korean bosses seeing me, but she was worried the other Peruvians would see me and start rumors about why I was there. She only reluctantly let me out of the container so I could brush my teeth in the communal bathroom nearby. She tried to rush me past a small group of men who were chatting and smoking in the light coming from the building's open door.

"Who's that?" someone asked her in Spanish. She ignored them, but then they asked more questions.

"Is she going to work here?"

"She is my friend from America," Lucia told them with exasperation as we disappeared into the building. "Peruvians are gossips," she said.

They were not the only people who mistook me for a factory worker in this area. The following morning after everyone else had gone to work, Lucia and I slipped through the large factory gates. We walked down a narrow road flanked by bright green fields of crops for about ten minutes before the first vehicle, a white work truck, came along. Lucia flagged it down, and the young Korean man who was driving stopped alongside us. His passenger-side window was already rolled down, probably to let in the breeze.

"Train station?" Lucia asked in Korean. He reached over and opened the passenger door for us. I had never hitchhiked in my life, but before I could ask Lucia if this was really OK, or protest, she had jumped in. I got in behind her and shut the door. Probably sensing my reluctance, she reassured me that this was how the factory workers always got to town. The driver heard us speaking Spanish and asked us where we were from. When Lucia said *Peru*, his eyes got wide. When I said *Miguk*, "the United States," he turned to look at us. After a moment he said that he hadn't seen any factory workers from the United States around there before. We both laughed, but neither of us corrected him. We just smiled as we bounced down the rough road toward the train station.

Once we got to Seoul, I led Lucia on a minitour of the city hall area where I had worked as an English teacher years earlier. We visited Cheonggyecheon stream, Deoksugung Palace, took photos of each other standing in front of the fountains near city hall, bought key chains at Namdaemun market, and ate a late lunch at a Peruvian restaurant. Around 5:00 p.m., I took her back home. That night I emailed her the photos we had taken, and she sent them to her children in Peru. She said they were very happy to see her *"paseando como turista."* From our conversation I took this to mean both "sightseeing" and literally "walking around like a tourist," as opposed to hiding in the factory.

When I flew to Peru the next month, Lucia had asked her parents and children to pick me up in their family taxi and take me on a similar tour in Lima. They took me to the Plaza de Armas, and to see a church, and then I treated them to a meal of *pollo a la brasa* (Peruvian rotisserie chicken) in central Lima. When we got back to the family house, we emailed Lucia the photos we had taken of her children feeding pigeons in the Plaza de Armas. We talked to her over a crackling internet connection from a dial-up modem set up in a bedroom. Although she seemed very happy this outing had taken place, I remember feeling sad that she could not see her children, but I could.

Sitting in the bedroom talking to Lucia, I also recalled Jorge's pride in his container and was surprised by how nice the family home seemed in comparison to what I thought it would look like. It was spacious and in an established part of a pueblo joven that had paved roads. Unlike other migrant homes that were still under construction, this one had a lived-in look with two finished floors and a roof-top garden with a chicken coop and plants. It appeared these things predated their migration and did not come from their remittances. However, it was also not clear to me if this was the family home collectively owned by everyone, or if it just belonged to Lucia's parents and the couple was saving to build their own home.

No matter the full situation, Jorge's position toward this house—and his life in Korea—made more sense to me the next time I saw the couple. It was in Peru in 2008. After three years of living in Korea, he and Lucia had been deported a few months before.

Omar and I invited them out to lunch and they suggested we meet at Larcomar, an upscale mall overlooking the Pacific Ocean in Miraflores. They brought their children who wanted to eat Happy Meals at the McDonald's inside. We sat at a table near the counter and they talked about how much they missed living in Korea.

"Let's put it this way. This is one of the nicest places in Peru," he said indicating the dark stone structure of Larcomar, "but this wouldn't even be a subway station in Korea."

This was an exaggeration, especially since Larcomar has an ocean view and luxury stores. But, I understood what he meant. There were some fancy subway stations in Seoul with impressive architecture and walls covered in a similar dark stone that somewhat resembled this shopping center. But more importantly, what I took from this comparison was that being in Korea had changed his understanding of quality. No matter what happened here, after experiencing life in Korea, Peru was never going to be the same. The couple told me returning to Korea would be nearly impossible since they had been deported. They were also sad about the prospect of leaving their children again, but they were already devising plans to migrate to Chile. This was a family project, I realized, as Lucia's children happily discussed the newer cell phone models she would be able to bring them from abroad. The ones they had from Korea were getting old.

Lucia and Jorge experienced many changes to their worldviews during their time in Korea. In their migration, they experienced a shift in the way they and their family valued things and actions. David Graeber posits that value is what we see as "beautiful, or worthwhile or important."[11] The value of things, people, or actions is determined by where they "become meaningful to the actor by being incorporated in some larger, social totality—even if in many cases the totality in question exists primarily in the actor's imagination."[12] As a result of the couple's attempts to overcome the multiple barriers to feeling at home in the world they encountered during their time in Korea, as well as taking advantage of opportunities to partially surmount those barriers, they now viewed their migration as a success despite being abused and misled at the beginning. Their attitude toward their container and its furnishings picked from the recycling plant transformed what an outsider might view as an inhospitable living situation into an enviable paradise. That happened in the Korean factory life where their privacy and access to the recycling plant's contents made them privileged in comparison to their peers. Living in their container in Korea had also made them see their home in Peru as unacceptable. Within their family's projects for cosmopolitan conversions through a future migration to Chile, the parents and children had also collectively changed the way they saw another lengthy family separation. While in Korea, Lucia had discussed the loss of time with her children as an almost unendurable sacrifice, yet while together with her children in Peru, talked happily about the chance to be apart. Their family project of a cosmopolitan conversion to change their fortunes and provide them with remittances shifted the way they talked about separation—from being about loss to being about opportunity.

Since they had not achieved financial independence and were still intending to migrate, Lucia and Jorge had perhaps not experienced the permanent type of conversion to their status that they had hoped for when planning their travels to Korea. However, during my day of sightseeing with Lucia, I saw that her desire to be a tourist for a day was indicative of her larger cosmopolitan project for travel and to experience the world. She "passed" as a tourist, both in the city space of Seoul's tourist area and also when her children viewed photos of her standing in front of a palace. Her transformation did not seem so radical to me though, because she had always seemed to view her journey as an exciting experience that was not dissimilar from traveling for pleasure. However, that ability to transform—or even maintain a cosmopolitan appreciation of exploring the world through her experiences as a migrant worker in Korea—was insufficient to protect her and Jorge from eventually being detained and deported. I too experienced a conversion to my status while in the factory area when I was categorized as a factory worker, yet, as both Lucia and I were aware, my passport and cultural capital made that a temporary—yet not insignificant—conversion. Perhaps this couple's most significant cosmopolitan conversion was that even after they had returned to Peru without any hope of returning to Korea, they continued to experience the effects of their migration and see the world in a new way—full of new projects and barriers.

"MARRY AN ARMY"

One afternoon in 2009, Eva, a twenty-three-year-old single mother from Norte Chico, and I had been shopping in Namdaemun market when she told me about her sister's plans to find her a Korean husband so that she could become documented and stay in Korea.

"Do you have to pay the guy to marry you?" I asked.

"Of course!" Eva had said. "$2,000 to marry a Korean and $5,000 to marry an *army*," "Army" being the term local Peruvians used to refer to US military personnel. She implied that this was a fairly regular process.

"How do you set that up?" I asked.

"They do that kind of thing in Dongducheon. My brother-in-law keeps telling me he could introduce me to one of his friends," she said.

The particular marriage Eva spoke of, and the citizenship it implied, had a set market price, and it varied by the desirability of the citizenship received. US citizenship is more expensive than Korean, partly because US citizenship will get you further—access to more countries and it is more prestigious—and partly because the paperwork is more difficult to file. I later heard from other Peruvian women that US soldiers receive a higher rate of pay when they are married and so continue to benefit financially from marriages of convenience.

When I asked Hilda, a forty-year-old woman who lived in a small factory town, if marriages between Peruvian women and US military personnel were common, she said, rhetorically, "Wow, how many *Peruanas* have left their husbands and run off with a soldier?" Then she laughed and said, "¿*Quien sabe? ¡Una cantidad!*" [Who knows? A huge number!]." There was no way to count.

Eva's sister Carla had just recently married a Korean man herself. Ten years Carla's junior, he had proposed after her Peruvian husband, with whom she had migrated to Korea, had left her for another Peruvian woman. Heartbroken, she had accepted the proposal. They had thrown a large Korean-style wedding in a wedding hall for which some of the Peruvian guests, including Eva, had shown up at 1:00 p.m. instead of the official start time of 12:00 p.m. This type of perpetual lateness was known as *la hora Peruana,* or Peruvian time, and it turned out to be one hour too late for the ceremony, which had started at 12:00 p.m. Korea time— 12:00 p.m. on the dot. Wedding halls in Korea are typically booked in one-hour slots all day long, and when one ceremony ends, the next wedding party is already coming in through the back doors.

Months later Carla was still furious with Eva for missing the ceremony, but she said she would forgive her if she finally agreed to marry one of her husband's Korean friends. In total, Carla had spent four years and roughly $12,500 USD to put together the right connections so that Eva could come to Korea. Before successfully entering Korea by posing as a business traveler, Eva had flown to Seoul from Lima on two separate occasions only to be refused entry by immigration officials at Incheon Airport and immediately sent back to Peru. Carla had not only paid for her sister's three round-trip tickets to Korea (more than $7,500 in total), but also provided the $5,000 fee to the real Peruvian businesswoman who had agreed to pose as Eva's employer and help her get the business visa that had finally convinced the Korean officials to let her in the country. Now, Carla wanted Eva to marry a Korean man so she could become documented and stay with her in Korea permanently.

People discussed these marriage plans as strategies for how to earn institutionalized cultural capital, through visas and passports, as well as the embodied cultural capital of being a person with freedom of mobility. Through entering into a relationship with an American or Korean man, migrant women could gain the freedom to travel, or stay put, as they wished. The possibility for entering into these relationships also arose as a direct result of being in a place like Dongducheon where there were a large number of foreigners and Koreans who were engaging in their own cosmopolitan conversions, or plans to migrate or change their status. By marrying an *army,* a Peruvian woman helped an American man increase his cultural and economic capital. Not only did the marriage reduce the time it took for someone to acquire cultural capital, but within this space, the marriage was accelerated. There were offices both on and off the base that helped to facilitate the paperwork for international marriages. Sometimes people rushed into marriages because there was always a risk someone could be deported. Carla wanted Eva to marry a Korean for somewhat selfish reasons. By marrying a Korean man, Eva would help her sister achieve a cosmopolitan project of feeling at home in her new world of Korea, where she felt freedom of movement, without feeling totally isolated from her family in Peru.

These relationships and the changes they promised emerged at the intersection of multiple cosmopolitan conversions that diverged and converged in new ways as people interacted in this space.

DANGEROUS RELATIONSHIPS

By April 2009, the effects of the global financial crisis had started to recede, but it was still dangerous for undocumented Peruvian migrants to walk around outside in their factory towns. I found that while some people dealt with this increased danger by rarely leaving their homes, others continued to venture out to socialize in public spaces. For example, one Sunday afternoon I was supposed to attend the Dongducheon Mass with Eva, but she called me early in the morning to cancel, saying Carla had heard immigration officers were patrolling in the area and she did not want to risk being detected. As soon as I hung up, Oliver, a member of Friendship Church, called to see if I wanted to meet him at a factory worker soccer tournament held in Dongducheon. I had heard about these games for years and wanted to attend one, but I told him we had better stay home because immigration officers were patrolling the streets. He told me he understood if I could not go, but he had promised friends he would be there and could not cancel. Convinced by his blasé reaction to the warnings, I decided to go as well.

When we arrived, there were already dozens of other factory workers there too, playing soccer or hanging out around the edges of the field. From the beginning of the game and throughout the day people received calls from friends located nearby who were reporting sightings of immigration officers. However, the reports placed the immigration officers relatively far from the field itself, so no one stopped playing.

The tournament was held at an abandoned schoolyard next to a school that has since been torn down. The building was in bad condition—most of the windows and some of the walls had been knocked out or torn down, and there was graffiti in Spanish and Korean on the remaining walls. However gutted, the school's bones still obscured the field and players from the main road. The games lasted until after dark and attracted players and spectators from Peru, the United States, Bolivia, Nigeria, and countries in the former Soviet Union. Men and women watched the game from threadbare couches and chairs people had pulled out of the trash and dragged up to the sidelines. Everyone passed around big bottles of beer to share and mostly ignored two Peruvian women who were standing by a table trying to sell containers of Peruvian food they had made. People told me they thought it was too expensive at 7,000 won (about $7) a plate.

I spent most of the afternoon standing on the sidelines talking to a woman from Lima named Veronica who introduced herself to me. I told her about my project and she started telling me about the players and who they were dating. I cringed as she pointed out that two of the worst players on the field—a sweaty goalie who had just let three goals through in succession and a very tall guy who had gotten injured almost immediately at the start of the game—were Americans ("like you!" she told me). They were US soldiers stationed at the nearby base who were dating two Peruvian women sitting on the sidelines.

Veronica's eighteen-year-old daughter Gaby, who had recently arrived in Korea and now worked in a factory dying fabrics, arrived late to the games. She came up to her mother and asked her to hold a backpack that contained her volleyball clothes. Gaby and other women were planning to play volleyball next to the soccer field, but for some reason their game never happened. Veronica took the bag and then jokingly asked Gaby where she had been the night before. Gaby looked embarrassed and started to walk away. "She came home the other night with a mark on her neck [a hickey], and I honestly thought she had gotten a stain from the dye at her factory!" she told me laughing, as her daughter walked off to find her boyfriend, another Peruvian factory worker, whom she had met in Korea. Veronica herself was separated from her husband in Peru and had recently dated and then broken up with one of the players on the field. She said that he kept trying to get her back, but she refused because he was jealous and accused her of dating other men. She lowered her voice as she told me that one man on the field had slept with many of the women in town, recorded the encounters, and then uploaded the videos to the internet. We ran into someone she had flown over with on the plane from Peru and had not seen since as well as people I had met during fieldwork at various churches and nightclubs.

The games and conversation continued as the light of day faded. I caught the last subway train home, but Oliver and others stayed at the abandoned school late into the night. Then he and other players went to a Peruvian restaurant and Latin-themed nightclub where they danced until 2:00 a.m. with the Filipina women who worked there. Immigration officers never came. There was another tournament the following weekend.

That afternoon was simultaneously routine, dangerous, and something that promised excitement beyond anything possible in Peru. I got the feeling the attendees were not in denial about the danger of being deported, but that the possibility for loss through deportation was always in the background of their lives. Not only were they willing to risk the danger of detection if it allowed them to socialize with people they would otherwise not be able to meet at these events or have experiences they could probably not find in Peru, but the danger accelerated their inclusion in this community of international people. There was always a chance they could be deported, or would be deployed, so they entered into relationships quickly.

Their plans—and their lives—emerged and transformed along with the plans of the other people they met along the way. Even though they had come to Korea for work, people most wanted to discuss in their conversations with me, and seemed to value most about their time there, the relationships they formed with other migrants. They were willing to take great risks, in terms of being detected by immigration officers and with their families at home in Peru, to meet and interact with others. The relationships they formed and ended in Korea were complicated and overlapping and had beginnings and ends in both Peru and Korea.

STUCK IN LOVE

Oliver had entered into a relationship with someone who turned out to be both risky and transformative for him long after his relationship and migration ended. It had all started a few years after arriving in Korea in 1997 when he met and fell in love with Katya, a migrant worker from Russia. When Katya became pregnant, they decided to get married and raise their child together. Katya stayed home to take care of their daughter while Oliver worked fourteen-hour shifts at a glass factory. A few years later he was hit in the eye with broken glass while working in his factory and was partially blinded. After a period of hospitalization, he was released to discover Katya had emptied his bank account of the money he had earned while in Korea, stolen his passport, and taken their young daughter to Russia.

After the accident, Oliver was left blind in one eye, penniless, and with only sporadic phone and internet contact with his wife and daughter. Of this time, he said:

> What could she have been thinking? I don't know. I can't imagine. The thing was that she made that decision. Maybe she thought that I would be [injured] for a while. That I wouldn't be able to work. Maybe she thought she would have to work. . . . All the money that I had, she took. I was left with . . . what's the saying? Without even a dollar. And she took my daughter.

He soon learned that Katya had never registered their marriage in Russia and had quickly remarried there. She later returned to Korea under a false name, but without Oliver's daughter. She dated other Peruvian men before being detained by immigration officers and taken to a detention facility to await deportation. Oliver's pastor pressured him into paying for Katya's return ticket to Russia to spare her from having to wait for months or even a year in the detention center. The pastor argued that despite Katya's bad behavior, she was still his wife. Oliver reluctantly paid for her plane ticket back to Russia. However, since Katya's second departure, all of Oliver's efforts to reconnect with his daughter have failed. When I asked Oliver if his church could help him legally demand parental rights in Russia, he said that when they tried to do just that, Katya had changed their daughter's last name and moved. If he were to travel to Russia to find his daughter, he would not know where to start looking. If he found her, he would not be able to reenter Korea and would not have enough money to get back to Peru.

Over the years as I heard more details of this story from Oliver, I came to see that while he had been in love with Katya, it was also apparent that he was proud of her nationality as a Russian woman. When speaking of Katya, he frequently mention her nationality first before proceeding with the story. To understand the significance of this approach, it is important to note that among the Peruvian men I spoke to in Peru and Korea, Russian women were thought of as being extremely beautiful, and entering into a relationship with a Russian woman was considered to be prestigious and (particularly in Peru where there were not many Russian women) highly unlikely.

When I asked Cristina, a twenty-two-year-old Peruvian woman working in a factory town, whether she thought Peruvian men in Korea liked Russian women in particular, she said, "Of course. Because they are tall and blond. For their bodies. But they have a bad reputation." When I asked her if Russian women were popular in Peru as well, she said, "Yes, but I think here [in Korea] it is easier [to meet them]. And listen, Peruvian men who are working abroad, are not faithful [to their wives in Peru]. That is 100 percent certain." Perhaps for this reputation cited by Cristina, other Peruvian men envied and respected Oliver for his relationship with Katya. It appeared that having a relationship with her helped him gain a level of cultural capital in the form of prestige for being part of this enviable transnational family.

Oliver's marriage to Katya gave him a way to engage in a cosmopolitan conversion by becoming a member of an enviable transnational family, but it simultaneously left him entangled in new ways. Not only did Oliver's failed marriage leave him emotionally devastated, but it also caused him to become legally stuck—at least temporarily—in Korea. In 2009 he tried to file for divorce, but said that representatives from the Peruvian embassy told him that he could not do so without having his wife present. To request an exception to this rule, they told him, he would need to collect documents from Peru—either in person or with the help of an expensive lawyer. When I asked him about this situation, he said, "I told the embassy everything. But they said that basically I could not do it in Korea. That those things are done in Peru. That I had to send a person [a lawyer or agent] who had power of attorney, and do many other things." After months of attempting to maneuver the bureaucratic red tape, Oliver gave up and decided to remain married to a woman he had not seen in years.

As undocumented migrants, neither Oliver nor Katya had many legal options or ways of solidifying their presence in Korea besides formally registering their marriage, which made their union valid and recognized by the state and in their church. However, in this case, rather than opening up new possibilities for future migrations or making his relationship last, Oliver's cosmopolitan plan actually restricted his freedom of movement. Although Oliver's is an unusual case, being made both forever linked and removable by official documentation such as birth certificates and visas is common for transmigrants in the globalizing world.[13] Instead of supporting or validating their marriage and enabling the family to stay together, their legally documented marriage inhibited him from moving on.

When I talked to him in 2015, Oliver told me that he was only able to get a divorce after he was deported to Peru. When I asked him if it had been easier to obtain the divorce than it had been in Korea, his voice became sad. He said, "Well, now that I am here [in Peru], I could do it myself. Anyway, they [the Peruvian Ministry of the Interior] told me that with everything Katya had done to me, my marriage was not valid." So, by officially divorcing, Oliver learned that his marriage to Katya had never existed.

Katya apparently had her own plans to change her life and status that no longer involved Oliver. Their cosmopolitan conversions had intersected in important ways, but they were ultimately not compatible.

Although this experience had caused Oliver loss—his vision, his money, and his family—through his interactions with his church, he was able to change the value of that loss into cultural capital. He told me that a few years before he was deported, he gave his *testimonio* (testimony) or personal story of salvation at Friendship Church. His testimonio included his migration experience, conversion from Catholicism, and everything that had happened with Katya. He said that his experiences were so exciting to the Koreans in attendance that they invited him to speak at Yeouido Full Gospel Church, which has 763,000 members and claims to be the largest in the world.[14] Allowing foreigners to present their testimonies, especially shocking ones that mix the trials of undocumented migration, injury, and betrayal with miraculous conversion and redemption, is an effective way to raise money for mission churches. By performing his story of loss in front of this audience, waiting to hear about big setbacks before the rise of redemption, he helped to revalue the meaning of his loss. By converting his loss into a testimonio, he influenced others and gained cultural capital as a special migrant, social capital through an invitation to participate in a prestigious group, and most likely helped raise economic capital for the church through donations.

CONCLUSION

In this chapter I have discussed various examples of cosmopolitan conversions, or projects or plans that individuals or groups undertake in the effort to change their lives or future opportunities and help them become cosmopolitan. The seeds for these plans may sometimes originate in Peru, but they really emerge and transform within the context of Korea when migrants interact with so many other people and groups who are embarking on cosmopolitan conversions of their own. The plans converge and diverge in unexpected ways and can help people overcome barriers that typically prevent undocumented migrants from achieving the freedom of mobility and the recognition of belonging that they seek, but can also leave them stuck or excluded in new ways.

In attempting to be recognized as belonging in Korea, by pursuing institutional capital like marriage licenses or visas, undocumented people can make themselves visible and deportable. They can also become vulnerable to potential forms of loss when pursuing embodied cultural capital such as entering into a love affair, passing as a tourist, or even attempting to access desirable remittances for their children. However, in interacting with others who are also embarking on emerging plans for cosmopolitan conversions, they have the chance to create the world that they are participating in. Along with that, they help to construct the value or meaning of their actions, experiences, and themselves. Through sharing the stories of their plans, they help to revalue things like loss or risk into enviable outcomes, the markers of success, or even economic capital.

In essence, the globalized world is made up of countless cosmopolitan conversions: plans that are emerging in conjunction with other plans; plans that are constantly being realized and still taking form. As the projects meet barriers and opportunities, they convert along with the people, places, and connections that they touch and reveal the configuration of the global worlds created through transnational migration.

EPILOGUE

By now, many of the Peruvians I met in Korea have either been deported or decided to leave. However, there are also a large number who have managed to stay, including those who married Korean citizens as well as many long-term undocumented migrants who have evaded detection largely by having strong social networks in their factories and churches, and by limiting their movements outside of their homes. Over the years I have kept in touch via instant messenger, Skype, and various social media platforms with people still in Korea and those who already left. Many of the Peruvians I spent the most time with in Korea, such as Karina and her father Victor from chapter 1, Rafael and Lily from chapter 2, Paty and Camila from chapter 3, and Eva and Oliver from chapter 4, left Korea between 2008 and 2015. Others, like Jheremy, the translator from Friendship Ministry who was preparing to study to be a pastor in Mexico, still seemed settled in Korea. He had been there for seventeen years and had weathered both the Asian financial crisis and the global financial crisis by working at the same small factory the whole time. However, one day in 2016, I went on social media and saw photos he had posted of himself and his family at the Lima airport.

A few months after Jheremy's departure, we chatted over Skype. One of the first things he told me was that he had been unable to find work in Peru and had decided to move to Santiago, Chile, where his sister was a resident.

"I have been in Santiago for two months," he told me. His voice sounded positive. "I'm doing construction and trying to get a Chilean ID card so I can find a better job," he said.

Soon after arriving in Peru he had realized how difficult it would be for him to find work there as a forty-one-year-old. "Thirty years old is considered too old [in Peru]. They want someone who is twenty-five or twenty-six because they don't want to pay benefits. In Chile there is a lot of work. In a matter of weeks I found a job," he told me.

During our conversation it seemed that the lack of work was not the only thing that had made him leave Peru. He missed Korea, and living in Chile offered some consolation. "I felt unsettled in Peru," he said. "I felt comfortable in Korea. I miss Korea. I spent all of my youth there. I arrived when I was twenty-four. My original plan was to only be there two years, save money, and return to study. But I liked it. The life there is calm. Then I decided to stay one more year. And then I didn't want to return to Peru. I stay in touch with brothers from the church and my factory. I talk with my bosses from my factory all the time. When I talk to them they say, 'When are you coming back? You have to come back! We miss you at the factory.' If I could, I would."

"What do you miss about it?" I asked.

"The people who live there. I miss walking around Seoul. The church, Friendship Ministry. My friends from all over the world. In Peru I didn't find friends from other places, but in Chile, I can. Colombians, people from the Dominican Republic. Tons of different places. From what I can see, it's the same as Korea. We are foreigners. It is something that unites us," he said.

"Could you tell me how you left Korea?" I asked.

He told me was detained by immigration officers on his day off when he was resting in the container he shared with his documented co-workers. He sounded frustrated with them as he recounted the experience:

> I worked with three people from Nepal. Monday to Friday. They always worked on Saturdays to make extra money. I always told them to bring their IDs with them to work, because if immigration officers came, they would bring them to our room and they would find me and deport me. They always went to work and didn't bring their IDs. One afternoon, as soon as they started working, immigration officers arrived. They asked for their IDs, but the Nepalis didn't have them. They tried to take out their cell phones to call me, but the officers saw and took away their phones. They said their IDs were in their room and the officers should wait for them in the factory. [From that] the officers knew someone undocumented was in there. They said, "It's better if we go together." They went to the room and I was there. They came in and saw me and asked me, "Are you Korean?" I said, "No." "Where are you from?" they asked. "Peru." They said, "Show me your passport." Then they said, "You are illegal. Come with me." They deported me. I was only allowed to bring my documents. They handcuffed me like I was a criminal.

He paused. "Why handcuffs?" he said rhetorically. "I wasn't making trouble."

"It seems excessive," I agreed.

His factory boss paid for the $2,000 plane ticket as well as a 20 million won fine for employing an undocumented worker. However, he was detained for a week because there were very few countries that would allow a deported person to transfer in their airports. The only route open to him was through Europe. He went from Seoul to Frankfurt, to São Paulo, and then finally to Lima. "It took three days. It was exhausting," he told me. "Did you have to wear handcuffs the whole time?" I asked.

They took them off at the airport in Incheon when my flight was about to leave. They led me to the door of the plane and said to the flight attendant, "This person is being deported and you are now responsible for him." I boarded first before any other passenger. When we got to Frankfurt, they told me to wait in the plane. A person came to get me. I was the last person to get off the plane. I waited in Frankfurt for seven hours. They told me not to move. Then in Brazil for five hours.

"Did they give you food? Or a hotel?" I asked.

"No. There was no hotel available. I just had to wait. The same thing happened in Brazil as I waited to go to Lima. When I arrived they called the immigration officers in Peru. It was in Peru that they gave me my passport," he said.

When I asked him how he felt about that, he said, "The way I returned made me very embarrassed."

I asked him to elaborate on what he was embarrassed about. I assumed he would say something about perhaps being made to feel like a criminal by his own country's immigration officers, or I also wondered if he was returning with less money than he had hoped. Instead, he clarified that he had been referring to the sudden way he had left Korea in handcuffs.

"I was embarrassed because I could not say goodbye to my friends [in Korea]. I can't return either. I didn't leave in the right way," he said. "Now I wish I could return to Korea to see some friends and say goodbye in the right way. I just want to see them again."

We may have reached the end of this particular global moment of Peruvian migration to South Korea, but the end of this migration does not mean that the experience has ended.

My conversation with Jheremy highlights how even though many Peruvian migrants have left Korea, the experience continues to affect their daily lives through the various ways they have come to see the world and the choices available to them. A need for work and money certainly framed Jheremy's choices to migrate to Korea and then Chile, but his perspective on these choices challenges the idea that money is an objective point we are all starting from. When describing his life in Chile, he sounded relieved to have a job but joyous about finding a community of international friends that he saw as similar to the community he had experienced in Korea. Only through migrating to Korea and returning to Peru did he realize that the type of community he found in Korea was something he was looking for, and that Peru lacked that type of community. Perhaps Chile promised even more potential for inclusion than Korea as he saw a chance to receive recognition of belonging through getting a work visa and had the support of his sister who was documented.

Further, when he told me about his deportation experience, he did not focus on his loss of money but his loss of status and a misrecognition of his value. The embarrassment he felt at being deported was not about returning as a "failed" economic migrant, but about the way he was handcuffed and removed in front of his friends. He seemed to take this particular exit as an affront to the status he had gained during his time in Korea where in his church he was an official leader and in his factory he was regarded as a hard worker. Whereas in his church and workplace his actions and years in Korea had created his reputation as a good person, within the Korean legal system, his actions and years in Korea marked him as a "criminal." Through his migration to Korea, Jheremy has embarked on, and continues to grapple with, multiple conversions to his understanding of his religious identity, goals, and place in the world.

In this book I have argued that conversions—concerning money, religious beliefs, and cosmopolitan plans—are the way migrants negotiate the meaning of their lives in a constantly changing context of place, statuses, and relationships and continue to make meaningful impacts on their worlds even when their money has disappeared. Their situations are constantly changing because of their own transnational movements and connections between Peru and South Korea, their unstable legal statuses in Korea, relationships with others also in transit and at home, and their own changing worldviews and plans.

I have explored their emerging global plans through the lens of what I term cosmopolitan conversions, or the various projects or plans that individuals or groups undertake in the effort to change their situations by gaining the skills and abilities of cosmopolitanism—having "infinite ways of being"[1]—and also by being recognized as worthy and deserving of that status by others. I showed how Peruvian migrants made plans to defy the status of disenfranchised undocumented factory workers to also be tourists, students, family leaders, members of transnational love affairs, or even saviors of Peru. However, they also worked to show others the validity of those identities, either by spending time and energy to gain institutionalized capital such as visas, marriage licenses, or educational certificates, or embodied capital such as identifying and relaying their respuestas from God, entering into relationships with foreigners, or even trying to pass as tourists during encounters with immigration officers and in public spaces.

While I would suggest that migrants (and nonmigrants) everywhere embark on their own types of cosmopolitan conversions, I have shown that South Korea is vital to the ways these particular experiences developed. That is because the plans of Peruvian migrants emerged at a historical moment that put them at the convergence of other large- and small-scale cosmopolitan conversion projects headed by the Korean state, churches, and the Koreans and migrants with whom they interacted. For example, the Korean state's efforts to become globalized (*seghyewha*) and manage arriving foreigners through multicultural policies first allowed Peruvians and other foreign workers entry and temporary documentation (through an amnesty) and then left them legally excluded (because of the EPS). Simultaneously, the efforts of various Korean Protestant churches to engage in Korea's global moment by having multicultural parishioners as charity cases and foreign mission partners made Peruvians highly desirable members. The Peruvian migrants' efforts to negotiate the meaning of their lives through these multiple forms of conversion—money, religious, and cosmopolitanism—helped to shift their value in Korea. The chance they could be deported accelerated their membership in various social circles, which gave them new opportunities. They became coveted church members because of their exclusion from the state and found new opportunities for education and marriage because of the barriers they faced to their legal belonging in Korea. However, sometimes in their attempts to make themselves at home in the world, they also created new potential losses for themselves, including becoming entangled in the very legal and social barriers they wanted to overcome.

With any conversion—money, religion, or plans—there is always loss. This makes it nearly impossible to reach an equivalent, or something better. Yet, through conversion, loss became valuable. Migrants built loss into their plans for cosmopolitan conversions. They came to see that they had to lose things—such as time with their families, their youth in Peru, and feelings of security—to allow for other parts of their plans to succeed. In fact, loss and sacrifice was the mark of a successful migration. At other times, such as when sharing the dark moments and periods of their migrations and at the same time interpreting them as respuestas during their testimonios, they converted loss into capital.

Part of any successful cosmopolitan conversion is convincing others to participate in the project and accept the conversion as valid. Initially, many tried to do this with their families by sending money home. This became increasingly difficult because of the global financial crisis when even something as seemingly solid as the value of the dollar became unpredictable. From one moment to the next, the money migrants had earned lost and gained value depending on the day's conversion rate. However, I showed the creative ways migrants found to convert their economic remittances into other capital they hoped would be regarded as more valuable. Yet, they found that these systems of value were not always compatible. Respuestas may have earned Cristianos cultural capital in their churches in Korea, but they did not hold as much traction for their Catholic families in Peru, or even their Catholic friends in Korea. Further, as Bourdieu points out, a risk with trying to convert economic capital into social capital—by giving a gift in the hope of influencing others, for example—is that there will be an incommensurability.[2] If the people on the receiving end of the gift do not express the appropriate gratitude, some of the value is lost. This incommensurability happened with Rafael in chapter 2, whose family thwarted many of his attempts to give them the opportunity to gain cultural capital—through an education or becoming a store owner—by squandering his economic capital. However, Lily, from the same chapter, successfully converted her remittances into a family with a house and careers that would support them after her migration had ended.

For migrants trying to relay their new religious worldviews to their families in Peru, they often found that the systems they were converting between were too different to reach a successful negotiation. For example, Camila's family in chapter 3 understood her desire to influence them to improve their lives through embracing a Protestant sobriety and business strategy, but they had little reason to participate in her plan—especially after she had returned home and lost her authority as an economic remitter. This highlights another risk of trying to convert capital, as cited by Bourdieu, which is that it takes a long time and a lot of labor for others to accept cultural capital as valid.[3] Migrants needed to put forth a lot of time and effort to get others to accept their conversion from an undocumented migrant into a person who was a successful entrepreneur, or a family or religious leader worthy of respect. Yet, since they were in constant risk of being deported or not earning enough money to survive, they did not know how long they had left in Korea to realize these changes.

That said, even deportation could not fully end these cosmopolitan conversions. That is because they are ongoing projects that constantly change direction depending on the particular configuration of barriers and opportunities that emerge as people make their way through the world. Also, the process of pursuing a cosmopolitan conversion has already made a person cosmopolitan, even if the project does not go as planned.

This particular global configuration has most likely finished, and with it the large-scale migration of Peruvians to South Korea. However, as I have shown, the migration acts as a thread linking all of these global and transnational flows together, and its impact continues.

At the end of my conversation with Jheremy I asked him what had happened to his plan of becoming a pastor in Mexico. He told me that after leaving Korea, he realized his true calling was to be a missionary—in Chile. He had met many Koreans living in Chile through a pastor friend in Korea but did not attend their church because it was too far away. Instead, he had found a new church and decided to use his gift of talking with people to evangelize there.

Rosa, the student who hoped to stay long enough in Korea to learn English and get a scholarship to study in the United States, ended up returning to Peru. However, she recently graduated from a university in Peru.

Rafael returned to Peru at fifty years old to find that in his eight-year absence, all of his friends had moved to Spain and he no longer had anyone to recommend him for a job. When I talked with him in 2016, he described his shock at returning. "The companies were different. The opportunities were different. We bought a taxi, and that went badly. I tried construction, but found it was too difficult [at my age]. I had forgotten many things."

He had been disappointed to be deported before saving enough money to complete a goal he had set for himself in Korea: to buy a farm in Peru. He said, "If you go to another country you have a goal (*una meta*). To make money and complete a project. I couldn't complete my project."

Then, after two years of what he described as "suffering," a new opportunity emerged. His family owned a large piece of land in the countryside, which he had nearly lost a claim to while in Korea. However, he regained control over it and learned that an electrical company wanted to build a plant there. He said, "We negotiated with the plant that if we sold them the land, they had to do something for us. We knew they would need workers. They gave us [Rafael, his son, and his brother] jobs. We've been working there for five years. It's stable there. We sold it all."

Then, although he could not afford to buy the large farm he had dreamed of, he used his earnings from Korea to buy a small piece of land and build a little farm. His mother lived there during the week and took care of the place, including his guinea pigs and turkeys. Every other week, he took a trip to Lima to visit his girlfriend, whom he had met in Korea. They had constructed another floor on her house to rent out to tenants and planned to retire soon.

These are not simple conversions—they involve negotiating emerging forms of loss and gain with multiple actors in a constantly changing context of configurations. However, conversions cannot fail because any barriers are chances to find a new opportunity, and any losses are chances to attempt more creative conversions. Just as there is no direct route from Peru to Korea and back, or when converting won to soles, there is no direct route for completing cosmopolitan conversions, which are plans that are yet to be realized. Whether a conversion involves capital, religion, or worldview, changes in direction do not negate the experience but rather inform it.

NOTES

INTRODUCTION

1. To protect people's anonymity, throughout this book I have omitted or merged some identifying details of my interlocutors' lives and used pseudonyms for all people, churches, and businesses. All translations between Spanish and English are mine unless otherwise specified. For Korean transliteration I followed the Revised Romanization of Korean and the official Korean spellings of place names.

2. Many Peruvians in Korea come from Lima's *pueblos jóvenes* (new villages). These places started out as squatter communities to accommodate internal migrants coming from rural areas in Peru in the 1970s. A few have become established areas, and others are still struggling to improve their infrastructures. I do not refer to them by name, but when significant to the context, I specify whether a particular *pueblo joven* was developed or developing. Otherwise, I try to keep the details vague to help protect people's anonymity.

3. The Peruvians I knew rarely used the word *Protestant* or *Protestante* as an identifier. They called Protestants *Cristianos* and Catholics *Católicos*. I have followed that distinction in this book.

4. Although there is no publication date, a summary of the 2007–8 global financial crisis, also known as the world economic crisis, by the Global Policy Forum sounds like it was written in the midst of the chaos. It says, "An economic and financial crisis has engulfed the world. Banks have collapsed, stock prices have slumped and there has been an unprecedented decline in economic activity. The crisis began in 2007, in the wake of financial and real estate speculation in the United States, but it came after a long period of international financial instability, trade imbalances and several local or regional crises. By late 2008, the crisis had spread to many countries. Governments responded with massive emergency measures, but the crisis continued to spread and large numbers of workers have been laid off all over

the world." Global Policy Forum, "The World Economic Crisis," www.globalpolicy.org/social-and-economic-policy/the-world-economic-crisis.html, last accessed July 9, 2019.

5. For details on the Employee Permit System refer to the Employee Permit System, www.eps.go.kr/en/view/view_01.jsp, last accessed July 26, 2018. The Peruvian embassy repeatedly asked to be given a Memorandum of Understanding to participate in the Employee Permit System. However, instead of a yes or no answer, their request went unanswered. The materials circulated to attendees at the Ministry of Labor's 6th Immigration Policy Forum in 2005 stated: "A sending country's departure state of legalized foreign workers and illegal residents in 2005 will be a determining factor in renewing and newly concluding MOU in 2006." This meant that if a country wanted its citizens to continue with or be invited to join the EPS, it needed to "proactively encourage voluntary departure" of migrant workers before they became undocumented. This note was addressed to "all countries concerned," and a member of the embassy told me that although representatives from Peru and Nigeria were invited to attend this forum, they were not considered to be one of the "countries concerned" and did not really have a chance to join.

6. Dong-Hoon Seol, "Past and Present of Foreign Workers in Korea, 1987–2000," *Asia Solidarity Quarterly* 2 (2000): 6–31; Timothy C. Lim, "Racing from the Bottom in South Korea? The Nexus between Civil Society and Transnational Migrants," *Asian Survey* 43, no. 3 (2003): 423–42; and Dong-Hoon Seol and John D. Skrentny, "Ethnic Return Migration and Hierarchical Nationhood," *Ethnicities* 9, no. 2 (2009): 147–74.

7. From an internal embassy memo. This book focuses on the 85 percent who arrived with the intention of finding work in Korea's factories and became undocumented.

8. This particular point is not new. In 1979's *Birds of Passage*, Michael Piore wrote, "This book starts from the proposition that income is not the critical analytical variable.... One can better understand migration by ignoring income differences and recognizing instead that people are rooted in a social context in ways that other commodities are not." Michael J. Piore, *Birds of Passage: Migrant Labor and Industrial Societies* (Cambridge: Cambridge University Press, 1979), 8.

9. I am drawing from Mei Zhan's concept of "worlding" here. Mei Zhan, *Other-Worldly: Making Chinese Medicine through Transnational Frames* (Durham, NC: Duke University Press, 2009), 6.

10. Nina Glick Shiller, Linda Basch, and Cristina Blanc-Szanton, "Towards a Definition of Transnationalism," *Annals of the New York Academy of Sciences* 645 (1992): ix–xiv, ix; they use the term "transmigrants." See also Jeffrey H. Cohen, "Migration, Remittances, and Household Strategies," *Annual Review of Anthropology* 40 (2011): 103–14.

11. Bruce Carruthers and Wendy Nelson Espeland, "Money, Meaning, and Morality," *American Behavioral Scientist* 41, no. 10 (1998): 1384–408; and Arjun Appadurai, *The Social Life of Things: Commodities in Cultural Perspective*, Cambridge Studies in Social and Cultural Anthropology (Cambridge: Cambridge University Press, 1986).

12. Diane Austin-Broos, "The Anthropology of Conversion: An Introduction," in *The Anthropology of Religious Conversion*, ed. Andrew Buckser and Stephen D. Glazier (Oxford: Rowman and Littlefield, 2003), 1–12, 2.

13. Susan Bibler Coutin, *Exiled Home: Salvadoran Transnational Youth in the Aftermath of Violence*, Global Insecurities (Durham, NC: Duke University Press, 2016), 22.

14. Carol A. Breckenridge and Sheldon Pollock, eds., *Cosmopolitanism*, A Public Culture Book (Durham, NC: Duke University Press, 2002); So Jin Park and Nancy Abelmann,

"Class and Cosmopolitan Striving: Mothers' Management of English Education in South Korea," *Anthropological Quarterly* 77, no. 4 (2004): 645–72.

15. Aiwha Ong, *Flexible Citizenship: The Cultural Logics of Transnationality* (Durham, NC: Duke University Press, 1999).

16. Cosmopolitanism has a particular resonance in the daily life of people and in scholarship on South Korea. It is an aspiration to be at home in the world—by being a fluent English speaker, or by doing study abroad—and it is common for these efforts to be part of family projects. Helene Lee notes that Korean Americans and Korean Chinese "return" to South Korea and, facing multiple forms of exclusion, retaliate by claiming a cosmopolitan citizenship. She writes, "'Their narratives shift toward a discourse of global citizenship and a cosmopolitan Koreanness only accessible to transnational actors like themselves." Helene Lee, *Between Foreign and Family: Return Migration and Identity Construction among Korean Americans and Korean Chinese* (Newark, NJ: Rutgers University Press, 2018), 137.

17. Anna Tsing, *Friction: An Ethnography of Global Connection* (Princeton, NJ: Princeton University Press, 2005).

18. This original meaning of *convert* comes from Middle English via the Latin *convertere*. Lexico, Powered by Oxford, "convert," www.lexico.com/en/definition/convert, last accessed July 14, 2019.

19. Lewis R. Rambo, "Anthropology and the Study of Conversion," in *The Anthropology of Religious Conversion,* ed. Andrew Buckser and Stephen D. Glazier (Oxford: Rowman and Littlefield, 2003), 213; and Timothy Steigenga and Edward L. Cleary, eds., *Conversion of a Continent: Contemporary Religious Change in Latin America* (New Brunswick, NJ: Rutgers University Press, 2007).

20. Steigenga and Cleary, *Conversion of a Continent,* 7.

21. Austin-Broos, "Anthropology of Conversion."

22. Pierre Bourdieu, "The Forms of Capital," in *Handbook of Theory and Research for the Sociology of Education,* ed. J. G. Richardson (New York: Greenwood Press, 1986), 241–58.

23. Bourdieu, "Forms of Capital."

24. Laura Bear, Karen Ho, Anna Lowenhaupt Tsing, and Sylvia Yanagisako, "Gens: A Feminist Manifesto for the Study of Capitalism," Editors' Forum: Theorizing the Contemporary, *Fieldsights,* March 30, 2015, https://culanth.org/fieldsights/gens-a-feminist-manifesto-for-the-study-of-capitalism. These authors argue, "Structure itself is not pre-formed, but heterogeneously made through processes of aligning multiple projects, converting them toward diverse ends that include (but are not limited to) the accumulation and distribution of capital."

25. Nancy D. Munn, *The Fame of Gawa: A Symbolic Study of Value Transformation in a Massim Society,* Henry Louis Morgan Lecture Series (Durham, NC: Duke University Press, 1986), 8.

26. See Eleana Kim, *Adopted Territory: Transnational Korean Adoptees and the Politics of Belonging* (Durham, NC: Duke University Press, 2010).

27. Caren Freeman, *Making and Faking Kinship: Marriage and Labor Migration between China and South Korea* (Ithaca, NY: Cornell University Press, 2011); and EuyRyung Jun, "'The Frog That Has Forgotten Its Past': Advocating for Migrant Workers in South Korea," *Positions: East Asia Cultures Critique* 24, no. 3 (2016): 669–92.

28. Mae M. Ngai, *Impossible Subjects: Illegal Aliens and the Making of Modern America* (Princeton, NJ: Princeton University Press, 2004), 5.

29. Ju Hui Judy Han, "'If You Don't Work, You Don't Eat': Evangelizing Development in Africa," in *New Millennium South Korea: Neoliberal Capitalism and Transnational Movements*, ed. Jesook Song (New York: Routledge, 2011).

30. Nina Glick Schiller et al., "Pathways of Migrant Incorporation in Germany," *Transit* 1, no. 1 (2004): 1–18.

31. Pierrette Hongdagneu-Sotelo, ed., *Religion and Social Justice for Immigrants* (New Brunswick, NJ: Rutgers University Press, 2007).

32. Leo Chavez, "Outside the Imagined Community: Undocumented Settlers and Experiences of Incorporation," *American Ethnologist* 18, no. 2 (1991): 257–78; Linda Bosniak, "Universal Citizenship and the Problem of Alienage," *Northwestern University Law Review* 94, no. 3 (2000): 963–84; Cecilia Menjívar, "Liminal Legality: Salvadoran and Guatemalan Immigrants' Lives in the United States," *American Journal of Sociology* 111 (2006): 999–1037; and Leisy Abrego and Sarah Lakhani, "Incomplete Inclusion: Legal Violence and Immigrants in Liminal Legal Statuses," *Law & Policy* 37, no. 4 (2015): 265–93.

33. Melanie B. E. Griffiths, "Out of Time: The Temporal Uncertainties of Refused Asylum Seekers and Immigration Detainees," *Journal of Ethnic and Migration Studies* 40, no. 12 (2014): 2003.

34. Nicholas P. De Genova, *Working the Boundaries: Race, Space, and "Illegality" in Mexican Chicago* (Durham, NC: Duke University Press, 2005).

35. Victor Turner, *The Ritual Process: Structure and Anti-Structure* (New York: Aldine de Gruyter, 1995).

36. David Graeber, *Toward an Anthropological Theory of Value: The False Coin of Our Own Dreams* (New York: Palgrave Macmillan, 2001), xii.

37. Julie Chu, *Cosmologies of Credit: Transnational Mobility and the Politics of Destination in China* (Durham, NC: Duke University Press, 2010), 5.

38. Tsing, *Friction;* Inderpal Grewal, *Transnational America: Feminisms, Diasporas, Neoliberalisms* (Durham, NC: Duke University Press, 2005); and James Clifford, *Routes: Travel and Translation in the Late Twentieth Century* (Cambridge, MA: Harvard University Press, 1997).

39. Zhan, *Other-Worldly,* 6.

40. Pnina Werbner, "Global Pathways: Working-Class Cosmopolitans and the Creation of Transnational Ethnic Worlds," *Social Anthropology* 7, no. 1 (1999): 19; Michele Ruth Gamburd, "Money That Burns Like Oil: A Sri Lankan Cultural Logic of Morality and Agency," *Ethnology*, 43, no. 2 (2004): 167–84; and David Pedersen, *American Value: Migrants, Money, and Meaning in El Salvador and the United States* (Chicago: University of Chicago Press, 2013).

41. David Pedersen, "The Storm We Call Dollars: Determining Value and Belief in El Salvador and the United States," *Cultural Anthropology* 17, no. 3 (2002): 431–59; and Gamburd, "Money That Burns Like Oil," 168.

42. It was also not an accident that China was the place that first emerged in my idea of Asian destinations. In the beginning of her ethnography about consumer nationalism in South Korea, anthropologist Laura Nelson wrote that since 1991, when she too arrived in Seoul as an English teacher "on a whim," there has been a change in the ways Americans see and discuss Asia. Rather than reflecting an increased appreciation of geography among Americans, she points out that a growing geopolitical appreciation and fear of things

surrounding the Chinese economic "behemoth" is "remapping international space, in both reality and imagination." Laura Nelson, *Measured Excess: Status, Gender, and Consumer Nationalism in South Korea* (New York: Columbia University Press, 2000), viii.

43. John Cho, "Global Fatigue: Transnational Markets, Linguistic Capital, and the Return Migration of Korean-American Male English Teachers to Seoul," *Journal of Sociolinguistics* 16 no. 2 (2012): 218–37.

44. Seol, "Past and Present of Foreign Workers in Korea," 3.

45. Seol, "Past and Present of Foreign Workers in Korea," 1.

46. Lim, "Racing from the Bottom," 426. In the December 2008 newsletter to Korea's Catholic Spanish-speaking community, Hermana Pilar, who worked closely with migrant workers from 2002 to 2008, wrote, "When I [first] arrived in Korea in April 1991, I did not imagine that I would meet so many people from so many countries." She then listed the different countries where the people she had met and helped came from, including Peru, Korea, Bolivia, Colombia, Mexico, Chile, Spain, Brazil, Ecuador, Paraguay, Guatemala, Puerto Rico, the Philippines, Argentina, Belgium, Dominican Republic, Thailand, France, and Poland. While not all of those people were necessarily migrant workers, this list speaks to the diverse international community in South Korea in the early 2000s.

47. The Peruvian embassy attempted to collect a list of the types of jobs Peruvians held in the hopes of using that data to argue they should be included in the EPS, but the consul general told me the migrants were suspicious of the embassy's motives, and everyone wrote down the generic *obrero* (worker).

48. Interviewees mentioned that there were many Peruvians employed in recycling in regions outside of my field sites.

49. Some Peruvians who had suffered injuries in these laundries lived with the Catholic clergy while they recovered. Peruvians told me particular nationalities of people often worked in one kind of factory. One man told me he had worked at a leather-curing factory for a couple of days, but the work was too intense for him to endure. In his opinion, the only people who could handle work that hard were migrants from China.

50. Two people told me separate examples of foreign workers burning down factories as a result of not being paid. Padre Ignacio, who had been in Korea since the 1970s, told me that factory conditions had improved drastically since 1991 and 1992 when there were many foreign workers and little control. At that time, there were many accidents, cases of beatings by factory bosses, and very low pay for foreign workers. It was his opinion that the government had become ashamed by the bad press around these incidents from Human Rights Watch and other international sources and worked to improve conditions. Since most Peruvians arrived in the mid-1990s onward, I only heard about a handful of cases of abuse and accidents happening to Peruvians. In contrast, at least 50 percent of the people I interviewed told me that at some point they had worked at a factory where they ultimately were not paid. A twenty-six-year-old man I interviewed in 2006 told me that usually the best place to find a new job was by asking for referrals from friends who were already working at a particular factory. Otherwise, there was no guarantee they would ever pay. However, he said that it was very difficult for men to find work at all anymore. He said only women could find work. I do not know if it was because jobs were gendered differently, or because the factories paid women at a lower rate and so sought them out because they were less expensive.

51. *Arbeit* is German for job and is commonly used to refer to part-time work in South Korea. It is usually spelled *arbeit* 아르바이트. A few Peruvians I met thought it was an English word and seemed a little disappointed when I told them it was not.

52. Katharine Moon, *Sex among Allies: Military Prostitution in U.S. Korea Relations* (New York: Columbia University Press, 1997).

53. Ethnographers have described camp towns as transnational spaces where global economic inequalities and cold war politics interact via sex tourism. Sealing Cheng, *On the Move for Love: Migrant Entertainers and the U.S. Military in South Korea* (Philadelphia: University of Pennsylvania Press, 2010); and Hae Yeon Choo, *Decentering Citizenship: Gender, Labor, and Migrant Rights in South Korea* (Stanford, CA: Stanford University Press, 2016).

54. Choo, *Decentering Citizenship*, 74.

55. From what my interviewees told me, the factory paid the same amount per worker, but for the EPS workers, 400,000 won went to their insurance and benefits, and 600,000 was their salary. In contrast, undocumented workers received no benefits but took home the whole 1,000,000 won. This take-home pay discrepancy resulted in some people abandoning their official EPS jobs and finding jobs as undocumented migrants elsewhere.

56. The EPS requires a Korean language test, but these men were unable to speak Korean well.

57. I keep the names and locations of these areas intentionally vague in an effort to protect my interviewees and other communities of migrants. When significant to a story or vignette, I specify whether the setting was an urban area in Seoul or in a semirural area near or adjacent to a factory or camp town. The only area I name is Dongducheon, because people frequently invoked it in their migration and conversion narratives. The place where migrants played soccer had already been torn down or went out of business prior to this book's publication.

58. In an effort to protect people's anonymity, I use "pueblo joven" and "Norte Chico" instead of the individual names of places where people are from. Norte Chico refers to a group of coastal towns about 200 kilometers north of Lima. It includes Barranca, Puerto Supe, Huaral, and Huacho. Norte Chico is a term local people use, but mostly interviewees referred to the individual towns when discussing their points of origin.

59. I was an intermediate-level Korean speaker.

60. Lila Rodriguez, my good friend from the English school where I had previously worked—who also happens to be of Peruvian Japanese descent—introduced me to the Peruvian consul general, who led to more contacts in the Peruvian embassy and the Korean Ministry of Justice.

61. Padre Ignacio had been in Korea from 1974 to 1991, and then returned in 2001. Hermana Pilar had first arrived in Korea in 1991. When she left Korea in 2008, she wrote in the Catholic newsletter that she had been working with the Spanish-speaking community since 2001. Through multiple one-on-one interviews with Padre Ignacio and reading Hermana Pilar's contributions in the Catholic newsletter, I was able to develop a long-view and historical perspective on Peruvian migration to Korea.

62. A priest told me this was because the number of foreign migrants were on the rise, but also because Korean workers had gained legal protections through protest movements over the past decades and no longer needed their help in the way they had at the beginning of the labor movement.

63. When Hermana Pilar left Korea in December 2008, she wrote a goodbye letter in the Catholic newsletter. In it she described the kinds of things she had helped migrants with. She said, "I have suffered a great deal in sharing the problems and difficulties for painful situations at work, in the factories, in the prison, in the hospital, for illness, for work-related accidents, motorcycle accidents, even sharing the pain of people who had to get surgery. The list is endless and could fill a thick book. Far from family one suffers loneliness, right? But I have also been blessed to have lived intense moments . . . [of faith]."

64. The prayer she gave me to read was typed on a slip of paper and said in Spanish, "#2. For the intellectuals, professors and journalists who live and work inspired by Jesus and the Gospel, so that they are never assaulted by doubts and remain faithful to the Churches of God WE PRAY." Every week she handed out a few prayers to parishioners to read and seemed excited that this particular prayer was the perfect one for me.

65. Online, some churches in Korea and the United States accuse Nazarene of being a cult.

66. As with chain migration, often these churches had groups of migrants from one particular hometown.

67. George E. Marcus, "Ethnography in/of the World System: The Emergence of Multi-Sited Ethnography," *Annual Review of Anthropology* 24 (1995): 95–117, 113.

68. On the back of the programs I received at the Sunday worship service at Nazarene, there was a list of prayer topics. Number 4 was "May God raise up [*levante*] translators, interpreters, and materials for the message in the trainings."

69. Susan F. Harding, "Convicted by the Holy Spirit: The Rhetoric of Fundamental Baptist Conversion," *American Ethnologist* 14, no. 1 (1987): 178.

1. PERU, SOUTH KOREA, PERU . . .

1. See Geon-Soo Han, "African Migrant Workers' Views of Korean People and Culture," *Korea Journal* 43, no. 1 (2003).

2. In their research on Nepalis looking for work in Korea, Heather Hindman and Robert Oppenheim found that although the Employee Permit System was meant to eliminate "middlemen" like the private labor recruiters who charged fees to help Nepalis apply for the now-defunct Industrial Trainee System, the EPS's Korean-language requirement essentially creates another middleman where applicants must pay for language lessons. Heather Hindman and Robert Oppenheim, "Lines of Labor and Desire: 'Korean Quality' in Contemporary Kathmandu," *Anthropological Quarterly* 87, no. 2 (2014): 465–95, 479.

3. Kentucky Fried Chicken is popular in both Peru and South Korea. The first KFC in Seoul opened in 1984 (see www.kfckorea.com/company/kfc_is.asp for a timeline). A KFC opened in Peru in the late 1990s and was considered a prestige food by some of the people I knew in Peru. When I invited people out, they often asked to go to KFC or McDonald's. I got the feeling they would not have paid to go there on their own, and also, since I was an American, they thought that is what I would want to eat.

4. Jason De León, *The Land of Open Graves: Living and Dying on the Migrant Trail*, California Series in Public Anthropology (Oakland: University of California Press, 2015).

5. Chung In Moon, "Korean Contractors in Saudi Arabia: Their Rise and Fall," *Middle East Journal* 40, no. 4 (1986): 614–33.

6. Cited by Timothy C. Lim, "Racing from the Bottom in South Korea? The Nexus between Civil Society and Transnational Migrants," *Asian Survey* 43, no. 3 (2003): 423–42, 426, from an internal report from the Foreign Workers' Labor Counseling Office (Seoul, Korea).

7. Lim, "Racing from the Bottom," 426.

8. Estimation from interviews with the Catholic clergy in Seoul.

9. See Timothy C. Lim, "The Changing Face of South Korea: The Emergence of Korea as a 'Land of Immigration,'" *Korea Society Quarterly* (Summer/Fall 2002): 16–21.

10. See Yong Wook Lee and Hyemee Park, "The Politics of Foreign Labor Policy in Korea and Japan," *Journal of Contemporary Asia* 35, no. 2 (2005): 143–65.

11. From email correspondence with the embassy.

12. In 2007 the Peruvian embassy estimated that 85 percent of Peruvians in Korea were undocumented. From internal embassy memo.

13. From an English-language document given to me by the Catholic Church titled "Act on Foreign Workers' Employment, Etc.: Act No. 6967, Aug. 16, 2003," 696. Quotes from an Addendum on Article 2 (Special Cases concerning Illegal Foreign Workers).

14. Not my translation. Cited from the English transcription of Director Min Hee Lee's remarks created for the forum. Obtained from a participant.

15. Caren Freeman, *Making and Faking Kinship: Marriage and Labor Migration between China and South Korea* (Ithaca, NY: Cornell University Press, 2011).

16. Statistics cited from Nora Hui-Jung Kim, "Korea: Multiethnic or Multicultural?" in *Multiethnic Korea? Multiculturalism, Migration, and Peoplehood Diversity in Contemporary South Korea*, ed. John Lie (Berkeley: Institute of East Asian Studies, University of California, 2014), 58–78.

17. Eleana Kim, *Adopted Territory: Transnational Korean Adoptees and the Politics of Belonging* (Durham, NC: Duke University Press, 2010).

18. Timothy Lim, "Late Migration, Discourse, and the Politics of Multiculturalism in South Korea: A Comparative Perspective," in *Multiethnic Korea? Multiculturalism, Migration, and Peoplehood Diversity in Contemporary South Korea*, ed. John Lie (Berkeley: Institute of East Asian Studies, University of California, 2014), 31–57.

19. Hyun Mee Kim, "The State and Migrant Women: Diverging Hopes in the Making of 'Multicultural Families' in Contemporary Korea," *Korean Journal* 47, no. 4 (2007): 100–122.

20. EuyRyung Jun, "'The Frog That Has Forgotten Its Past': Advocating for Migrant Workers in South Korea," *Positions: East Asia Cultures Critique* 24, no. 3 (2016).

21. John Lie, "Introduction: Multiethnic Korea?" in *Multiethnic Korea? Multiculturalism, Migration, and Peoplehood Diversity in Contemporary South Korea*, ed. John Lie (Berkeley: Institute of East Asian Studies, University of California, 2014), 1–27.

22. People in Seoul would probably refer to where Beatriz lived currently as being rural and "provincial," but I got the feeling, by her use of this term, that she thought her old place was both far away from the city and extremely unsophisticated.

23. Susan Bibler Coutin, "Being En Route," *American Anthropologist* 107, no. 2 (2005): 195–206. Coutin argues that while unauthorized migrants occupy the same physical spaces as everyone else, they are socially absented. Of this, she writes, "Absenting is often partial in that, alongside those who are legally present, unauthorized migrants travel, work, take up residence, shop, and so forth. There is, therefore, a sense in which the 'underground,' occupied by the unauthorized, is a dimension of social reality rather than a separate place."

As the unauthorized are both absent and not, this dimension is both totalizing and partial, hidden and visible" (196).

24. Jorge Durand, "The Peruvian Diaspora: Portrait of a Migratory Process," special issue, "Peruvian Migration in a Global Context," *Latin American Perspectives* 37, no. 5 (2010): 12–28.

25. Kimberly Theidon, *Violence and Reconciliation in Peru*, Pennsylvania Studies in Human Rights (Philadelphia: University of Pennsylvania Press, 2012).

26. Attractive for its (perhaps imagined) job and settlement opportunities, the United States was the principal destination for Peruvian migration until 1986, when the passing of the Immigration Reform and Control Act (IRCA) resulted in a tightening of the borders and a decrease in benefits offered to migrants. See Ayumi Takenaka and Karen A. Pren, "Leaving to Get Ahead: Assessing the Relationship between Mobility and Inequality in Peruvian Migration," special issue, "Peruvian Migration in a Global Context," *Latin American Perspectives* 37, no. 5 (2010): 29–49.

27. Sarah Mahler, *American Dreaming: Immigrant Life on the Margins* (Princeton, NJ: Princeton University Press, 1995). See also Elena Sabogal, "*Viviendo en la Sombra*: The Immigration of Peruvian Professionals to South Florida," *Latino Studies* 3, no. 1 (2005): 113–31.

28. Ulla Berg, *Mobile Selves: Race, Migration, and Belonging in Peru and the U.S.*, Social Transformations in American Anthropology (New York: New York University Press, 2017).

29. Durand, "Peruvian Diaspora"; "LAMP: Latin American Migration Project," Princeton University, http://lamp.opr.princeton.edu, accessed September 2019.

30. Statistics as of 2007, courtesy of OECD, Ministry of Justice 2008; and Teofilo Altamirano Rua, *Migration, Remittances, and Development in Times of Crisis* (Lima: Pontifica Universidad Católica del Perú, 2010).

31. Karsten Paerregaard, *Return to Sender: The Moral Economy of Peru's Migrant Remittances* (Berkeley: University of California Press, 2014), 27.

32. Vanessa Fong, *Paradise Redefined: Transnational Chinese Students and the Quest for Flexible Citizenship in the Developed World* (Stanford, CA: Stanford University Press, 2011).

33. Takenaka and Pren, "Leaving to Get Ahead."

34. De León, *Land of Open Graves*.

35. Japan also had agreements with other countries, including Brazil. See Takeyuki Tsuda, *Strangers in the Ethnic Homeland: Japanese Brazilian Return Migration in Transnational Perspective* (New York: Columbia University Press, 2003).

36. Ayumi Takenaka, "Transnational Community and Its Ethnic Consequences: The Return Migration and the Transformation of Ethnicity of Japanese Peruvians," *American Behavioral Scientist* 42, no. 9 (1999): 1462; and Wayne Cornelius, "Japan: The Illusion of Immigration Control," in *Controlling Immigration: A Global Perspective*, ed. Wayne A. Cornelius, Phillip L. Martin, and James F. Hollifield (Stanford, CA: Stanford University Press, 1994), 375–410, 397.

37. Andrew Eungi Kim, "Characteristics of Religious Life in South Korea: A Sociological Survey," *Review of Religious Research* 43, no. 4 (2002): 291–310.

38. Jun, "'The Frog That Has Forgotten Its Past.'"

39. KRIM (Korea Research Institute for Mission), http://krim.org/2010/english.html, last accessed September 30, 2013.

40. Sung-Deuk Oak, *The Making of Korean Christianity: Protestant Encounters with Korean Religions, 1876–1915* (Waco, TX: Baylor University Press, 2013).

41. Ju Hui Judy Han, "'If You Don't Work, You Don't Eat': Evangelizing Development in Africa," in *New Millennium South Korea: Neoliberal Capitalism and Transnational Movements,* ed. Jesook Song (New York: Routledge, 2011).

42. Han, "'If You Don't Work, You Don't Eat,'" 149.

43. Cecilia Blondet, "Villa El Salvador," in *The Peru Reader: History, Culture, Politics,* ed. Orin Starn, Carlos Ivan Degregori, and Robin Kirk (Durham, NC: Duke University Press, 2005), 287–92.

2. MONETARY CONVERSION

1. Peggy Levitt, "Social Remittances: Migration Driven Local-Level Forms of Cultural Diffusion," *International Migration Review* 32, no. 4 (1998): 926–48.

2. Data from self-reporting in interviews.

3. In 2004, one dollar bought 3.31 soles. In 2006, one dollar bought 3.07 soles, and in 2011, one dollar bought 2.7 soles.

4. Memo from the Peruvian embassy in Seoul, May 12, 2008, to the Catholic Church.

5. The rate went from 1,034 won per dollar to 1,393 won per dollar.

6. At a conversion of one dollar per 939 won in February 2008 using www.x-rates.com/historical.

7. Michele Ruth Gamburd, "Money That Burns Like Oil: A Sri Lankan Cultural Logic of Morality and Agency," *Ethnology* 43, no. 2 (2004): 168.

8. Jorge Durand, Emilio A. Parrado, and Douglas S. Massey, "Migradollars and Development: A Reconsideration of the Mexican Case," *International Migration Review* 30, no. 2 (1996): 423–44; Douglas S. Massey and Emilio Parrado, "Migradollars: The Remittances and Savings of Mexican Migrants to the USA," *Population Research and Policy Review* 13, no. 1 (1994): 3–30.

9. Ester Hernandez and Susan Bibler Coutin, "Remitting Subjects: Migrants, Money, and States," *Economy and Society* 35, no. 2 (2006): 201.

10. Ulla Dalum Berg and Carla Tamango, "El Quinto Suyo from Above and from Below: State Agency and Transnational Political Practices among Peruvian Migrants in the US and Europe," *Latino Studies* 4, no. 3 (2006): 258–81.

11. Caroline Melly finds that in Senegal, half-finished houses built with migrant remittances are "defining features" of Dakar and "stand as witnesses to and evidence of transnational movements of labor and capital." Caroline Melly, *Bottleneck: Moving, Building, and Belonging in an African City* (Chicago: University of Chicago Press, 2017), 78–79. In Peru it was unclear to me whether the homes were in an active building process, or decaying. Melly writes that this half-finished quality and the speculation it sparks from viewers shows how the houses are *"turned inside out:* their insides are neither private nor contained" (79, Melly's italics), and are open to the elements and rumor.

12. A pseudonym for his real nickname.

13. See Jeffrey H. Cohen, "Migration, Remittances, and Household Strategies," *Annual Review of Anthropology* 40 (2011): 103–14.

14. Lisa Akesson, "Making Migrants Responsible for Development: Cape Verdean Returnees and Northern Migration Policies," *African Spectrum* 41, no. 1 (2011): 61–83.

15. Sarah Mahler, *American Dreaming: Immigrant Life on the Margins* (Princeton, NJ: Princeton University Press, 1995), 88.

3. RELIGIOUS CONVERSION

1. There was good reason for this little window. On a separate occasion I talked with the sister of another one of my contacts in Korea who told me that a few months earlier, four or five people had robbed the pharmacy where she was working. This pharmacy, which was also in a pueblo joven, had a door to allow customers in. This door was left locked during business hours, and she was only supposed to let in people who looked trustworthy. One man came to the door and knocked. She thought he looked OK, and opened the door. He came in and pulled out a gun. Then three or four other people who also had guns followed him through the door. She said, "They stole all the medicine, the money, the phone cards, everything." After the incident, she left that pharmacy and started working at a different one where the owner slept inside the building at night to protect it from break-ins.

2. Many of the evangelical churches Peruvians belong to in Korea resemble what Glick Schiller and colleagues refer to as a Christian Modernist–style church, in that they follow a prosperity theology, where economic success is attributed to having a good relationship with God, and its members do not see themselves as part of a Korean church but as a part of a larger movement bringing "real Christianity" to the world. Nina Glick Schiller, Boris Nieswant, Gunther Schlee, Ayse Calglar, Evangelos Karagiannis, Tsypylma Darieva, Lale Yalcin-Heckmann, and Laszlo Foszto, "Pathways of Migrant Incorporation in Germany," *Transit* 1, no. 1 (2004): 1–18, 2.

3. He told me this invitation would come from a church affiliated with Friendship and that the church would have to be financially stable enough to support him with a scholarship and remuneration for his missionary services.

4. They organized big events for the church, including an event welcoming visiting Latin American missionaries, and what seemed like a dress rehearsal for the missionary event. At that event they invited the Catholic clergy, who sat uncomfortably next to the Peruvian consul. The consul read a letter aloud from the ambassador who was unable to attend.

5. Elizabeth E. Brusco, *The Reformation of Machismo: Evangelical Conversion and Gender in Colombia* (Austin: University of Texas Press, 1995); Anna L. Peterson and Manuel A. Vasquez, eds., *Latin American Religions: Histories and Documents in Context* (New York: New York University Press, 2008); and Kimberly Theidon, *Violence and Reconciliation in Peru*, Pennsylvania Studies in Human Rights (Philadelphia: University of Pennsylvania Press, 2012).

6. Ju Hui Judy Han, "'If You Don't Work, You Don't Eat': Evangelizing Development in Africa," in *New Millennium South Korea: Neoliberal Capitalism and Transnational Movements*, ed. Jesook Song (New York: Routledge, 2011), 148. In their work on West African migrants in "Christian Modernist" churches in Germany, Nina Glick Schiller and colleagues found that the migrant churches they worked in shared these ideas that "prosperity and success are perceived as proof of a 'righteous' Christian life" ("Pathways of Migrant Incorporation in Germany," 2). They traced these ideas to a kind of Christianity that emerged from the United States and moved worldwide starting in the 1980s and 1990s.

7. Han, "'If You Don't Work, You Don't Eat,'" 148.

8. Glick Schiller et al., "Pathways of Migrant Incorporation in Germany," 2.

9. It was also a term I found in the scriptures commonly included in the English- and Korean-language versions of the sermon program distributed at Nazarene. For example, "You must receive your *answer* [응답 eung dap] through evangelism every day" (Philippians 4:7). "The *answers* will accurately come. He will guard your hearts and your minds in Christ Jesus" (1 John 2:20–27) (my italics). It also appears to be a term used in other Spanish-speaking evangelical communities, but not everywhere. Over email I asked a friend whose husband is a pastor in Tijuana, Mexico, about the use of *respuestas* in their church. She and her husband discussed it and told me that instead of using the term *respuesta* when they are referring to a conversation with God, their parishioners use terms like "me contestó, me escuchó me oyó [he answered me, heard me, listened to me]."

10. Robert Shanafelt, "Magic, Miracle, and Marvels in Anthropology," *Ethnos* 69, no. 3 (2004): 317–40.

11. In the Friendship newsletter, one American member wrote, "You must listen to God's guidance even if it seems unreasonable. His plan may be different from yours but you must listen and follow." Also in the Friendship newsletter, one of the five Peruvian leaders wrote in his *testimonio* about his fear of not being able to get a visa during the amnesty and having to leave Korea prematurely. Of this memory, he said, "What if I can't return to Korea? Or what if I deviate from the path of GOD when I am in my country?" After asking his pastor for advice and praying, he received his visa.

12. James Clifford, *Routes: Travel and Translation in the Late Twentieth Century* (Cambridge, MA: Harvard University Press, 1997), 3.

13. James Peacock and Dorothy C. Holland, "The Narrated Self: Life Stories in Process," *Ethos* 21, no. 4 (1993): 367–83.

14. Elinor Ochs and Lisa Capps, "Narrating the Self," *Annual Review of Anthropology* 25 (1996): 22.

15. Nina Glick Schiller, Linda Basch, and Cristina Blanc-Szanton, "Towards a Definition of Transnationalism," *Annals of the New York Academy of Sciences* 645 (1992): 926–48.

16. Robert A. Orsi, *Between Heaven and Earth: The Religious Worlds People Make and the Scholars Who Study Them* (Princeton, NJ: Princeton University Press, 2005); Mei Zhan, *Other-Worldly: Making Chinese Medicine through Transnational Frames* (Durham, NC: Duke University Press, 2009).

17. The Peruvians who were free during this time sold accessories at night or had lost their jobs and were looking for work.

18. They prayed for each of these individually and together as a group at church. Asking God to help inspire workers (*los obreros*) to bring the gospel to Latin America and to raise money for Cristo Vive were prayer topics nos. 2 and 3 on the back of the Nazarene Sunday pamphlets.

19. In the "Good News" evangelization pamphlet they gave me later, I read more about what Paty was referring to. It said that once a person had accepted the message (of the gospel as laid out in the booklet), they would receive blessings and would be "a witness of these blessings," which meant they could become missionaries or "participate in the ministry of the Word in [their] field."

20. Simon Coleman, "Continuous Conversion? The Rhetoric, Practice, and Rhetorical Practice of Charismatic Protestant Conversion," in *The Anthropology of Religious Conversion*, ed. Andrew Buckser and Stephen D. Glazier (Lanham, MD: Rowman and Littlefield, 2003), 17.

21. The booklet outlined the church's teachings; suggested the receiver had a series of problems including illness, financial issues, or depression; and gave a reason why—listing a series of scriptures. It then suggested a solution to these spiritual and physical problems and offered a way to find blessing through specific scriptures. There was a place at the front of the booklet where the giver could write their name and phone number in case the receiver needed guidance.

22. There was one exception to the Korean church-sponsored visits. One year in November, a church from an American military base sponsored the food. The pastor gave a sermon in English and then we shared a traditional Thanksgiving dinner with turkey, stuffing, mashed potatoes, and the rest. While I happily ate my food, which had been prepared on the base and tasted exactly like Thanksgiving food from the United States, the Peruvians I was sitting with found it almost impossible to eat. "What was that thing?" one woman asked me, sadly, pointing at the stuffing with her fork. "I couldn't even get it past my throat." Everyone said they preferred the Korean food they usually had.

23. RPP Noticias, "Peruanos en Corea del Sur." On the program "Peruanos en el Exterior," RPP Noticias, www.rpp.com.pe/2010-02-22-peruanos-en-corea-del-sur-(20-02-10)-noticia_244423.html, accessed September 29, 2013 (as of 2019, the site is no longer available).

24. A Peruvian consul who had previously been appointed in Japan told me that it was easier to help the Peruvian community in Japan because the majority of the Peruvians were documented professionals.

4. COSMOPOLITAN CONVERSION

1. So Jin Park and Nancy Abelmann, "Class and Cosmopolitan Striving: Mothers' Management of English Education in South Korea," *Anthropological Quarterly* 77, no. (2004): 645–72, 650.

2. Carol A. Breckenridge and Sheldon Pollock, eds., *Cosmopolitanism*, A Public Culture Book (Durham, NC: Duke University Press, 2002).

3. Here I refer to Park and Abelmann's discussion of "cosmopolitan striving." They follow Ann Anagnost's definition of cosmopolitanism as being "citizens[s] capable of being at home in the world." Anagnots (2000: 412), as cited in Park and Abelmann, "Class and Cosmopolitan Striving," 650.

4. Pierre Bourdieu, "The Forms of Capital," in *Handbook of Theory and Research for the Sociology of Education*, ed. J. G. Richardson (New York: Greenwood Press, 1986), 241–58.

5. Bourdieu, "Forms of Capital."

6. Breckenridge and Pollack, *Cosmopolitanism*.

7. Breckenridge and Pollack, *Cosmopolitanism*.

8. Nancy D. Munn, *The Fame of Gawa: A Symbolic Study of Value Transformation in a Massim Society*, Henry Louis Morgan Lecture Series (Durham, NC: Duke University Press, 1992), 8.

9. They were expensive at the original price, but must have cost even more on the black market. Undocumented migrants were not able to shop at Costco on their own because the store required a valid visa to get a membership card.

10. They had been scammed by a Peruvian woman and Korean man posing as job brokers in Peru. They were left abandoned at a hotel in Seoul without jobs or housing and made their way to the Peruvian embassy, which directed them to Padre Ignacio. He helped them

press charges, which eventually led to the arrest of the brokers, but they only recovered $300 of their money.

11. David Graeber, *Toward an Anthropological Theory of Value: The False Coin of Our Own Dreams* (New York: Palgrave Macmillan, 2001), ix.

12. Graeber, *Toward an Anthropological Theory of Value*, xii.

13. Barbara Yngvesson and Susan Bibler Coutin, "Backed by Papers: Undoing Persons, Histories, and Return," *American Ethnologist* 33, no. 2 (2006): 177–90.

14. Yeouido Full Gospel Fact Sheet, http://english.fgtv, last accessed October 31, 2010.

EPILOGUE

1. Carol A. Breckenridge and Sheldon Pollock, eds., *Cosmopolitanism, A Public Culture Book* (Durham, NC: Duke University Press, 2002); So Jin Park and Nancy Abelmann, "Class and Cosmopolitan Striving: Mothers' Management of English Education in South Korea," *Anthropological Quarterly* 77, no. 4 (2004).

2. Pierre Bourdieu, "The Forms of Capital," in *Handbook of Theory and Research for the Sociology of Education*, ed. J. G. Richardson (New York: Greenwood Press, 1986), 241–58, 255.

3. Bourdieu, "Forms of Capital."

BIBLIOGRAPHY

Abrego, Leisy, and Sarah Lakhani. "Incomplete Inclusion: Legal Violence and Immigrants in Liminal Legal Statuses." *Law & Policy* 37, no. 4 (2015): 265–93.

Akesson, Lisa. "Making Migrants Responsible for Development: Cape Verdean Returnees and Northern Migration Policies." *African Spectrum* 41, no. 1 (2011): 61–83.

Altamirano Rua, Teofilo. *Migration, Remittances, and Development in Times of Crisis.* Lima: Pontifica Universidad Católica del Perú, 2010.

Appadurai, Arjun. *The Social Life of Things: Commodities in Cultural Perspective.* Cambridge Studies in Social and Cultural Anthropology. Cambridge: Cambridge University Press, 1986.

Austin-Broos, Diane. "The Anthropology of Conversion: An Introduction." In *The Anthropology of Religious Conversion,* edited by Andrew Buckser and Stephen D. Glazier, 1–12. Oxford: Rowman and Littlefield, 2003.

Berg, Ulla. *Mobile Selves: Race, Migration, and Belonging in Peru and the U.S.* Social Transformations in American Anthropology. New York: New York University Press, 2017.

Berg, Ulla Dalum, and Carla Tamango. "El Quinto Suyo from Above and from Below: State Agency and Transnational Political Practices among Peruvian Migrants in the US and Europe." *Latino Studies* 4, no. 3 (2006): 258–81.

Blondet, Cecilia. "Villa El Salvador." In *The Peru Reader: History, Culture, Politics,* edited by Orin Starn, Carlos Ivan Degregori, and Robin Kirk, 287–92. Durham, NC: Duke University Press, 2005.

Bosniak, Linda. "Universal Citizenship and the Problem of Alienage." *Northwestern University Law Review* 94, no. 3 (2000): 963–84.

Bourdieu, Pierre. "The Forms of Capital." In *Handbook of Theory and Research for the Sociology of Education,* edited by J. G. Richardson, 241–58. New York: Greenwood Press, 1986.

Breckenridge, Carol A., and Sheldon Pollock, eds. *Cosmopolitanism.* A Public Culture Book. Durham, NC: Duke University Press, 2002.

Brusco, Elizabeth E. *The Reformation of Machismo: Evangelical Conversion and Gender in Colombia*. Austin: University of Texas Press, 1995.

Carruthers, Bruce G., and Wendy Nelson Espeland. "Money, Meaning, and Morality." *American Behavioral Scientist* 41, no. 10 (1998): 1384–408.

Chavez, Leo. "Outside the Imagined Community: Undocumented Settlers and Experiences of Incorporation." *American Ethnologist* 18, no. 2 (1991): 257–78.

Cheng, Sealing. *On the Move for Love: Migrant Entertainers and the U.S. Military in South Korea*. Philadelphia: University of Pennsylvania Press, 2010.

Cho, John. "Global Fatigue: Transnational Markets, Linguistic Capital, and the Return Migration of Korean-American Male English Teachers to Seoul." *Journal of Sociolinguistics* 16, no. 2 (2012): 218–37.

Chong, Kelly H. *Deliverance and Submission: Evangelical Women and the Negotiation of Patriarchy in South Korea*. Cambridge, MA: Harvard University Press, 2008.

Choo, Hae Yeon. *Decentering Citizenship: Gender, Labor, and Migrant Rights in South Korea*. Stanford, CA: Stanford University Press, 2016.

Chu, Julie Y. *Cosmologies of Credit: Transnational Mobility and the Politics of Destination in China*. Durham, NC: Duke University Press, 2010.

Clifford, James. *Routes: Travel and Translation in the Late Twentieth Century*. Cambridge, MA: Harvard University Press, 1997.

Cohen, Jeffrey H. "Migration, Remittances, and Household Strategies." *Annual Review of Anthropology* 40 (2011): 103–14.

Coleman, Simon. "Continuous Conversion? The Rhetoric, Practice, and Rhetorical Practice of Charismatic Protestant Conversion." In *The Anthropology of Religious Conversion*, edited by Andrew Buckser and Stephen D. Glazier, 15–27. Lanham, MD: Rowman and Littlefield, 2003.

Cornelius, Wayne A. "Japan: The Illusion of Immigration Control." In *Controlling Immigration: A Global Perspective*, edited by Wayne A. Cornelius, Phillip L. Martin, and James F. Hollifield, 375–410. Stanford, CA: Stanford University Press, 1994.

Coutin, Susan Bibler. "Being En Route." *American Anthropologist* 107, no. 2 (2005): 195–206.

———. *Exiled Home: Salvadoran Transnational Youth in the Aftermath of Violence*. Global Insecurities. Durham, NC: Duke University Press, 2016.

De Genova, Nicholas P. *Working the Boundaries: Race, Space, and "Illegality" in Mexican Chicago*. Durham, NC: Duke University Press, 2005.

De León, Jason. *The Land of Open Graves: Living and Dying on the Migrant Trail*. California Series in Public Anthropology. Oakland: University of California Press, 2015.

Durand, Jorge. "The Peruvian Diaspora: Portrait of a Migratory Process." Special issue, "Peruvian Migration in a Global Context." *Latin American Perspectives* 37, no. 5 (2010): 12–28.

Durand, Jorge, Emilio A. Parrado, and Douglas S. Massey. "Migradollars and Development: A Reconsideration of the Mexican Case." *International Migration Review* 30, no. 2 (1996): 423–44.

Employee Permit System website. www.eps.go.kr/en/view/view_01.jsp. Last accessed July 26, 2018.

Espeland, Wendy Nelson, and Mitchell L. Stevens. "Commensuration as a Social Process." *Annual Review of Sociology* 24 (1998): 313–43.

Fong, Vanessa. *Paradise Redefined: Transnational Chinese Students and the Quest for Flexible Citizenship in the Developed World*. Stanford, CA: Stanford University Press, 2011.

Freeman, Caren. *Making and Faking Kinship: Marriage and Labor Migration between China and South Korea*. Ithaca, NY: Cornell University Press, 2011.

Gamburd, Michele Ruth. "Money That Burns Like Oil: A Sri Lankan Cultural Logic of Morality and Agency." *Ethnology* 43, no. 2 (2004): 167–84.

Glick Schiller, Nina. "Transnational Social Fields and Imperialism: Bringing a Theory of Power to Transnational Studies." *Anthropological Theory* 5, no. 4 (2005): 439–61.

Glick Schiller, Nina, Linda Basch, and Cristina Blanc-Szanton. "Towards a Definition of Transnationalism." *Annals of the New York Academy of Sciences* 645 (1992): ix–xiv.

Glick Schiller, Nina, Boris Nieswant, Gunther Schlee, Ayse Calglar, Evangelos Karagiannais, Tsypylma Darieva, Lale Yalcin-Heckmann, and Laszlo Foszto. "Pathways of Migrant Incorporation in Germany." *Transit* 1, no. 1 (2004): 1–18.

Global Policy Forum. "The World Economic Crisis." www.globalpolicy.org/social-and-economic-policy/the-world-economic-crisis.html. Last accessed July 9, 2019.

Graeber, David. *Toward an Anthropological Theory of Value: The False Coin of Our Own Dreams*. New York: Palgrave Macmillan, 2001.

Grewal, Inderpal. *Transnational America: Feminisms, Diasporas, Neoliberalisms*. Durham, NC: Duke University Press, 2005.

Griffiths, Melanie B. E. "Out of Time: The Temporal Uncertainties of Refused Asylum Seekers and Immigration Detainees." *Journal of Ethnic and Migration Studies* 40, no. 12 (2014): 1991–2009.

Han, Geon-Soo. "African Migrant Workers' Views of Korean People and Culture." *Korea Journal* 43, no. 1 (2003): 154–73.

Han, Ju Hui Judy. "'If You Don't Work, You Don't Eat': Evangelizing Development in Africa." In *New Millennium South Korea: Neoliberal Capitalism and Transnational Movements*, edited by Jesook Song, 142–58. New York: Routledge, 2011.

Harding, Susan F. "Convicted by the Holy Spirit: The Rhetoric of Fundamental Baptist Conversion." *American Ethnologist* 14, no. 1 (1987): 167–81.

Hernandez, Ester, and Susan Bibler Coutin. "Remitting Subjects: Migrants, Money and States." *Economy and Society* 35, no. 2 (2006): 185–208.

Hondagneu-Sotelo, Pierrette, ed. *Religion and Social Justice for Immigrants*. New Brunswick, NJ: Rutgers University Press, 2007.

Jun, EuyRyung. "'The Frog That Has Forgotten Its Past': Advocating for Migrant Workers in South Korea." *Positions: East Asia Cultures Critique* 24, no. 3 (2016): 669–92.

Kearney, Michael. "The Local and the Global: The Anthropology of Globalization and Transnationalism." *Annual Review of Anthropology* 24 (1995): 547–65.

Kim, Andrew Eungi. "Characteristics of Religious Life in South Korea: A Sociological Survey." *Review of Religious Research* 43, no. 4 (2002): 291–310.

Kim, Eleana. *Adopted Territory: Transnational Korean Adoptees and the Politics of Belonging*. Durham, NC: Duke University Press, 2010.

Kim, Hyun Mee. "The State and Migrant Women: Diverging Hopes in the Making of 'Multicultural Families' in Contemporary Korea." *Korean Journal* 47, no. 4 (2007): 100–122.

Kim, Nora Hui Jung. "Korea: Multiethnic or Multicultural?" In *Multiethnic Korea? Multiculturalism, Migration, and Peoplehood Diversity in Contemporary South Korea*, edited by John Lie, 58–78. Berkeley: Institute of East Asian Studies, University of California, 2014.

Korean Ministry of Labor. "Plan to Induce Voluntary Departure and Changes in the EPS." Conference Report, Seoul, 6th Annual Immigration Policy Forum, April 20, 2005.

KRIM (Korea Research Institute for Mission). http://krim.org/2010/english.html. Last accessed September 30, 2013.

LAMP (Latin American Migration Project). http://lamp.opr.princeton.edu/. Last accessed September 2019.

Lee, Helene K. *Between Foreign and Family: Return Migration and Identity Construction among Korean Americans and Korean Chinese.* Newark, NJ: Rutgers University Press, 2018.

Lee, Yong Wook, and Hyemee Park. "The Politics of Foreign Labor Policy in Korea and Japan." *Journal of Contemporary Asia* 35, no. 2 (2005): 143–65.

Levitt, Peggy. "Social Remittances: Migration Driven Local-Level Forms of Cultural Diffusion." *International Migration Review* 32, no. 4 (1998): 926–48.

Lie, John. "Introduction: Multiethnic Korea?" In *Multiethnic Korea? Multiculturalism, Migration, and Peoplehood Diversity in Contemporary South Korea,* edited by John Lie, 1–27. Berkeley: Institute of East Asian Studies, University of California, 2014.

Lim, Timothy C. "The Changing Face of South Korea: The Emergence of Korea as a 'Land of Immigration.'" *Korea Society Quarterly* (Summer/Fall 2002): 16–21.

———. "Racing from the Bottom in South Korea? The Nexus between Civil Society and Transnational Migrants." *Asian Survey* 43, no. 3 (2003): 423–42.

———. "Late Migration, Discourse, and the Politics of Multiculturalism in South Korea: A Comparative Perspective." In *Multiethnic Korea? Multiculturalism, Migration, and Peoplehood Diversity in Contemporary South Korea,* edited by John Lie, 31–57. Berkeley: Institute of East Asian Studies, University of California, 2014.

Mahler, Sarah. *American Dreaming: Immigrant Life on the Margins.* Princeton, NJ: Princeton University Press, 1995.

Marcus, George E. "Ethnography in/of the World System: The Emergence of Multi-Sited Ethnography." *Annual Review of Anthropology* 24 (1995): 95–117.

Massey, Douglas S., and Emilio Parrado. "Migradollars: The Remittances and Savings of Mexican Migrants to the USA." *Population Research and Policy Review* 13, no. 1 (1994): 3–30.

Melly, Caroline. *Bottleneck: Moving, Building, and Belonging in an African City.* Chicago: University of Chicago Press, 2017.

Menjívar, Cecilia. "Liminal Legality: Salvadoran and Guatemalan Immigrants' Lives in the United States." *American Journal of Sociology* 111 (2006): 999–1037.

Moon, Chung In. "Korean Contractors in Saudi Arabia: Their Rise and Fall." *Middle East Journal* 40, no. 4 (1986): 614–33.

Moon, Katharine. *Sex among Allies: Military Prostitution in U.S. Korea Relations.* New York: Columbia University Press, 1997.

Munn, Nancy D. *The Fame of Gawa: A Symbolic Study of Value Transformation in a Massim Society.* Henry Louis Morgan Lecture Series. Durham, NC: Duke University Press, 1992.

Nelson, Laura. *Measured Excess: Status, Gender, and Consumer Nationalism in South Korea.* New York: Columbia University Press, 2000.

Ngai, Mae M. *Impossible Subjects: Illegal Aliens and the Making of Modern America.* Princeton, NJ: Princeton University Press, 2004.

Oak, Sung-Deuk. *The Making of Korean Christianity: Protestant Encounters with Korean Religions, 1876–1915.* Waco, TX: Baylor University Press, 2013.

Oanda Solutions for Business website. www.oanda.com/currency/historical-rates/. Last accessed March 1, 2014.

Ochs, Elinor, and Lisa Capps. "Narrating the Self." *Annual Review of Anthropology* 25 (1996): 19–43.

Ong, Aiwha. *Flexible Citizenship: The Cultural Logics of Transnationality.* Durham, NC: Duke University Press, 1999.

Paerregaard, Karsten. *Return to Sender: The Moral Economy of Peru's Migrant Remittances.* Berkeley: University of California Press, 2014.

Park, So Jin, and Nancy Abelmann. "Class and Cosmopolitan Striving: Mothers' Management of English Education in South Korea." *Anthropological Quarterly* 77, no. 4 (2004): 645–72.

Peacock, James L., and Dorothy C. Holland. "The Narrated Self: Life Stories in Process." *Ethos* 21, no. 4 (1993): 367–83.

Pedersen, David. *American Value: Migrants, Money, and Meaning in El Salvador and the United States.* Chicago: University of Chicago Press, 2013.

———. "The Storm We Call Dollars: Determining Value and Belief in El Salvador and the United States." *Cultural Anthropology* 17, no. 3 (2002): 431–59.

Peterson, Anna L., and Manuel A. Vásquez, eds. *Latin American Religions: Histories and Documents in Context.* New York: New York University Press, 2008.

Piore, Michael J. *Birds of Passage: Migrant Labor and Industrial Societies.* Cambridge: Cambridge University Press, 1979.

Rambo, Lewis R. *Understanding Religious Conversion.* New Haven, CT: Yale University Press, 1995.

———. "Anthropology and the Study of Conversion." In *Anthropology of Religious Conversion,* edited by Andre Buckser and Stephen D. Glazier. Lanham, MD: Rowman and Littlefield, 2003.

Rouse, Roger. "Making Sense of Settlement: Class Transformation, Cultural Struggle, and Transnationalism among Mexican Migrants in the United States." *Annals of the New York Academy of Sciences* 645 (1992): 25–52.

RPP Noticias. "Peruanos en Corea del Sur." On the program "Peruanos en el Exterior," 2010. RPP Noticias. www.rpp.com.pe/2010-02-22-peruanos-en-corea-del-sur-(20–02–10)-noticia_244423.html. Last accessed September 29, 2013.

Sabogal, Elena. "Viviendo en la Sombra: The Immigration of Peruvian Professionals to South Florida." *Latino Studies* 3, no. 1 (2005): 113–31.

Seol, Dong-Hoon. "Past and Present of Foreign Workers in Korea, 1987–2000." *Asia Solidarity Quarterly* 2 (2000): 6–31.

Seol, Dong-Hoon, and John D. Skrentny. "Ethnic Return Migration and Hierarchical Nationhood." *Ethnicities* 9, no. 2 (2009): 147–74.

Shanafelt, Robert. "Magic, Miracle, and Marvels in Anthropology." *Ethnos* 69, no. 3 (2004): 317–40.

Steigenga, Timothy, and Edward L. Cleary, eds. *Conversion of a Continent: Contemporary Religious Change in Latin America.* New Brunswick, NJ: Rutgers University Press, 2007.

Takenaka, Ayumi. "Transnational Community and Its Ethnic Consequences: The Return Migration and the Transformation of Ethnicity of Japanese Peruvians." *American Behavioral Scientist* 42, no. 9 (1999): 1459–74.

Takenaka, Ayumi, and Karen A. Pren. "Leaving to Get Ahead: Assessing the Relationship between Mobility and Inequality in Peruvian Migration." Special issue, "Peruvian Migration in a Global Context," *Latin American Perspectives* 37, no. 5 (2010): 29–49.

Takenaka, Ayumi, Karsten Paerregaard, and Ulla Berg. "Peruvian Migration in a Global Context." Special issue, "Peruvian Migration in a Global Context," *Latin American Perspectives* 37, no. 5 (2010): 3–11.

Theidon, Kimberly. *Violence and Reconciliation in Peru.* Pennsylvania Studies in Human Rights. Philadelphia: University of Pennsylvania Press, 2012.

Tsing, Anna. *Friction: An Ethnography of Global Connection.* Princeton, NJ: Princeton University Press, 2005.

Tsuda, Takeyuki. *Strangers in the Ethnic Homeland: Japanese Brazilian Return Migration in Transnational Perspective.* New York: Columbia University Press, 2003.

Turner, Victor. *The Ritual Process: Structure and Anti-Structure.* New York: Aldine de Gruyter, 1995.

Vogel, Erica. "Predestined Migrations: Undocumented Peruvians in South Korean Churches." *City & Society* 26, no. 3 (2010): 331–51.

———. "Ongoing Endings: Migration, Love, and Ethnography." *Journal of Contemporary Ethnography* 45, no. 6 (2016): 673–91.

Werbner, Pnina. "Global Pathways: Working-Class Cosmopolitans and the Creation of Transnational Ethnic Worlds." *Social Anthropology* 7, no. 1 (1999): 17–35.

———. "The Predicament of Diaspora and Millennial Islam." *Ethnicities* 4, no. 4 (2004): 451–76.

XE Corporation. www.xe.com/currencytables/?from=KRW&date=2017-08-04. Last accessed July 14, 2019.

Xrates.com. www.x-rates.com/d/KRW/USD/hist1996.html. Last accessed June 20, 2011.

———. www.x-rates.com/d/KRW/USD/hist1998.html. Last accessed July 25, 2011.

Yeouido Full Gospel Fact Sheet. http://english.fgtv.com. Last accessed October 31, 2010.

Yngvesson, Barbara, and Susan Bibler Coutin. "Backed by Papers: Undoing Persons, Histories, and Return." *American Ethnologist* 33, no. 2 (2006): 177–90.

Zhan, Mei. *Other-Worldly: Making Chinese Medicine through Transnational Frames.* Durham, NC: Duke University Press, 2009.

INDEX

155